STAND YOUR GROUND

Black Bodies and
the Justice of God

Kelly Brown Douglas

ORBIS BOOKS

Maryknoll, New York 10545

ORBIS BOOKS
Maryknoll, New York 10545

Fathers and Brothers
MARYKNOLL™

Founded in 1970, Orbis Books endeavors to publish works that enlighten the mind, nourish the spirit, and challenge the conscience. The publishing arm of the Maryknoll Fathers and Brothers, Orbis seeks to explore the global dimensions of the Christian faith and mission, to invite dialogue with diverse cultures and religious traditions, and to serve the cause of reconciliation and peace. The books published reflect the views of their authors and do not represent the official position of the Maryknoll Society. To learn more about Maryknoll and Orbis Books, please visit our website at www.maryknollsociety.org.

Douglas, Kelly Brown.
    Stand your ground : Black bodies and the justice of God / Kelly Brown Douglas.
        pages cm
    Includes index.
    ISBN 978-1-62698-109-6 (pbk.)
    1. Racism—United States. 2. Racism—Religious aspects—Christianity—History. 3. African Americans—Social conditions. 4. United States—Race relations. I. Title.
    E185.615.D664   2015
    305.800973—dc23
                                                        2014041240

I write this book for my son,
Desmond

Contents

PART TWO

Prologue

The date was February 26, 2012. It was a Sunday evening in Sanford, Florida. It was a rainy evening. Seventeen-year-old Trayvon Benjamin Martin, who lived in Miami Gardens, Florida, with his mother, was visiting his father. Trayvon was walking back to his Sanford residence from a store, where he had just purchased a can of ice tea and a pack of Skittles candy. Trayvon was wearing a hoodie. A neighborhood "watch captain" spotted Trayvon. He called 911 to report a "suspicious" person in the gated neighborhood. The 911 operator advised the caller to remain in his car, not to follow the person, and police would be there. The "watch captain" did not follow instructions. Armed with a gun, he left his car. Shortly thereafter, shots were fired, and Trayvon was left dead on the Florida sidewalk. Trayvon was African American. The "watch captain" was not. Trayvon possessed ice tea and Skittles. The "watch captain" possessed a gun. Trayvon's body was taken to a morgue. The "watch captain" was freed to go home. The next day, Tracy Martin identified his son's lifeless body from a photo. The "watch captain" was not charged with a crime. The killer was seemingly protected under Florida's Stand Your Ground law. Almost two months later, after black communities across the country launched protest rallies calling for the arrest of the "watch captain"; he was finally arrested and charged. However, he claimed he killed Trayvon in self-defense.

A year and a half later, on Saturday night, July 13, 2013, a six-woman jury found Trayvon's killer not guilty. They acquitted him of both second-degree murder and second-degree manslaughter. He was a free man. The only person seemingly responsible for Trayvon's slaying was Trayvon himself.

The story of Trayvon Martin was an all-too-familiar story in the black community. It was eerily reminiscent of the 1955 lynching of fourteen-year-old Emmitt Till, which also garnered national media attention. Emmitt was brutally murdered for allegedly "flirting" with a white woman in a convenience store. Like Trayvon's killer, Emmitt's killers were found not guilty. The only person held responsible for Emmitt's death was Emmitt. And so it was that the story of Trayvon would go down in history as that of another young black male killed for no other reason than the fact of his blackness being perceived as "threatening," with his killer getting away with it.

The story of Trayvon was the catalyst for this book. But since then, there have been many other stories like Trayvon's—stories of unarmed black teenagers killed because they were perceived as a threat.

On November 23, 2012, seventeen-year-old Jordan Russell Davis was shot and killed at a Jacksonville, Florida, gas station after an exchange over loud music that was being played in the SUV in which he was a backseat passenger. Believing Jordan had a gun, the white male killer said he felt threatened. The killer, therefore, returned to his vehicle, retrieved a gun, and fired ten shots into Jordan's fleeing vehicle. Three of the shots hit Jordan. Jordan did not have gun. Neither did the other three black male teens in the SUV with Jordan. Jordan was killed. His killer left the scene of the crime. The killer was eventually charged and found guilty of attempted murder for firing at the other teens in the vehicle. The jury hung on the murder charge. Once again, it seemed as if Jordan was responsible for his own murder. A retrial for the murder was scheduled.

On September 14, 2013, an unarmed twenty-four-year-old Jonathan Ferrell was killed by a white police officer. Jonathan's slaying took place after he knocked on a door for help following a single car crash in which he was involved. Frightened, the homeowner called the police. After arriving, a white police officer fired twelve shots at Jonathan, ten of which struck him, causing his death. After an initial grand jury ruled not to indict the officer, a second grand jury indicted him on voluntary manslaughter charges.

Almost two months after Jonathan Ferrell's slaying, a similar fate would befall a nineteen-year-old black female. On the Saturday night of November 2, 2013, Renisha Marie McBride knocked on a door seeking help after a single car accident in which she was injured. The homeowner, a white male, perceived her to be a threat. He opened his door and, with shotgun in hand, killed Renisha. He pleaded self-defense. He was charged with second-degree manslaughter.

These incidents were becoming all too frequent. Why is it becoming increasingly acceptable to kill unarmed black children, I wondered? Why are they so easily perceived as a threat? How are we to keep our black children safe? As a mother of a black male child, I find these to be urgent questions. The slaying of Trayvon struck a nerve deep within me. After Jordan, then Jonathan, then Renisha I was practically unnerved. I knew that I had to seek answers. This book reflects my search for those answers.

Introduction

There has been no story in the news that has troubled me more than that of Trayvon Martin's slaying. President Obama said that if he had a son he would look like Trayvon. I do have a son, and he does look like Trayvon. Raising a black male child is not an easy matter in this society. As a parent, you encourage him to dream, to go for his dreams, and to believe in himself. At the same time, however, you have to make him aware of the society of which he is a part. This is a society in which black males are perceived as suspicious or dangerous. I was certainly aware of this from my son's earliest school days. Expectations were frequently lowered in terms of his academic abilities, while trouble was often anticipated. Whether the bias against black males is spoken or unspoken, conscious or unconscious, it is palpable. As President Obama observed in his July 19, 2013, press conference following the verdict in the trial of Trayvon's killer, there is virtually a visceral reaction to the black male presence—from locking car doors to clutching one's purse on an elevator.

Parents of black male children know that the world poses a much greater danger to our sons than they do to the world. We raise our black sons to be aware of their surroundings and to know how they are being perceived—whether they are shopping in a store, or walking down the street with a group of friends, or even wearing a hoodie over their heads. After hearing what happened to Trayvon as he was walking home from a store wearing a hoodie and carrying Skittles and ice tea, I was once again reminded of what a dangerous world this is for our sons. And I thought about Trayvon's mother. She sent her son on a trip to visit family, only to have him fall victim to the unfounded fears and stereotypes grafted onto black male bodies. Something must be said, I thought, about what is happening to our black children, especially our sons. This book is my attempt to do that.

But there is more. The killing of Trayvon was followed on July 13, 2013, by the acquittal of his killer.

On the morning following the Saturday night verdict, black congregations across the United States were united by profound feelings of hurt, disbelief, anger, confusion, and fear. In my own congregation that Sunday morning, men were shaken and women cried. "How could they have let him completely off the hook?" people asked. "Is not a black boy's life worth anything?" "How are we supposed to protect our children?" As the reality of the verdict sank in, black church people wondered if there would ever be justice for Trayvon. They also wondered if the world would ever be a just place for their children. As they shared stories of how their own bodies had been disrespected, harassed, stopped and frisked, just because of their blackness, they questioned if black bodies could ever enjoy peace in our American society. Indeed, when the judge read the verdict, black Americans were once again confronted with the harsh reality that their lives were virtually unprotected, if not dispensable. The Trayvon Martin case was a jarring "reality check" of how far we still had to go in the struggle for racial justice in America.

At the same time, on that Sunday morning, black congregations wrestled with issues of faith. Just as members of my congregation wanted to know what would become of their children, they also wanted to know what God was saying. They asked, "What is the message from God that we are to hear in this midst of this injustice?" "What does it mean to be faithful in times such as these?" "What are we to hope for?" Even as they affirmed their faith in a God that had brought them "a mighty long way," on that particular Sunday morning black church people contemplated the meaning of their faith in this time of "stand your ground." Black churchwomen and men recognized that in such a time, God has to be saying something. They yearned to know, however, what precisely this might be. And so this book also attempts to address such questions of faith concerning the justice of God.

Fifty years ago, in response to President Kennedy's assassination, Martin Luther King Jr. wrote: "Our nation should do a great deal of soul-searching. . . ." He went on to say, "While the question 'Who killed President Kennedy?' is important, the question 'What killed him?' is more important." King's words are instructive as we respond to this current crisis. Our responses must go far beyond a concern for convicting Trayvon's killer. If, indeed, there is to be "justice for Trayvon," we must examine "what killed him." While the answer to this question certainly involves the Stand Your Ground law, which was a backdrop to the Trayvon Martin case, it goes beyond this law.

The Stand Your Ground law is an extension of English Common Law that gives a person the right to protect his or her "castle." Stand Your Ground law essentially broadens the notion of castle to include one's body. It permits certain individuals to protect their embodied castle whenever and wherever they feel threatened. Essentially, a person's body is his or her castle. In this regard, a person does not have to retreat from the place in which he or she is "castled"; they can stand their ground. While this law was initially invoked as a reason for Trayvon's slaying, it was not used as a formal defense. Nevertheless, Stand Your Ground law signals a social-cultural climate that makes the destruction and death of black bodies inevitable and even permissible. It is this very climate that also sustains the Prison Industrial Complex, which thrives on black male bodies. Most disturbing, this stand-your-ground climate seems only to have intensified as it continues to take young black lives such as those of Renisha McBride, Jonathan Ferrell, and Jordan Davis. The repeated slaying of innocent black bodies makes it clear that there is an urgent need for soul searching within this nation.

This book will explore the social-cultural narratives that have given birth to our stand-your-ground culture and the religious canopies that have legitimated it. This stand-your-ground culture has produced and sustained slavery, Black Codes, Jim Crow, lynching, and other forms of racialized violence against black bodies. This book is an attempt to untangle the web of social, cultural, and theological discourse that contributes to stand-your-ground culture as well as to provide a theological response to the ideological assumptions that undergird this culture.

This book is divided into two parts. Part I examines the stand-your-ground culture that took Trayvon's life. This part explores the origins of this deadly culture and the social-cultural and religious narratives that foster it. These narratives have surfaced during the current stand-your-ground crisis. The underlying assumption of Part I is that what happened to Trayvon is about more than what took place one evening on a Florida sidewalk. Trayvon's slaying has its roots in the backwoods of ancient Germany and was set in motion with the founding of this nation.

Chapter 1 addresses America's grand narrative of exceptionalism. This chapter explores the way in which the Anglo-Saxon myth has shaped this narrative and the way in which this narrative provides the essential foundation for a stand-your-ground culture. In the end, this chapter explores the various ideologies spawned by American exceptionalism that have led to the "hypervaluation" of whiteness and the denigration of blackness. This chapter also explores the theological implication of these narratives, namely, God's presumed "preferential option" for Anglo-Saxon exceptionalism.

Chapter 2 explores the construction of the black body as perpetually guilty chattel. This chapter identifies a natural-law theo-ideology that provides religious legitimation for this construction. The underlying assumption is that the black body as chattel is the foundation upon which all other racially stereotypic perceptions of the black body are grafted. In the end, the chapter shows how the suspicious pursuit of Trayvon was a result of the black body being constructed as guilty chattel.

Chapter 3 examines the relationship between the narrative of Manifest Destiny and stand-your-ground culture. This chapter argues that America's sense of Manifest Destiny has resulted in the declaration of a "just war" on black bodies. The various manifestations of this war, such as Black Codes, Jim Crow, lynching, and the war on drugs, will be examined. In the end, this chapter argues that a deadly stand-your-ground culture is practically inevitable when it comes to the black body.

Part II of this book addresses the meaning of God for these stand-your-ground times. It seeks to understand the message of black faith in the wake of the deaths of Trayvon, Jordan, Renisha, and Jonathan. In doing so, it further explores the theological and faith concerns raised in Part I. In the end, this part will show the strength of the black faith tradition and suggests where God is and what God is saying in a stand-your-ground war.

Chapter 4 addresses the strength of black faith and the freedom of God. This chapter explores the theological narratives that have provided the fundamental understanding of God within the black faith tradition. It revisits black faith understandings of the Exodus tradition. It pays particular attention to black faith as it emerged during slavery and was informed by the African faith tradition. In the end, this chapter explores the paradox of maintaining black faith in the midst of a stand-your-ground-culture war.

Chapter 5 explores the theological and faith dynamics between Jesus and Trayvon. Through an examination of the cross and resurrection, it specifically addresses the justice of God. In the end, this chapter answers the question, "Where was God when Trayvon was slain?"

Chapter 6 explores black prophetic testimony and the time of God. With Martin Luther King's "I Have a Dream" speech as the backdrop, this chapter revisits America's narrative of exceptionalism and the black faith tradition to discern the message of God to us in this stand-your-ground time. In the end it recognizes this time of crisis in the black community as a *kairos* moment.

Throughout this book, I highlight a mother's perspective, and I conclude with an epilogue that reviews the stand-your-ground cases discussed throughout this book with reference to the Michael Brown case, with appreciation for the paradox of a mother's grief and hope.

In the end, I do not attempt to resolve the many issues of stand-your-ground culture. This book is an invitation to engage in the hard soul searching needed if our country is ever to become a safer place for our black sons and daughters, and if we are to end the stand-your-ground-culture war on the Trayvons, Jordans, Renishas, and Jonathans of our world.

PART ONE

1

America's Exceptionalism

"If Trayvon was of age and armed, could he have stood his ground on that sidewalk?" This is the question that President Barack Obama asked during a July 19, 2013, press conference in which he tried to help the nation understand the black community's response to Trayvon Martin's killer being found not guilty. For black people it was a rhetorical question. They had asked and answered it well before President Obama posed it. It was a topic of conversation within black households, barbershops, beauty parlors, and churches not long after the circumstances of Trayvon's murder came to light. While black women and men may not have known the details of the Stand Your Ground law that provided the rhetorical backdrop for Trayvon's slaying, within their historical consciousness they understood the reason for it. The black community instinctively knew this law was concerned with defending and protecting property—and not just any property. It was meant to safeguard America's most cherished property—the property at the very heart of American identity and America's sense of self. This law concerns the property that keeps America "exceptional."

In the end, the details of Stand Your Ground law do not matter. It is not significant that this law was not used in the legal defense for Trayvon's killer. What happened to Trayvon Martin on his way home from the store that deadly evening was not about a law. Rather, it was about cherished property and the culture that was forged to preserve that property. Whether or not Trayvon "could have stood his ground on that sidewalk" rested upon his right to possess such property. This is considered a "divine right." Yet, it is a right not established in a

3

church or even in a courtroom. It was established somewhere in the woods of ancient Germany.

This chapter, like this book, is not about the Stand Your Ground law. Rather it is about the culture that produced the law. The underlying assumption of this book is that the seeds for Stand Your Ground law were planted well before the founding of America. These seeds produced a myth of racial superiority that both determined America's founding and defined its identity. This myth then gave way to America's grand narrative of exceptionalism. This narrative, replete with its own sacred canopy, in turn constructed cherished property and generated a culture to shelter that property, thus insuring that America remain "exceptional." I identify this culture as "stand-your-ground culture." This culture is itself generative. It has spawned various social-cultural devices—legal and extralegal, theoretical and ideological, political and theological—to preserve America's primordial exceptional identity.

What happened to Trayvon Martin on February 26, 2012, is a result of America's narrative of exceptionalism. In order to answer whether or not Trayvon had the right to stand his ground, one must understand the complex meaning of this narrative. It is through understanding this that the significance of a stand-your-ground culture becomes clear. This chapter attempts to discern the meaning of America's exceptionalism by tracing the process through which it was established. In the space of a chapter, it is impossible to explore all the aspects of that process and thus the many implications of America's exceptionalism. This chapter does not pretend to do so. The purpose of this chapter is to answer the question of how we got here to this stand-your-ground moment, so to answer the question of Trayvon's rights. The answer to both questions begins with the words of an ancient Roman historian.

The Making of the Anglo-Saxon Myth

Tacitus's Germania

In 98 C.E. the Roman historian Tacitus published *Germania*, which has been called "one of the most dangerous books ever written."[1] Perhaps it is. The danger is not so much in what Tacitus said, but in how

---

1. Quote from Christopher B. Krebs, *A Most Dangerous Book: Tacitus's*

his words have been construed. In the brief space of thirty pages, he offered an ethnological perspective that would have tragic consequences for centuries to come. This perspective played a significant role in the Nazi's monstrous program for "racial purity." It is the racial specter behind the stand-your-ground culture that robbed Trayvon of his life.

In *Germania* Tacitus provides a meticulous portrait, based on others' writings and observations, of the Germanic tribes who fended off Rome's first-century empire-building agenda. He identifies the tribes as an "aboriginal" people "free from all taint of intermarriages."[2] They are, he says, "a distinct unmixed race, like none but themselves," with "fierce blue eyes, red hair, huge frames."[3] Tacitus commended these Germans for their bravery and strong moral character. "No one in Germany," he explained, "laughs at vice." He went on to say that for these Germans "good [moral] habits" were more effectual than "good laws."[4] Perhaps what is most significant, at least in garnering the attention of political architects for centuries to come, is that Tacitus portrayed these ancient Germans as possessing a peculiar respect for individual rights and an almost "instinctive love for freedom."[5] This was evident, he said, by the way in which they governed themselves. According to Tacitus, within the various tribes "the whole tribe" deliberated upon all important matters, and most final "decision[s] rest with the people."[6] Tacitus seemed to be describing a community that encouraged the participation of its members (at least the male members) in governance and criminal procedures. According to many later interpreters, Tacitus was describing the perfect form of government. This was one that respected "common law," trial by jury, and individual liberties. Tacitus's description of these tribal governing systems influenced the nature of various Western systems of

Germania from the Roman Empire to the Third Reich (New York: W. W. Norton & Company, 2012), 16.

2. Tacitus, *Germania*, Medieval Sourcebook, http://www.fordham.edu/halsall/source/tacitus1.html.

3. Tacitus, *Germania*.

4. Tacitus, *Germania*.

5. Reginald Horsman, *Race and Manifest Destiny: The Origins of American Racial Anglo-Saxonism* (Cambridge, MA: Harvard University Press, 1981), 26.

6. Tacitus, *Germania*.

government throughout history. As we will see, it played no small role in America's form of democracy. But this was not the only way in which the *Germania* influenced the shape of various Western societies. Along with playing a role in determining systems of governance, it laid the foundation for the subjugation, if not elimination, of certain peoples: those people who were not members of the "unmixed race" that Tacitus described.

Even though the precise ethnic make-up of these Germanic tribes was not certain, they are considered the progenitors of the Anglo-Saxon race. Tacitus's ethnological description spawned the construction of the Anglo-Saxon myth. This myth has been a ubiquitous, even if unspoken, ideology in the modern world. Initially, this myth highlighted Anglo-Saxon forms of governing. Building on Tacitus's admiration for the way these Germanic tribes ruled their communities, the myth stressed the unique superiority of Anglo-Saxon religious and political institutions. Eventually, and perhaps inevitably, the myth shifted its focus to Anglo-Saxon blood. In so doing, it seized upon Tacitus's characterization of the ancient Germans as "free from taint," and it suggested that the superiority of their institutions was a result of their blood. It argued that strong moral qualities and a high regard for freedom flowed uniquely through Anglo-Saxon veins. In due course, the superiority and purity of blood became the focus of the Anglo-Saxon myth. The way in which this myth became transformed is as important to the meaning of America's exceptionalism and its production of a stand-your-ground culture as the myth itself. In order, therefore, to appreciate the complex impact of this myth on America's social-cultural consciousness, we must first understand how it came to America and later spawned America's grand narrative. To do this, we must begin in England.[7]

An Anglo-Saxon Identity

This myth, replete with reverence for Tacitus, arrived in America by way of England's post-Reformation struggles. The English

---

7. In interpreting the impact of the Anglo-Saxon myth on American identity, I am indebted to the analysis of Reginald Horsman, *Race and Manifest Destiny: The Origins of American Racial Anglo-Saxonism* (Cambridge, MA: Harvard University Press, 1981).

fascination and overt identification with Tacitus's Germans began in the aftermath of the sixteenth-century Reformation. In an effort to establish the antiquity of the Church of England and to justify the 1559 Elizabethan Settlement, Archbishop Matthew Parker encouraged research into the culture, history, and politics of Anglo-Saxons. This research continued for at least two centuries. If the Elizabethan Settlement was concerned with finding an acceptable "middle way" between Roman Catholicism and Protestantism, then Anglo-Saxonist studies were concerned with substantiating the connection of the English Church and government with the governing practices of ancient Germans.

The English considered themselves the descendants of the Germanic tribes identified by Tacitus. They believed that these tribes were their Anglo-Saxon ancestors. They, therefore, traced their systems of governance back to the ancient German woods. Even non-English scholars recognized this connection. In *The Spirit of the Laws* (1748), a book popular in both England and colonial America, French nobleman Montesquieu wrote, "In perusing the admirable treatise of Tacitus *On the Manners of the Germans* we find it is from that nation the English have borrowed the idea of their political government. This beautiful system was invented first in the woods."[8] Fueled with this understanding of their ancestral lineage, the early English reformers were intent on restoring English church and society to their free Anglo-Saxon past.

Notwithstanding the fact that some of Tacitus's ancient tribes were probably of Norse heritage, these reformers generally agreed that corruptions entered into English church and society with the Norman conquest in 1066. Popular belief held that the Normans adulterated the very English laws and institutions that served to protect individual liberties. Thus, the English Reformation was about more than just a struggle between King Henry VIII and the Roman papacy. It was concerned with cleansing English church and society of Norman contaminations and restoring both to their true Anglo-Saxon ways. The road to restoration was not, however, without contention.

---

8. Charles de Secondat, Baron de Montesquieu, *Complete Works,* vol. 1. *The Spirit of the Laws,* 1748, Online Library of Liberty, http://oll.libertyfund.org/titles/837. Original Source: Charles de Secondat, "Of the Constitution of England," bk. XI, chap. VI, in Charles de Secondat, Baron de Montesquieu, *The Complete Works of M. de Montesquieu,* 4 vols. (London: T. Evans, 1777), I, paragraph 212.

There were reformers who believed that the church and government was not sufficiently cleansed of Norman taint. The reformers who would have the greatest impact on America's religious
and political culture, and thus transport the Anglo-Saxon myth to
America, were the Pilgrims, Puritans, and even radical Whigs, such
as the Levelers. Both the Pilgrims and Puritans thought the Church
of England did not go far enough in the eradication of Catholic and
Norman abuses. The Pilgrims, the more radical of the two groups,
severed their ties with the church, while the Puritans remained an
agitating force within it. Given the fact that the king of England was
head of both church and state, to rebel against the church was also to
rebel against the state. This, of course, would have consequences for
America. Both groups fled England and made their exodus across
the Atlantic.

The Levelers, a prominent group of protestors during the English
Civil War (1642–1648), were more directly focused on state matters.
They believed that radical reform was needed in the English system of
governance, more radical than what they had seen. They were guided
by the principle that all people possessed natural rights, especially the
right to be free. They also insisted that the government not place limits on this freedom—unless such limits were necessary to protect the
freedom of another. At issue were common law, trial by jury, and the
overall relationship between the Parliament and the Crown. Leveler
political ideology influenced American political sensibilities.

The Anglo-Saxon myth came to America through these radical
English reformers. In transporting this myth across the Atlantic they
actually imported the cornerstone for stand-your-ground culture.
This myth was the essential piece in the construction of America's
exceptional identity. The religious reformers were the ones who guar-
anteed this myth a decisive role in defining that identity.

An Anglo-Saxon Remnant

The Pilgrims and Puritans fled from the Church of England to build a
religious institution more befitting Anglo-Saxon virtue and freedom.
They considered themselves the Anglo-Saxon remnant that was continuing a divine mission. They traced this mission beyond the woods
of Germany to the Bible. Thus, they saw themselves "as the Israelites

in God's master plan."[9] Upon arriving at Plymouth, Massachusetts, in 1620, the Pilgrims drafted the Mayflower Compact. This compact clarified that their "undertaking" to "plant a colony" was for the "glory of God." The Pilgrims' radical separatist ways led to their demise as a distinct and identifiable group. The Puritans, on the other hand, had a more enduring and pervasive impact on American religious and political culture.

Arriving ten years after the Pilgrims, the Puritans understood their mission to be like that of their radical predecessors, except they were not separatists, and they arrived with a royal charter. No one better expressed the views of the Puritans than Reverend Francis Higginson. During a farewell addresses to the people of London he reportedly said, "We do not go to New England as separatists from the Church of England; though we cannot but separate from the corruptions in it: but we go to practise the positive part of church reformation and propagate the gospel in America."[10] Echoing these same themes Puritan leader John Winthrop crafted "A Model of Christian Charity" while still aboard the *Arabella*. In it he declared, "We must consider that we shall be as a city upon a hill. The eyes of all people are upon us, so that if we shall deal falsely with our God in this work we have undertaken, and so cause Him to withdraw His present help from us, we shall be made a story and a byword through the world."[11] These words gave birth to two legitimating canopies for American identity, one civil and one Christian. The wider theological implications of these canopies will be discussed throughout this chapter. The important point for now, however, is to recognize that these reformers' exodus from England was first and foremost a religious mission. They were fleeing the Church of England because of its perceived corruption, notably its Roman Catholic tendencies. A part of their mission, therefore, was not simply to build a nation that was in keeping with their Anglo-Saxon political heritage, but also to build a religious nation.

---

9. Martin E. Marty, *Pilgrims in Their Own Land: 500 Years of Religion in America* (New York: Penguin Books, 1984), 59.

10. Thomas Wentworth Higginson, *Life of Francis Higginson: First Minister in the Massachusetts Bay Colony, and Author of "New England's Plantation" (1630)* (New York: Dodd, Mead and Co., 1891), 29.

11. Governor John Winthrop, "A Model of Christian Charity," *Collections of the Massachusetts Historical Society* (Boston, 1828), 3rd series 7:31-48.

In fact, for them, building an Anglo-Saxon nation was virtually synonymous with building a religious nation. And, according to one of these legitimating canopies, it meant building a Protestant Christian nation. In general, the Pilgrims and the Puritans not only insured that the Anglo-Saxon myth was the defining piece of American identity, but they provided this myth with religious legitimation. They gave it sacred authority. The importance of this becomes apparent as America's grand narrative is enacted.

These first Americans, Pilgrims and Puritans alike, believed that a straight line could be drawn from the "freedom loving Anglo-Saxons" in the woods of ancient Germany to them. They carried their Anglo-Saxon heritage across the Atlantic Ocean with a self-righteous pride. Believing that they were the true and chosen heirs to a divine Anglo-Saxon mission, they were determined not to betray their Anglo-Saxon roots, as they thought the English had done. This determination initially expressed itself as a resolve to establish the Anglo-Saxon forms of governance that cherished freedom and individual rights. From its earliest beginning, therefore, America's political identity was an Anglo-Saxon identity. Its sense of democracy and freedom was inextricably linked to the Anglo-Saxon myth and Tacitus's Germans. America's democracy was conceived of as an expression of Anglo-Saxon character.

In his book *The Racial Contract,* Charles Mills argues that America's democracy is qualified by an unspoken subaltern contract that is defined by race.[12] He essentially argues that the liberty America promises to its citizens is intended only for its white citizens. Mills's observations are perhaps apt. However, what will become clear, particularly as the narrative of America's exceptionalism is established, is that the racial limitations of America's democracy are not the result of a subaltern contract. Rather, they result from the palpable Anglo-Saxon chauvinism that defined America's beginnings.

The "city on the hill" that the early Americans were building was nothing less than a testament to Anglo-Saxon chauvinism. This chauvinism would be consequential for non–Anglo-Saxons in America centuries later, as Mills suggests. It ushered forth America's grand nar-

---

12. Charles Mills, *The Racial Contract* (Ithaca, NY: Cornell University Press, 1997).

rative. That it would be a defining force in determining America's identity was practically assured, given the ethnocentrism of the founding
fathers. There was no one who evinced Anglo-Saxon chauvinism more
than the "Father of America's Democracy," Thomas Jefferson.

The Making of America's Grand Narrative

Anglo-Saxon Chauvinism

"Tacitus I consider as the first writer in the world without exception,"
wrote Jefferson to his granddaughter Anne.[13] Jefferson's reverence for
Tacitus is befitting for one as admiring of Anglo-Saxons as Jefferson.
Jefferson was a thoroughgoing and unabashed Anglo-Saxonist, to
the point of studying Anglo-Saxon language and grammar. Though
he referred to this study as "a hobby," it was really much more than
that.[14] In "An Essay on the Anglo-Saxon Language," he wrote, "The pure
Anglo-Saxon [language] constitutes . . . the basis of our language. . . .
Hence the necessity of making the Anglo-Saxon a regular branch of
academic education."[15] In an attempt to do just that, Jefferson produced
a grammar to make this language available to students. In a "Report
of the Commissioners for the University of Virginia" he proposed the
Anglo-Saxon language as one of "the branches of learning . . . [that]
should be taught in the University." He argued, "Anglo Saxon is of peculiar value" because it is "the first link in the chain of . . . our language
through all its successive changes to the present day."[16] Jefferson's focus
on language foreshadows the place that language will have in the formation of stand-your-ground culture. As for Jefferson, his fascination
perhaps renders him particularly vulnerable to a belief in the supremacy of Anglo-Saxon peoples. We will explore this connection later.

---

13. Thomas Jefferson, "From Thomas Jefferson to Anne Cary Randolph
Bankhead," December 8, 1808, http://www.founders.archives.gov.

14. Thomas Jefferson, "Letter to the Honorable J. Evelyn Denison,
M.P.," Monticello, November 9, 1825, American History from Revolution to
Reconstruction and Beyond, http://www.let.rug.nl/usa.

15. Thomas Jefferson, "An Essay on the Anglo-Saxon Language," in *The Life
and Selected Writings of Thomas Jefferson,* ed. Adrienne Koch and William Peden
(New York: Random House, 1998), 158.

16. Thomas Jefferson, "Report of the Commissioners for the University of
Virginia, August 4, 1818," http://www.vindicatingthefounders.com.

What are clear are Jefferson's Anglo-Saxon chauvinism and his strong conviction concerning the superiority of Anglo-Saxon institutions.

Echoing the attitudes of Saxonist scholars a century before him, Jefferson avowed that the "rightful root" of the English constitution was "the Anglo-Saxon." He also shared in the opinion that the English constitution "was violated and set at naught by Norman farce."[17] Jefferson went so far as to associate the Whigs with Anglo-Saxons and the Tories with the Normans.[18] Jefferson was, therefore, resolute in his thinking that Americans were obligated to establish a form of government commensurate with their Anglo-Saxon political past. In his mind, to do anything less would not only betray their heritage, but also lead to an inferior form of governing. He conveyed this sentiment in a discussion he had with a friend concerning the right of individuals to own property. Jefferson writes, "Has not every restitution of the ancient Saxon laws had happy effects? Is it not better now that we return at once into that happy system of our ancestors, the wisest & most perfect ever yet devised by the wit of man. . . ."[19] It is worth noting that associating the right to own property with an Anglo-Saxon heritage portends the nature of America's cherished property. It is interesting to note that what will be two of the pivotal aspects of a stand-your-ground culture are critical to Jefferson's political philosophy. What this again suggests is the inevitable emergence of this culture in America, given the ideological biases of its preeminent founding father.

Sacred Canopies of Legitimation

Jefferson justified his high regard for Anglo-Saxon systems of government with another fundamental element of America's identity. He believed, like his Pilgrim and Puritan forebears, that Americans were chosen by God to implement an Anglo-Saxon system of governing.

---

17. Thomas Jefferson, "Letter to Major John Cartwright, Monticello, June 5, 1824," American History from Revolution to Reconstruction and Beyond, http://www.let.rug.nl/usa.

18. Ibid.

19. Thomas Jefferson, "Letter to Edmund Pendleton, Philadelphia, August 13, 1776," American History from Revolution to Reconstruction and Beyond, http://www.let.rug.nl/usa.

He too considered Americans the New Israelites. The seal that he proposed for America symbolized his understanding of America's divine Anglo-Saxon heritage and mission. John Adams described it in a letter to his wife. He said, "Mr. Jefferson proposed. The Children of Israel in the Wilderness, led by a Cloud by day, and a Pillar of fire by night, and on the other Side Hengist and Horsa, the Saxon Chiefs, from whom We claim the Honour of being descended and whose Political Principles and Form of Government We have assumed."[20]

Jefferson was not the only founding father to believe that America had a divine purpose. Benjamin Franklin believed the same and also expressed this in his proposed seal. John Adams says of Franklin's suggestion, "Dr. F[ranklin] proposes a Device for a Seal. Moses lifting up his Wand, and dividing the Red Sea, and Pharaoh, in his Chariot overwhelmed with the Waters.—This Motto. Rebellion to Tyrants is Obedience to God."[21]

While Jefferson's and Franklin's beliefs that America was the New Israel and Americans the New Israelites reflected the religious narrative introduced by the Pilgrims and Puritans, they did so in a nonsectarian way. For Jefferson and Franklin, this religious narrative was not about Christianity. It was about the sacred nature of Anglo-Saxonism. It would become known as American civil religion.[22] If Jefferson's and Franklin's expressions of America's religious canopy were sectarian, they were sectarian in terms of race, not religion. In many respects, Anglo-Saxonism was their religion. However, the Christian aspect of the Puritan and Pilgrims religious narrative would not be lost in the formation of America's identity. It was manifested through another canopy that the Puritans spawned. Like its parent canopy this one would also serve to legitimate the Anglo-Saxon myth. It, however, would bring race and Christianity together as defining pieces of America's identity and mission. It initially expressed itself as a way to explain the revival spirit that spread across New England known as the Great Awakening. This religious canopy is best identified as a

---

20. "Letter from John Adams to Abigail Adams, August 14, 1776," Massachusetts Historical Society, http://www.masshist.org.

21. Ibid.

22. See Robert Bellah, *The Broken Covenant: American Civil Religion in Time of Trial* (New York: Seabury Press, 1975; 2nd ed., Chicago: University of Chicago Press, 1992).

Protestant evangelical canopy. A leading Puritan revivalist, Jonathan Edwards, gave voice to this evangelical canopy.

Edwards was convinced that the "glorious work of God," which would culminate in the Second Coming of Christ, was destined to begin in America. Based on his interpretation of the prophecy of Isaiah, Edwards said, "It is signified that it shall begin in some very remote part of the world, with which other parts have no communication but navigation. . . . I cannot think that any thing else can be here intended but America." Edwards went on to say that "this new world is probably now discovered, that the new and most glorious state of God's church might commence there; that God might in it begin a new world in a spiritual respect, where he creates the new heavens and the new earth." According to Edwards, America was carrying forth the true church of God. He notes, "America was discovered about the time of the reformation," in which God was trying to rescue the world from the "depths of darkness and ruin" into which it had sunk. Yet, "in order to introduce a new and more excellent state of the church" where "the power of God might be more conspicuous," God had to start all over in a new world, America. "*America*, and especially in *New England*," Edwards argued, was the "forerunner of something vastly great" that God was doing with the world.[23]

While the canopies of civil religion and Protestant evangelicalism were different in terms of their sectarianism, they both functioned in the same way. They legitimated America's Anglo-Saxon mission; at the same time they gave sacred validity to the Anglo-Saxon myth. They connected both to God. Such legitimation would valorize America's sense of "Manifest Destiny." While Manifest Destiny will be explored more fully later, it is worth noting that it is another aspect of America's sense of self that flows from the Anglo-Saxon myth. As such, it will play a significant role in what happened to Trayvon on the Florida sidewalk. The point of the matter is, a myth that declares the "supra-status" of a group of people compels a sense of destiny that is bound to turn deadly.

---

23. Jonathan Edwards, "Some Thoughts concerning the Present Revival of Religion in New England, and the Way in Which It Ought to Be Acknowledged and Promoted. Humbly Offered to the Public, In a Treatise on the Subject," in *Works of Jonathan Edwards, Volume 1*, Christian Classics Ethereal Library, http://www.ccel.org.

America's Exceptionalism

What is becoming clear thus far on the road toward the emergence of a stand-your-ground culture is the formation of the narrative that will demand it. This is the grand narrative of American identity. It is fitting, therefore, that America's preeminent founding father, Thomas Jefferson, personified this narrative and that his proposed seal was emblematic of it. Born from the Anglo-Saxon myth, the grand narrative is the story of Anglo-Saxon exceptionalism. The narrative of Anglo-Saxon exceptionalism *is* America's exceptionalism. This grand narrative is responsible for the culture that has determined the history of particular peoples in America, notably black people. It is vital to America's identity if not existence.

American exceptionalism has long been debated.[24] The phrase has become a consistent part of America's twentieth- and twenty-first-century political discourse. However, its contemporary usage does not truly reflect the intricacies of its original meaning, at least as the first Americans as well as founding fathers shaped that meaning. Even though the precise phrase "American exceptionalism" likely did not enter into American discourse until the twentieth century, the culture of exceptionalism emerged with the dawning of America. While most contemporary understandings associate America's exceptionalism with its form of democratic governing and its mission to spread democratic principles across the world, to understand it as simply about politics and mission does not capture the racial or divine character of America's narrative of exceptionalism. To be sure, in America's earliest beginnings its sense of exceptionalism focused on the nature of its institutions, as we have seen. It must not be overlooked, however, that what made America's institutions exceptional was their Anglo-Saxon character. America's exceptional identity was grounded in the Anglo-Saxon myth. To reiterate, this myth stressed that it was Anglo-Saxon institutions that best respected individual rights and liberty. Inasmuch as America stayed true to its Anglo-Saxon character when forming its governing institutions, then it would maintain its excep-

---

24. For a more thorough discussion of the debate concerning American exceptionalism and its use in political discourse, see James W. Ceasar, "American Exceptionalism: Is It Real, Is It Good?: The Origins and Character of American Exceptionalism," http://www.polisci.wisc.edu/uploads/documents/ceasar.pdf.

tional identity. This exceptionalism was initially expressed as a chosen identity. With the formation of America's grand narrative, the two key pieces of America's sense of self come together: its Anglo-Saxon character and its "chosen" nature. Both of these things are fundamental to American identity. Both are defining factors in America's exceptionalism. Thus, America's grand narrative of exceptionalism is the narrative of America's identity. To be a chosen nation is to be an Anglo-Saxon nation. To be an Anglo-Saxon nation is to be a chosen nation. It is this constructed racial-religious synchronicity that makes America exceptional. And, it is this synchronicity that demands a stand-your-ground culture. To appreciate the inexorable reality of stand-your-ground culture, one must recognize that America's exceptionalism is deeply rooted in the Anglo-Saxon myth. Even if this myth initially had an institutional focus, its Anglo-Saxon qualifier was always its defining feature when it came to American identity. This fact becomes even clearer as the myth itself undergoes the inauspicious transformation from an institutional focus to a decidedly racial focus. To comprehend the tremendous impact this change had on America's collective consciousness and hence its continuing sense of exceptionalism, we will explore the catalysts for this transformation more carefully. This exploration will bring us even closer to understanding the determining factors in Trayvon's right to stand his ground on that sidewalk.

A Matter of Blood

In 1751 Benjamin Franklin wrote a short essay on demography that, similar to Tacitus's treatise, had influence far beyond its length. Franklin's observations concerning the significance of available labor and natural resources for population growth influenced theories on population nearly a century later.[25] As prescient as his demographic observations may have been, other remarks within that essay are more telling when it comes to America's exceptionalism and the stand-your-ground culture that it has spawned. Franklin's concern for population was not primarily about numbers. It was about the Anglo-Saxon myth. Franklin said this:

---

25. Thomas Malthus quoted Franklin in his 1802 "Essay on the Principle of Population."

Why should Pennsylvania, founded by the English, become a colony of Aliens, who will shortly be so numerous as to Germanize us instead of our Anglifying them, and will never adopt our language or customs, any more than they can acquire our complexion?

Which leads me to add one remark: That the number of *purely* [emphasis mine] white people in the world is proportionately very small. All Africa is black or tawny. Asia chiefly tawny. America (exclusive of the new comers) wholly so. And in Europe, the Spaniards, Italians, French, Russians and Swedes are generally of what we call a swarthy complexion; as are the Germans also, the Saxons only excepted, who with the English make the principal body of white people on the face of the earth. I could wish their numbers were increased. And while we are . . . scouring our planet, by clearing America of woods, and so making this side of our globe reflect a brighter light to the eyes of inhabitants in Mars or Venus, why should we in the sight of superior beings, darken its people? Why increase the sons of Africa, by planting them in America, where we have so far an opportunity, by excluding all black and tawneys, of increasing the lovely white and red?[26]

Franklin's comments presage what is to come as America tries to make good on its exceptional identity. They reflect a menacing shift in the Anglo-Saxon myth. Franklin makes clear that the purity of Anglo-Saxon institutions is not his chief concern. His overwhelming anxiety involves the purity of the nation. The people who inhabit the nation are the measure of its purity. Franklin therefore emphasizes the need to protect the language, customs, and complexion of "pure white people." Most telling in his remarks is the way in which he speaks about the Germans. There are for Franklin "superior beings" for whom an increase in population is desired. They were decidedly not the Germans, at least not those who were now streaming into America in droves. Franklin's regard for the Germans points to problems to come as the matter of blood becomes more central to America's sense

---

26. Benjamin Franklin, "Observations concerning the Increase of Mankind, Peopling of Countries, &c." (Tarrytown, NY: S. Kneeland, 1775), 223 (emphasis mine).

of exceptionalism. Again, Franklin's remarks reflect the fact that the matter of blood had already become the focus of the Anglo-Saxon myth.

This myth began to stress that the "secret of [Anglo] Saxon success lay not in the institutions but in the blood."[27] It was now not enough for a people to carry on Anglo-Saxon institutions. They had to also be carriers of Anglo-Saxon blood. In fact, the ability to build Anglo-Saxon institutions was a function of blood.

Perhaps this shift in focus to blood was inevitable. When so high a premium is placed on the institutions of a people, eventually the people themselves will be regarded as extraordinary. However, what no doubt hastened this shift was the coming together of two eighteenth- and nineteenth-century cultural occurrences: romanticism and philological studies. These cultural events helped to transform the Anglo-Saxon myth from one that projected an institutional chauvinism to one that promoted racial bigotry. In so doing, these two historical events also influenced the ways in which America's exceptionalism was enacted and subsequently the construction of America's cherished property. Characteristic features of each influenced the way America's grand narrative of exceptionalism was expressed in relation to certain peoples, thus, again, tilling the social-cultural soil for a stand-your-ground culture. It is for this reason that I will look at these two events more closely.

Two Pivotal Cultural Events

Romanticism cultivated a reverence for the individual. It eschewed the Enlightenment focus on universals for a focus on particularities. The romantic movement highlighted the differences, as opposed to the similarities, between peoples. It emphasized the unique qualities and spirit of nations and cultures. Romanticism fueled cultural and national chauvinism as it specified exceptional gifts and qualities of certain groups of people. The romantic movement thus fed into the Anglo-Saxon myth. It stoked the fires that were already burning and lauded the special qualities of the Anglo-Saxons first identified by Tacitus: qualities such as the love of liberty and high moral character. There is perhaps no better representative of the way in which roman-

---

27. Horsman, *Race and Manifest Destiny*, 24.

ticism and the Anglo-Saxon myth coalesced in American culture than Ralph Waldo Emerson.

Emerson was clearly well versed in the Anglo-Saxon myth, including its origins in Tacitus. His book *English Traits* includes several references to Tacitus. In this book he describes various branches of the Saxon race, with the primary attention given to the English. He does, however, make a special effort to reinforce the connection between Tacitus's Germans and Americans. He says that when reading Tacitus he "found abundant points of resemblance between the Germans of Hercynian forest, and our *Hoosiers, Suckers,* and *Badgers* of the American woods.[28] As for the Saxon race, Emerson credits it with having a "democratic principle."[29] He referred to the "moral peculiarity of the Saxon race" in an 1847 speech to the Manchester Athenaeum. He went on to describe Saxons as having a "commanding sense of right and wrong."[30] With his romantic emphasis on the specialness of peoples, Emerson wonders if the unique traits are in the blood. He asks, "Is this power due to their blood, or to some other cause? Men hear gladly," he says, "of the power of blood or race." While Emerson may not have been quite sure from whence the traits of particular peoples were derived, he was certain that those traits were distinctive enough to warrant a differentiation between races. Moreover, he was confident that the "oldest blood of the world" belonged to the Celts, one of the three sources from which all Saxon stocks derive.[31]

Emerson's discussion of the blood origins of racial traits reflected the ongoing interest in the origins of humankind that flourished simultaneously with the romantic movement. This search for human origins was the second cultural event that contributed to the transformation of the Anglo-Saxon myth. Before examining this search for humanity's origins, it is important to note another aspect of Emerson's romanticism.

Having once been a Unitarian minister, Emerson had theological concerns. In terms of his theology he is best described as a transcendentalist. Reflective of both his romantic and his transcendentalist

---

28. Ralph Waldo Emerson, *English Traits,* chapter IV, paragraph 6, http://www.bartleby.com.

29. Ibid., chapter V, paragraph 1.

30. "Speech at Manchester," in Emerson, *English Traits.*

31. Emerson, *English Traits,* chapter IV, paragraphs 4, 19.

beliefs he viewed humans as virtually a "divine reality." He placed great stock in the goodness of humankind and thought that humans possessed a certain "intuition" that allowed them, without a mediator, to connect with God. This intuition manifests itself as virtue/justice. Emerson said, "If a man is at heart just, then in so far is he God. . . ."[32] This almost complete identification between God and humans, while reflecting the romantic spirit, resonates with the American sense of chosenness and the sacred legitimation of its exceptional character. We will see later how it perhaps made Emerson vulnerable to notions of Anglo-superiority in such a way that it diminished the worth of other people. It is in this way that Emerson will exemplify how the American cultural ethos, shaped by romanticism and saturated with the Anglo-Saxon myth, again created the perfect soil for a stand-your-ground culture to thrive and grow.

Let us return to the second decisive event for transforming the Anglo-Saxon myth: the quest for human origins. This quest actually clarified how much of a difference blood made. It was aided by a similar search—the search for the roots of Anglo-Saxon languages, specifically German and English. This linguistic search flourished in the late eighteenth century with the appearance of the *Asiatic Research Journal*. Through this journal philological findings and theories were disseminated across Europe. Various philologists began to overtly associate language with race. They generally agreed that Anglo-Saxon languages emerged from an Indo-European family of languages that originated with a people from the Asian steppes. As German and British scholars developed this theory, they eventually constructed a myth "of a specific, gifted people—the Indo-Europeans—who spilled out from the mountains of central Asia to press westward following the sun," carrying with them their language.[33] Nineteenth-century French historian Jules Michelet explained their movement this way:

Trace the movements of humankind from east to west along the path of the sun and the magnetic currents of the globe, observe humankind on this long journey from Asia to Europe, from

32. Ralph Waldo Emerson, "Divinity School Address: Delivered at Harvard Divinity School before the Senior Class," July 15, 1838, Ralph Waldo Emerson Texts, http://www.emersoncentral.com/divaddr.htm.

33. Horsman, *Race and Manifest Destiny*, 33.

India to France. . . . At the point of departure, in India, in the cradle of all races and religions—*the womb of the world. . . .*[34]

A prevailing notion began to take hold that catapulted a change in the Anglo-Saxon myth, and subsequently created a new urgency in the enactment of America's exceptionalism. This notion suggested that an Urfolk, Indo-Europeans, emerged from the Asian steppes. These were the original people. An elite branch of these Urfolk came to be known as Caucasians. These Caucasians, following the sun as Michelet explained, migrated westward into Germany. These were Tacitus's Germans. The ancient Germans were considered the most gifted of the Caucasians. But Anglo-Saxons were the elite of the Germans.

As for language, these Urfolk gave birth to the Indo-European languages, one of which was Anglo-Saxon. Just as Anglo-Saxons were the elite descendants of the Indo-Europeans, Anglo-Saxon language was the superlative Indo-European language. The Anglo-Saxon language was the language of a gifted people, the people who eventually founded America.

The Sanctity of Blood

With the culmination of the searches for origins, the table was now set for the transformation of the Anglo-Saxon myth. Taking their cues from the romantics and the philologists, the stewards of the Anglo-Saxon myth were compelled to realize that the Anglo-Saxon capacity for morality and free institutions was not an accident. It was an innate capacity. It was in the blood. Morality and freedom flowed through Anglo-Saxon veins. The instinct for liberty was essentially genetic. It had been passed down through the generations, starting presumably with the Urfolk Indo-Europeans. To be Anglo-Saxon, then, was to be a moral and freedom-loving people. Morality and freedom literally belonged to them. It was in their blood as if it were a genetic marker. Language, thanks to philological studies, became an indication of one's stock. One's language indicated what branch of

---

34. Jules Michelet, *On History: Introduction to World History (1831); Opening Address at the Faculty of Letters, 9 January 1834 Preface to History of France (1869)* (Open Book Publishers, 2013), 26.

the Indo-Europeans one was from, that is, if one was merely Caucasian or Anglo-Saxon.

This emphasis on blood was not lost on America's founding fathers. It is behind both Jefferson's and Franklin's fixation on language. A marker of America's exceptionalism, therefore, was the language of the nation. For Jefferson this meant insuring that Americans were familiar with their mother tongue, thus keeping it alive in the nation. Franklin took this a step further. He was not so much concerned with keeping the mother tongue alive as he was concerned with making sure that English remain the predominate, if not only, language spoken in the country. Clearly for him, as well as for others, English was the modern equivalent to Anglo-Saxon. Again, the language of the nation indicated the "stock" of the nation, and it was America's stock that made it exceptional. To the degree that America's exceptionalism was defined by the Anglo-Saxon myth, and it was, then the "stock" of people that populated America mattered. America's divine exceptionalism was now a matter of blood, a matter of Anglo-Saxon blood. Benjamin Franklin understood this; thus, his attitude toward the Germans. Franklin's anti-German bigotry actually presaged, as suggested earlier, the way in which America would begin to exert its exceptionalism.

Language would become the indicator of the kind of blood flowing through a people's veins. The precedent was set for this through the search for human origins. In the final analysis, as language became associated with race in the quest for human origins, it took on new meaning for the stewards of Anglo-Saxon exceptionalism. Language was another necessary link toward forming a stand-your-ground culture. It was decisive in the construction of America's cherished property. It was with this construction that a stand-your-ground culture became real. Essentially, the construction of America's cherished property is America's exceptionalism, exerting itself with stand-your-ground culture acting as its shield. Let us dig deeper to see how this is the case, and how it all comes to a deadly head on a Florida sidewalk. Before we do this, however, let us review how we got here.

The Anglo-Saxon myth was a fundamental part of America's founding identity. This myth extolled the virtues of Anglo-Saxon institutions. This myth, along with America's sense of being chosen, produced America's grand narrative of exceptionalism. It is this defining narrative of exceptionalism, invested with sacred legitimation, that necessitates a stand-your-ground culture. With the decidedly racial turn, this narrative will exert itself in the construction of cherished property, the final piece in the puzzle for the formation of a fully formed stand-your-ground culture. It is to the construction of cherished property that we will now turn.

The Making of Cherished Property

The Underside of Romanticism

The romantic recognition of the peculiar traits of a people does not necessarily suggest the superiority or inferiority of that people in relation to others. However, as mentioned earlier, when inordinate recognition is given to the peculiar character and genius of a people, this can easily morph into arrogance and condescension, especially when that recognition comes in contact with ethnocentric perspectives, such as the Anglo-Saxon myth. This was what happened in America, thus providing the impetus for the construction of cherished property. Emerson exemplifies how easy it is for racial chauvinism to emerge when a romanticist spirit arises in a social-cultural context defined by racial exceptionalism.

Emerson's previously cited book, *English Traits,* epitomizes the troubling amalgam of romanticism and the Anglo-Saxon myth, and in so doing points toward America's cherished property. In this book, even though he acknowledges that the English are of "mixed origin," Emerson extolls them as "collectively a better race than any from which they are derived."[35] He goes so far as to call the English "the best stock in the world."[36] Earlier in his treatise he comments on other Anglo-Saxon branches of people. As he does so, he can't help but to comment on a race decidedly not Anglo-Saxon, the "Negro." No doubt influenced by the Anglo-Saxon myth, Emerson says, "Race in the negro is of appalling importance."[37] What is clear is that even though Emerson's romanticism led him to stress the inherent virtue of humans, he did not believe that all humans were equal. The qualifying

---

35. Emerson, *English Traits*, chapter IV, paragraph 11, 12.
36. Ibid., chapter VIII, paragraph 9.
37. Ibid., chapter IV, paragraph 6.

factor to his romanticist disposition seemed to be the insidious sway of the Anglo-Saxon myth. Thus, he placed a high premium on the race of a nation's people. "But it is in the deep traits of a race," Emerson said, "that the fortunes of nations are written. . . ."[38]

Fellow Unitarian preacher and romantic transcendentalist thinker Theodore Parker was even more direct in expressing his belief in the racial superiority of certain peoples. He thus provides another example of the lethal combination of romanticism and racial preferentialism.[39] He said, "The Caucasian differs from all other races: he is humane; he is civilized and progressive. . . . The Caucasian has often been master of other races—never their slave."[40] In a sermon in which he was sure to point out that Americans were Anglo-Saxon, he counted Anglo-Saxons (and Americans by implication) as "Caucasian's best." He went on to say, "No other nation had ever as fair a beginning as [America]." He argued that this was the case given the fact that "the Anglo-Saxon is a good hardy stock for national welfare to grow on. . . . Human nature had never anything so good," he continued, "for popular liberty to be grafted into."[41] In another sermon, even after recognizing America's many faults, Parker asserted, "The peculiar characteristics of the Anglo-Saxon appear now more prominent in the American than in the Britons."[42] As Emerson's and Parker's

---

38. Ibid., chapter VIII, paragraph 9.

39. It should be noted that Emerson and Parker were both romantics and transcendentalists. While Romanticism emerged early in the nineteenth century and transcendentalism later in the period, these movements overlapped. Moreover, the former was more a philosophical and literary movement, while the latter was a theological religious movement. Transcendentalism erupted as a protest in the Unitarian Church, in which Emerson and Parker were ordained members. Indeed, they came from the same congregation, though Parker came after Emerson. Emerson's transcendentalism was most manifest in his theology. Nevertheless, their perspectives were similar in their regard and emphasis on the individual.

40. Theodore Parker, quoted in Augustus C. L. Arnold and Edward Augustus Samuels, *The Living World: Containing Descriptions of the Several Races of Men and the Different Groups of Animals, Birds, Fishes, Insects*, I, xi.

41. Theodore Parker, "A Sermon of Dangers Which Threaten the Rights of Man in America," preached at the Music Hall on Sunday July 2, 1854, in *The Collected Works of Theodore Parker: Discourses of Slavery* (1864), II:110.

42. Theodore Parker, "The Nebraska Question: Some thoughts on the new

romanticism morphed into racial chauvinism, they show how easily the Anglo-Saxon myth, with its emphasis on Anglo-Saxon superiority, had become a part of the American ethos and thus accepted in a taken-for-granted fashion. They are both illustrative of the fact that America's grand narrative of Anglo-Saxon exceptionalism had become ingrained in the collective American psyche. They signal that it was a given that America's exceptionalism was all about the blood. Not even their romantic perspectives, which valued the unique qualities of people, could overcome it.

By the mid-eighteenth century various scientific productions all but declared the exceptionalism of Anglo-Saxon blood a scientific fact. As scientists developed systems to classify human beings, as well as to measure human skulls and facial features, they provided the scientific "data," specious as it was, for affirming Anglo-Saxon superiority, if not their necessary supremacy over other races of people. Needless to say, Anglo-Saxons were at the top or near the top of most of these questionable measures. It was the people with the least amount of Anglo-Saxon blood coursing through their veins that fell to the bottom, that is, black Americans. It would not, however, be science that provided the most compelling or even prominent legitimation of America's exceptionalism. It was religion.

The Underside of America's Sacred Canopies

It bears repeating that in the very beginning, Americans "made a liturgy out of their history."[43] As pointed out earlier, the first Pilgrim and Puritan Americans were certain that the American story was God's story. They were the progenitors of America's predominant sacred canopies. Both canopies, the civil and Christian, assumed that God was acting in and through American history to bring about God's vision for the world. This vision was effectively indistinguishable from the Anglo-Saxon/American vision for freedom and democracy.

---

assault upon freedom in American, and the general state of the country in relation thereunto," discourse preached at the Music Hall in Boston, on Monday, February 12, 1854, in *The Collected Works of Theodore Parker: Discourses of Slavery* (1864), I:245.

43. Martin E. Marty, *Righteous Empire: The Protestant Experience in America* (New York: Dial Press, 1970), 17.

America's religious canopies viewed the American story as if it were a historical divine incarnation. As the Anglo-Saxon myth became more about blood than institutions and the narrative of America's Anglo-Saxon exceptionalism really began to exert itself, the implicit underside of America's religious legitimation became apparent. This troubling underside was actually prefigured in the national seals that Jefferson and Franklin proposed.

Both seals featured the nation's people, not the nation's institutions. As these seals suggest, the divine and sacred character of the nation that determined its chosen status was found not in its institutions but in its people. Whether spoken or not (and it will soon be spoken) chosenness was always understood to be a matter of blood, that is, Anglo-Saxon blood. As shown earlier, it was the coming together of these two concepts that actually cemented America's narrative of exceptionalism. This narrative of racial-religious synchronicity suggested "a kind of mystical unity" between the Anglo-Saxon people and God.[44] Jefferson's seal in particular suggests as much with the Israelites on one side of it and Saxon chiefs on the other. The theological implication, and certainly one that no doubt lingered in the American consciousness, was that divinity was one of the special qualities of Anglo-Saxons. Indeed, their presumed instinct for morality and liberty could be seen as nothing less than proof of this. From this perspective, John Winthrop's "Model of Christian Charity" takes on even deeper meaning. For as he delineates the behavior and demeanor that he expects the Puritans to exhibit, it is as if he is admonishing them to follow their divine Anglo-Saxon instincts. A belief that Anglo-Saxons were gifted with a divine instinct was undoubtedly assumed by Theodore Parker, thus prompting him to assert that there was nothing better for human nature to graft liberty and virtue onto than Anglo-Saxons. From the perspective of transcendentalism, one might even suggest that the divine instinct about which Emerson spoke flows uniquely in Anglo-Saxon blood. Jonathan Edwards implies as much in a sermon in which he interprets the claim in the First Epistle of Peter that Christians are a peculiar people. He says, "True Christians are a distinct race of men. They are of a peculiar descent or pedigree, differ-

---

44. Marty, *Righteous Empire*, 16.

ent from the rest of the world."[45] Given his esteem for Anglo-Saxons, even as he speaks of this peculiar race as a people descended from God, especially New Englanders, one can presume that these people are in reality Anglo-Saxons. The fact of the matter is that in a nation saturated with the Anglo-Saxon myth and where national identity is intimately tied to the notion of Anglo-Saxon exceptionalism, what it means to be a chosen people is unavoidably and intricately related to Anglo-Saxon blood. In short, it is the blood that makes one chosen.

During the eighteenth and nineteenth centuries there were plenty of accounts of the Genesis creation myth in support of such an idea. These accounts virtually pronounced Anglo-Saxons as a "special" divine creation, distinct from other races of people, most notably darker races. With science and God on its side, Anglo-Saxon America could not go wrong. It was certainly an exceptional country. But, there was a dogged incongruity in the narrative of Anglo-Saxon exceptionalism. It is this incongruity that prompts the aggressive exertion of America's grand narrative and the subsequent construction of cherished property replete with the determination of stand-your-ground rights.

The Immigrant Paradox

Not everybody in America who looked like an Anglo-Saxon was actually Anglo-Saxon. There were even those who came from Europe that not only did not share Anglo-Saxon language and customs, but, like Franklin's "swarthy Germans," did not even share Anglo-Saxon complexion. America's exceptionalism faced an immigrant problem. This was a problem that was not going to go away. It is an inherent problem for America. It is the vexing paradox intrinsic to America's very identity as an Anglo-Saxon nation.

America is an Anglo-Saxon nation because it is an immigrant nation. Anglo-Saxons are not native to American soil. They immigrated to it from across the Atlantic. Those native to America are decidedly not Anglo-Saxon (about which more will be said in a later chapter). And so, America's quintessential Anglo-Saxon identity is fundamentally an immigrant identity. Nevertheless, the grand nar-

---

45. Jonathan Edwards, "Christians a Chosen Race, a Royal Priesthood, a Holy Nation, a Peculiar People," http://www.biblebb.com/files/edwards/chosen.htm.

rative of America's Anglo-Saxon exceptionalism prevailed over its immigrant character, thus creating a jingoistic immigration posture.

As immigrants from across Europe began to flood into America, the preferred immigrants, it is clear, were those from western and northern Europe. These would become known as the "old stock." All other European immigrants, those from eastern and southern Europe, were considered of "mixed blood." These would become known as the "new stock." This new stock began pouring into America in the nineteenth century. According to the 1790 census, 83.5 percent of the nation was of English stock, with only 5.6 percent German and 1.6 percent Irish. By 1850, 42.8 percent of the "foreign born" in America were from Ireland, 26 percent were from Germany, and only 13.7 percent were from England. These numbers were seen as cause for alarm to the nation's Anglo-Saxon exceptionalism. Most alarming of all were those "new stock" Americans, such as the Germans, who did not speak English.

While the ancient Germans were idolized in the American imagination, such was not the case with the modern Germans. These were not Tacitus's Germans. Their language and their complexion defied their ancient stock—at least in the eyes of Franklin and many who shared his view. Franklin's concern that his state of Pennsylvania would be so overwhelmed by "new stock" immigrants (for him that meant Germans) that it would cost Pennsylvania its Anglo-Saxon status would be voiced throughout history with regard to the nation as a whole.

President Theodore Roosevelt became so obsessed with the number of "new stock" immigrants compared to the low birthrate of "old stock" Anglo-Saxons that he feared "race suicide." His obsession was fed by theories that suggested "contact with inferior people somehow caused lower birth rates among the native born."[46] This was in fact the theory Francis Walker, the chief of the U.S. Bureau of Statistics at the time, put forth. The only way to avoid such a dire end, Roosevelt argued, was for Anglo-Saxons to have children, and lots of them. He said that the "man or woman who deliberately avoids marriage," and chooses not to have children, is a "criminal against the race, and

---

46. David R. Roediger, *Working toward Whiteness: How America's Immigrants Became White* (New York: Basic Books, 2005), 65.

should be an object of contemptuous abhorrence by all healthy people."[47] He echoed these same sentiments in a 1905 speech delivered before the Congress of Mothers. In that speech he said "the first and greatest duty of womanhood" is to have children "numerous enough so that the race shall increase and not decrease."[48] Roosevelt was even more unrelenting in an address he delivered before the National Congress when he said, "willful sterility is, from the standpoint of the nation, from the standpoint of the human race, the one sin for which the penalty is national death, race death; a sin for which there is no atonement. . . ."[49] Later, President Woodrow Wilson expressed a similar fear when he wrote that "our Saxon habits of government" are threatened by the "corruption of foreign blood."[50] Henry Cabot Lodge recognized the panic the immigrants were creating in an 1882 article. He wrote,

> The question of foreign immigration has of late engaged the most serious attention of the country, and in a constantly increasing degree. The race changes which have begun during the last decade among the immigrants to this country, the growth of the total immigration, and the effects of it upon . . . the quality of our citizenship, have excited much apprehension and aroused a very deep interest.[51]

The fear of "Germanizing," "race suicide," "willful sterility," and "corruption of foreign blood" are the fears that will give birth to a stand-your-ground culture as it emerges from America's narrative of

---

47. Theodore Roosevelt's 1902 letter to Marie Van Horst on "race suicide," http://www.progressingamerica.blogspot.com/2013/06/theodore-rooseelts-19.

48. Theodore Roosevelt, "On American Motherhood: A Speech Given on March 13, 1905 before the National Congress of Mothers," http://www.nationalcenter.org/TRooseveltMotherhood.html.

49. Theodore Roosevelt, "Sixth Annual Message, December 3, 1906," The American Presidency Project, http://www.presidency.ucsb.edu/ws/?pid=2947.

50. Wilson quoted in Roediger, *Working toward Whiteness*, 69.

51. Quoted in David B. Lee, "A Great Racial Commission: Religion and the Construction of White America," in *Race, Nation, and Religion in the Americas*, ed. Henry Goldschmidt and Elisabeth McAlister (New York: Oxford University Press, 2004), 101.

exceptionalism. Ironically, this narrative was first enforced in relation to European immigrants. Hence, it was in relation to the threat that they posed to America's exceptional identity that what might be considered a proto-stand-your-ground culture emerged.

Language and Blood Revisited

An initial proving ground for the budding stand-your-ground culture was an old nemesis, language. Both the language used against "corrupting" immigrants as well as the native language spoken by the immigrants would be a tool used in this incipient culture. As if to make clear the distinction between "old stock" and "new stock," the narrative of Anglo-Saxon exceptionalism generated an obscene pejorative lexicon for identifying particular new stock ethnic groups. Dago, greaser, hunkie, wop, cracker, and guinea were some of the terms invented. The point of this derogatory language was to remind these non-Anglo-Saxon immigrants of their place in American society. Maintaining place and space, both cultural and actual, are key reasons for the construction of a stand-your-ground culture. It is meant to keep the inferior other in his/her own place, while preserving the exceptionality of the Anglo-Saxon space. We will return to this later. For now, let us continue to examine how language contributed to the formation of this culture.

At the same time that language was used to derogate "new stock" immigrants, it remained a measure of Anglo-Saxon stock and, thus, a sign of America's exceptionalism. As earlier explained, language was associated with race during the quest for human origins. People who did not speak an Anglo-Saxon language were viewed as inferior. If America was not to be viewed as an inferior nation, English had to be the predominant spoken language. Short of making English the official language, though efforts to do so have been made throughout American history, pains were taken to make sure it was the prevailing language. The language of an Anglo-Saxon nation had to be English. The bottom line was non-English languages were not to be tolerated, at least not in public. It was therefore imperative that the "new stock" immigrants learn and speak English, a fact that is reminiscent of Jefferson's obsession to develop an Anglo-Saxon grammar and to introduce the study of Anglo Saxon into university curricula. The upside of this language requirement for the new immigrants, if an upside was to be found, was that speaking English became a way for them to assimilate into Anglo-Saxon culture, or at least not to stand out (an important matter for later discussion).

Anglo-Saxon linguistic intransigence seemed to pay off, at least according to Census Bureau statistics. For instance, in 1916, 76.8 percent of south-central-east European borns in U.S. households reported "non-English use in their childhood home." For those born between 1916 and 1930 that decreased to 70.2 percent; between 1931-1945, to 45.5 percent, and for those born between 1946 and 1960, to 24.9 percent.[52]

Legislative Solutions

Another device of the incipient stand-your-ground culture was quota systems. Quota systems have been fundamental to guaranteeing America's exceptionalism. They emerged not as a means to let more immigrants in but in order to keep them out. Driven by U.S. Census Bureau statistics, numerous laws were passed to limit the number of immigrants flooding in from southern and eastern Europe and from other non-Anglo-Saxon countries. In many respects, the Census provided the "scientific" data to support the Anglo-Saxon fear that took flight with rapid immigration. It legitimated a proto-stand-your-ground culture the same way that the scientific racism of the nineteenth century legitimated notions of Anglo-Saxon superiority. The watershed moment for addressing Anglo-Saxon fears came in 1924 with the passing of the Johnson-Reed Act.

In an article titled "Whose Country Is This?" President Calvin Coolidge provided a lengthy rationale for restrictive immigration laws.[53] He argued that even though America was an immigrant nation, it could not allow sentimentality to get in the way of it accepting the "right kind" of immigrant. He explained that it was in the nation's best interest "to require of all those aliens who come here that they have a background not inconsistent with American institutions."[54] By now we know, as Coolidge's readers surely knew, that "American"

---

52. See Roediger, *Working toward Whiteness*, 153-54.

53. President Coolidge signed the Johnson Reed Act into law on May 26, 1924.

54. Calvin Coolidge, "Whose Country Is This?" *Good Housekeeping* 71.2 (February 1921): 13.

meant Anglo-Saxon. Coolidge made this clear when he said, "Such a background might consist either of a racial tradition or national experience."[55] He went on to say that just as there was no room in the country for the importation of cheap goods, there was "no room either for cheap men." Thus, America was obliged "to maintain that citizenship at its best."[56] This meant, for Coolidge, erecting some kind of quota system. He substantiated his bigotry with science. He said, "Biological laws tell us that certain divergent people will not mix or blend. The Nordics propagate themselves successfully. With other races, the outcome shows deterioration on both sides. . . . Observance of ethnic law is as great a necessity to a nation as immigration law."[57] The argument put forth by President Coolidge reflected the long-standing fear that was sweeping across the country, one expressed by presidents before him. It was the fear that the Anglo-Saxon would be wiped out in America. *Saturday Evening Post* correspondent Kenneth Roberts expressed it succinctly when he said in a 1922 article, "If a few more million members of the Alpine, Mediterranean and Semitic races are poured among us, the result must inevitably be a hybrid race of people as worthless and futile as the good-for-nothing mongrels of Central America and Southeastern Europe."[58] It was this type of reasoning, and fear of the adulteration of America's exceptionalism, that led to the 1921 Emergency Quota Act. This Act states, "the number of aliens of any nationality who may be admitted under the immigration laws to the United States in any fiscal year shall be limited to 3 per centum of the number of foreign-born persons of such nationality resident in the United States as determined by the United States census of 1910."[59] As many perceived this law to be insufficient to stem the tide of "cheap men" and "good-for-nothing mongrels" entering the country, so the Johnson-Reed Act was enacted in 1924. This Act states, "The annual quota of any nationality shall be 2 per centum of

55. Ibid.

56. Ibid., 14.

57. Ibid.

58. Kenneth Lewis Roberts, *Why Europe Leaves Home: A True Account of the Reasons Which Cause Central Europeans to Overrun America* (Bobbs Merrill, 1922), 22.

59. 1921 Emergency Quota Act, Pub. L. No. 67-5, 42 Stat. 5 (1921).

the number of foreign-born individuals of such nationality resident in the continental United States as determined by the United States census of 1890, but the minimum quota of any nationality shall be 100."[60] This Act remained in effect until 1965.

The purpose of these laws was to make sure that "new stock" did not overwhelm the "old stock." They were legislative efforts to reify America's narrative of Anglo-Saxon exceptionalism. They were endeavors to make real America's Anglo-Saxon identity.

An Evangelical Solution

Another community would come to the defense of Anglo-Saxon exceptionalism, namely, the Protestant evangelical community. It is here that the sectarian canopy mentioned earlier reveals its underside. That the early evangelicals equated an Anglo-Saxon identity with a Protestant identity cannot be emphasized enough. It was this composite identity that assured them of America's chosen status. Because of this assumption, the Protestant evangelical community was just as alarmed at the flood of non–Anglo-Saxon Europeans into the country as the secular community, if not more so. Most troubling was the fact that many of these new immigrants were Catholic, the very church that precipitated the Pilgrims and Puritans to flee the Church of England. The Protestant evangelical community thus declared its own plan for protecting America's sacred Anglo-Saxon exceptionalist identity. Convert them. They may not have been able to change their blood, but they could Christianize them. The editor of a monthly journal made this plain in an 1880 editorial when he wrote, "Only let these strangers be brought under the power of the Gospel and we may safely trust them with our civilization."[61] In 1844 church historian Robert Baird put the matter this way: "In a word, our national character is that of the Anglo-Saxon race," and he said, "essentially Germanic or Teutonic [are] the chief supports of the ideas and institutions of evangelical Christianity."[62]

---

60. 1924 Immigration Act, Pub. L. No. 68-139, 43 Stat. 153, 159 (1924).

61. Quoted in David B. Lee, "A Great Racial Commission: Religion and the Construction of White America," in *Race, Nation, and Religion*, 101.

62. Quoted in Marty, *Righteous Empire*, 23.

What was becoming clear during the eighteenth and nineteenth centuries was that inasmuch as evangelical Protestants were spreading their brand of Christianity, they believed themselves to be also spreading Anglo-Saxonism. Their mission was as much an Anglo-Saxon mission as it was a Christian mission. Converting "foreigners" to Christianity, therefore, was the way to protect the Anglo-Saxon identity of America. Sociologist David Lee says it best: "Conversion to Christianity was considered the only logical way to produce Anglo-Saxons out of the tired and huddled masses. . . . By accepting Christ, it was asserted, even Blacks could be made white as snow."[63] Evangelical Protestant Christianity and Anglo-Saxonism are intimately intertwined. This entanglement implicates evangelical Protestant Christianity in a stand-your-ground culture and will have an important bearing on how segments of the religious community will respond to the slaying of Trayvon and other related matters.

As for the immigrant problem of the late nineteenth and early twentieth centuries, legislating quotas, constructing and restricting language, as well as Protestant evangelism, are examples of the tools used to offset any challenge to the narrative of America's exceptionalism. It is worth reiterating, these rudiments of a stand-your-ground culture surfaced first in response to European immigrants. This culture was a secretion of the Anglo-Saxon racism that is endemic to America's grand narrative. However, the first targets of this racism and its proto-stand-your-ground culture fought back. They fought back with an asset they shared with their Anglo-Saxon bullies, namely, their whiteness. It was the exertion of the narrative of Anglo-Saxon exceptionalism that fostered the construction of whiteness and hence the concept of cherished property.

The Construction of Whiteness

"I'm White, I'm White!" That is what Joseph Loguidice, an Italian immigrant, remembered hearing a man yell as he was "running down the middle of the street" for fear "people would shoot him down."[64] The man actually was European, according to Loguidice, probably Italian. "I'm White, I'm White" represents the "new stock" immi-

---

63. Lee, "Great Racial Commission," 107.
64. This story is recounted in Roediger, *Working toward Whiteness*, 58.

grants' protest to Anglo-Saxon exceptionalism. They did not possess Anglo-Saxon blood, but they did have white skin. And, this made a difference.

The construction of whiteness for these European immigrants was admittedly a complicated one. Identifying as white was the way they negotiated their "real life context and social experience," which was riddled with contradictions, most notably in terms of their relationship with the black community.[65] As is pointed out by a group of researchers on the invention of ethnicity, such negotiation is in fact how ethnicities are constructed.[66] For these "new stock" immigrants, whiteness was a way "to reconcile the duality of the 'foreignness' and the 'Americanness' which [they] . . . experienced in their everyday lives."[67] It essentially provided them with security, power, and, most of all, an American identity in their "in-between" space.[68] While these Europeans may not have been the descendants of Anglo-Saxons, they were not the descendants of slaves either. And, they "quickly learned that the worst thing one could be in the Promised land was 'colored,' and they distanced themselves as best they could from this pariah population."[69]

Ironically, one of the ways the "new stock" immigrants tried to do this was by using a tool that had been used against them by the "old stock": language. A story is told that in 1807 a British investor went to visit a friend in New England. When he knocked on the door and a maid answered, he asked, "Is your master home?" With that inquiry the maid became indignant and replied that she had no master. She went on to say, "I am Mr. ___'s *help*. I'd have you to know, *man*, that I am no *servant*; none but *negers* are *servants*."[70] Another person

---

65. Kathleen Neils Conzen, David A. Gerber, Ewa Morawska, George E. Pozzetta, and Rudolph J. Vecoli, "The Invention of Ethnicity: A Perspective from the U.S.A.," *Journal of American Ethnic History* 12.1 (Fall 1992): 5.

66. Ibid.

67. Ibid., 6.

68. In *Working toward Whiteness*, Roediger refers to these "new stock" immigrants as in-betweeners.

69. Conzen et al., "The Invention of Ethnicity," 14.

70. Roediger, *Wages of Whiteness*, 47.

reported, "It is more than petty treason to the republic to call a free citizen a *servant*."[71]

The same type of discussion occurred around the word "master." White workers made clear that only black people had masters; thus they adopted the Dutch word "boss." In his book *The American Democrat*, James Fenimore Cooper seemed to mock such a distinction as one of the "common faults of American language" that result from "an ambition of effect, a want of simplicity, and a turgid abuse of terms."[72] He would no doubt consider the adoption of "boss" as a "turgid abuse of terms." For surely he found it a ridiculous pretension of language created by "race prejudice." He said, "In consequence of the domestic servants of America having once been negro-slaves, a prejudice has arisen among the laboring classes of whites, who not only dislike the term servant, but have rejected that of master. So far has this prejudice gone, that in lieu of the latter, they have resorted to the use of the word *boss*, which has precisely the same meaning in Dutch!"[73] Once again, language becomes a way to make distinctions between "desirable" and undesirable people. In this instance, it was the poor white workers, oftentimes immigrant, who distinguished themselves from the most undesirable of all—black people.

Whatever the specific twists and turns on the path to constructing whiteness, the construction was done in opposition to blackness. The "new stock" immigrants constructed their white identities as "not slaves" and as "not blacks."[74] For even if these immigrants were not, as some have suggested, "white on arrival," it did not take them long to become so.[75] Therefore, as soon as possible, in the words of James Baldwin, "*Giorgio* becomes *Joe*, *Pappavasiliu* becomes *Palmer*, *Evangelos* becomes *Evans*, *Goldsmith* becomes *Smith* or *Gold*, and *Avakian*

---

71. Ibid., 47.

72. James Fenimore Cooper, *The American Democrat or Hints on the Social and Civil Relations of the United States of America* (Cooperstown, NY: H. & E. Phinney, 1838), 117.

73. James Fenimore Cooper, *The American Democrat*, 122.

74. Roediger, *Wages of Whiteness*, 13.

75. See Roediger's discussion of "White on Arrival," in *Working toward Whiteness*, 110-19.

becomes *King*."[76] The new immigrants essentially sublimated their European ethnic identities in order to become white.

The claim to whiteness provided the "new stock" a pathway to Americanness. Whiteness marked them "fit" for citizenship. It indicated that they and especially their children could be assimilated into American—that is, Anglo-Saxon—culture. It did so in at least two significant ways. First, the very fact that they, for the most part, were similar in appearance to Anglo-Saxons indicated their potential for assimilation/civilization. In this regard "white skin mattered." (It is no accident that those Europeans considered having more "swarthy complexions," such as Italians, Greeks, and Germans—at least in Franklin's eyes—raised the most ire from the "old stock.") Second, the fact that they set themselves over and against black people, the truly uncivilizable, gave them more credence in Anglo-Saxon eyes. Toni Morrison says, "It is no accident and no mistake that immigrant populations . . . understood their 'Americanness' as an opposition to the resident black population. Race, in fact, now functions as a metaphor so necessary to the construction of Americanness. . . . Deep within the word 'American' is its association with race."[77] In the words of legal scholar Cheryl Harris, "The amalgamation of various European strains into an American identity was facilitated by an oppositional definition of Black as other."[78] Thus, while the "new stock" immigrants may not have had Anglo-Saxon blood, at least they had the requisite foundation—biological make-up (white skin) and cultural disposition (anti-black bigotry)—upon which Anglo-Saxon culture and customs could be grafted. Even President Theodore Roosevelt allowed that they could be properly assimilated within "the space of two generations."[79]

---

76. James Baldwin, *The Price of the Ticket* (New York: St. Martin's/Marek, 1985), xix.

77. Toni Morrison, *Playing in the Dark: Whiteness and the Literary Imagination* (Cambridge, MA: Harvard University Press, 1992), 47.

78. Cheryl I. Harris, "Whiteness as Property," *Harvard Law Review* 106.8 (June 1993): 1742. In this article Harris provides a comprehensive and insightful analysis of the meaning of whiteness as property through scrupulous examination of case law. Harris's article informs this discussion and description of "whiteness as cherished property."

79. Roediger, *Working toward Whiteness*, 64.

At the same time that "whiteness" created an American space for the "new stock," it ameliorated the panicked fear of the "old stock." The construction of whiteness allowed for flexibility within American identity without undermining its narrative of Anglo-Saxon exceptionalism. Inasmuch as whiteness signaled the adaptability of "old stock" immigrants and most importantly their willingness to adapt, then Anglo-Saxon customs and ways could continue to prevail and flourish in America—including the language. These "white" immigrants, once assimilated, could practically blend in with the "old stock" Americans, and no one would be the wiser.

The issue of blending in actually became the focus of a 1923 Supreme Court case, United States v. Bhagat Singh Thind. In this case, Thind petitioned for naturalized citizenship on the basis that he was ethnologically white. He argued that he was from a high caste of Indians, which meant he was Aryan and therefore "Caucasian," making him white. The courts ruled against him, denying his citizenship. The case actually turned on the fact that Thind could not blend in with other Americans, because he did not look white. Not looking white, in the eyes of the Supreme Court, rendered him unable to assimilate. He was missing a significant piece of the foundation upon which to graft Anglo-Saxonism, white skin. At this point, his willingness to adapt did not matter. His complexion marked him unable to adapt. It conflicted with America's exceptionalism. The majority opinion is worth quoting at length because it reveals the significance of socially constructed whiteness. It reads,

> What we now hold is that the words "free white persons" are words of common speech, to be interpreted in accordance with the understanding of the common man, synonymous with the word "Caucasian" only as the word is popularly understood. As so understood and used, whatever may be the speculations of the ethnologist, it does not include the body of people to whom the appellee belongs. It is a matter of familiar observation and knowledge that the physical group characteristics of the Hindus render them readily distinguishable from the various groups of persons in this country commonly recognized as white. The children of English, French, German, Italian, Scandinavian, and other European parentage, quickly merge into the mass of our population and lose the distinctive hallmarks of their European

origin. On the other hand, it cannot be doubted that the children born in this country of Hindu parents would retain indefinitely the clear evidence of their ancestry. . . . What we suggest is merely racial difference, and it is of such character and extent that the great body of our people instinctively recognize it and reject the thought of assimilation.[80]

In the final analysis, white skin weighed heavily in the Anglo-Saxon equation of American identity and the preservation of America's narrative of exceptionalism. The construction of whiteness helped to resolve the contradiction between America's Anglo-Saxon and immigrant identity. Whiteness signified that the immigrants were Anglo-Saxon enough. From all appearances, they were indistinguishable from blood-carrying Anglo-Saxons. In the end, "various immigrant groups of different ethnic origins were accepted into a white identity shaped around Anglo-American norms."[81] Moreover, their integration into an American identity showed just how exceptional Anglo-Saxons actually were. Instead of the "new stock" being lowered to the ways of "the old stock," as many guardians of Anglo-Saxon exceptionalism feared, the "new" elevated the "old." Anglo-Saxon blood was able to stand its ground against the threat of contamination. It had the power to extinguish identities. It *was* exceptional.

In many respects, the construction of whiteness marks another stage in the development of stand-your-ground culture. In fact, it is the penultimate stage to its full flowering. Whiteness is the line drawn between Anglo-Saxon exceptionalism and any other corrupting influences. As evidenced by the Thind case, it keeps out those who clearly are not white— people of color and most notably black people. Essentially, whiteness provides a protected space for America's Anglo-Saxon exceptionalism. It creates a distance between its most opposing

---

80. Majority Opinion, U.S. *v.* Bhagat Singh Thind (1923). Not All Caucasians Are White; The Supreme Court Rejects Citizenship for Asian Indians, History Matters, http://historymatters.gmu.edu/d/5067. Harris actually does not cite this case in her analysis. Noting the phenomenon of "passing," thus making appearance an unreliable measure of whiteness, she focuses on cases relating to the issue of blood as a determining factor as to who is black, which she says was in the end as subjective and unreliable as the matter of appearance. See Harris, *Whiteness as Property*, 1738-41.

81. Harris, *Whiteness as Property*, 1743.

force—blackness. If people cannot pass the test of whiteness there are certain spaces into which they cannot enter, certain rights that they cannot possess, hence an exceptionality that they cannot encroach upon. Whiteness was essentially the passport into the exceptional space that is American identity as defined by the narrative of Anglo-Saxon exceptionalism. Entrance into this space is "closely and grudgingly guarded" by whiteness itself.[82] It is in this way that whiteness is the cherished property of America's exceptionalism.

Whiteness as Cherished Property

That whiteness is cherished property does not suggest the commodification or objectification of white people or the white body, as has been the case for black people and their bodies. Whiteness in fact protects white people from ever being considered chattel. To speak of whiteness as cherished property points to the reality of whiteness as an esteemed attribute within Anglo-Saxon America. To reiterate, it is esteemed by the narrative of exceptionalism for the mere fact that it protects this narrative. The construction of whiteness as cherished property is the advent of the ideology of white supremacy. According to this ideology, whiteness itself is the marker of a superior people, if not an exceptional people. As others have pointed out, the idea of white supremacy becomes a "religion of sorts."[83] Deep faith is placed in it, as the supremacy of whiteness is that which provides the link to exceptionalism and, as we will soon see, the link to God. In short, the grand narrative of Anglo-Saxon exceptionalism is the wizard behind the curtain of white supremacy. White supremacy in fact guarantees that even if America's Anglo-Saxon identity has become more myth than fact, at least nothing will get on the other side of whiteness that is not Anglo-Saxon. In the end, white supremacy may mystify its existence, but it is America's narrative of Anglo-Saxon exceptionalism that constructs and sustains the ideology of white supremacy—that is, whiteness as cherished property.

Just as whiteness protects America's exceptional identity, the narrative of exceptionalism shelters whiteness. It does so by according to

---

82. Paraphrasing Harris, *Whiteness as Property,* 1736.

83. Michelle Alexander, *The New Jim Crow: Mass Incarceration in the Age of Colorblindness,* rev. ed. (New York: New Press, 2012), 26.

whiteness certain rights not granted to those who are not white. These rights serve to fortify further whiteness as the barrier between America's exceptional identity and those who most threaten it. W. E. B. DuBois, in his book *Black Reconstruction*, refers to these rights as "wages" of whiteness. These wages, he says, are not about income. In fact, they even supersede the instances when the white worker might not be compensated more than the black worker. The wages of whiteness are far more valuable than economic compensation, for they concretize the distinction between white people and black people. These wages, that is, rights, can only be possessed by white people. They are "a sort of public and psychological wage."[84] Charles Mills perhaps puts it best when he says, "No matter how poor one was, one was still able to affirm the whiteness that distinguished one from the subpersons on the other side of the color line."[85]

Essentially, the rights of whiteness as cherished property are the unspoken but understood privileges bestowed by America's narrative of Anglo-Saxon exceptionalism. They go beyond what it means to be a citizen. Again, they are the added bonuses for not only being an adopted Anglo-Saxon, but for protecting the sanctity of Anglo-Saxon space. They are the artifacts of what it means for whiteness to be cherished property. They are the rights that make whiteness an impregnable wall between Anglo-Saxon exceptionalism and those persons on the other side of whiteness.

While these rights may change in relationship to the historical context, there are those that are constant, and hence, fundamental to exceptionalism's cherished property. Moreover, they are the ones that ultimately usher in the stand-your-ground culture. The most fundamental is "the right to exclude." Cheryl Harris puts it this way: "Whiteness and property share a common premise—a conceptual nucleus—of a right to exclude."[86] This right to exclude inexorably gives way to other fundamental rights—the right to claim land and the right to stake out space. These rights, Harris points out, were actually "ratified" at America's beginnings with "the conquest, removal,

---

84. W. E. B. Dubois, *Black Reconstruction in America: An Essay toward a History of the Part Which Black Folk Played in the Attempt to Reconstruct Democracy in America, 1860-1880* (New York: The Free Press, 1935), 700.

85. Mills, *The Racial Contract*, 59.

86. Harris, *Whiteness as Property*, 1714.

and extermination of Native American life and culture."[87] From then on, she says, "Possession and occupation of land was validated and therefore privileged" as a white property right.[88] The establishment of these latter two rights with the removal and extermination of Native Americans from their land suggests something further about the nature of white space: it travels with white people. It is the space that white people occupy. This space is therefore not to be intruded upon, hence the right of whiteness to exclude. These rights of exclusion, land, and space are the defining characteristics of whiteness as cherished property. They are indicative of what it means for whiteness to be cherished at the same time that they strengthen whiteness as a protective, if not masking, shield for Anglo-Saxon exceptionalism. For again, even if the Anglo-Saxon identity of the nation is only nominal, the mask of whiteness insures that only Anglo-Saxons will enjoy certain rights, if not also power.

It is important to recall once again that the narrative of Anglo-Saxon exceptionalism is a religious narrative, be it the narrative of civil religion or Protestant evangelicalism. Not only did the early American Anglo-Saxons believe their mission to be one of erecting God's "city on a hill" but they also came to believe that they essentially had divinity running through their veins. The Protestant evangelicals in particular believed themselves to be as close a human manifestation of God on earth as one could get. In general, however, the religious legitimation of America's exceptionalist narrative suggests that to be against Anglo-Saxon America is to be against God. Moreover, it suggests that the further removed one may be from the Anglo-Saxon family tree, the further one is removed from God. Whiteness in this respect is not simply cherished property, but it is also sacred property. It is virtually the gateway to divinity, the key to salvation. As the evangelical Protestant hymn suggests, salvation requires one to be made "white as snow." Within the religious narrative of America's exceptionalism, anything that cannot pass the test of whiteness cannot get to God. In this regard, nonwhiteness is not simply an offense against Anglo-Saxon exceptionalism, it is an offense against God. For that which is on the other side of whiteness is on the other side of God.

---

87. Ibid., 1716
88. Ibid.

Inasmuch as one is alienated from Anglo-Saxon exceptionalism, one is alienated from God.

In effect, the construction of whiteness as cherished property is part and parcel of the construction of nonwhiteness as an expression of sin. Moreover, within this narrative of Anglo-Saxon exceptionalism, that which whiteness most opposes is also that which God most opposes—that is, blackness. The fact that new-stock immigrants constructed their whiteness in opposition to blacks is theologically consequential. Blackness itself is constructed as sin. The implications of this will be explored further in the next chapter.

Whiteness as the gateway to God has even more disquieting theological implications. If God is on the side of whiteness, God is by implication not simply white but Anglo-Saxon. An Anglo-Saxon God is the only God that Anglo-Saxon exceptionalism can admit. For if indeed Anglo-Saxon ethnicity, and hence blood, reflects the highest form of humanity, and all good things come from it, then "that of which nothing greater can be conceived" has to be an Anglo-Saxon God. Thus, as mentioned earlier, Anglo-Saxons are essentially human incarnations of a divine reality. From the perspective of the nineteenth-century German theologian Ludwig Feuerbach, this Anglo-Saxon God is but a projection of Anglo-Saxons' wishes for themselves. In this instance it reflects the wish that they are perfectly virtuous and just. Anglo-Saxon exceptionalism is virtually projected onto the sacred cosmos. To be sure, the sacred canopies that legitimate America's exceptionalism project an Anglo-Saxon God. The God that blesses America, in other words, is Anglo-Saxon. Essentially, what the religious legitimation of America's exceptionalism means for whiteness as cherished property is that one of the unspoken rights accorded to it is the right to determine what is or is not acceptable in the eyes of God—put simply, what is Christian and what is not. It is the right to name God.[89]

---

89. There was perhaps no better example of this than the controversy that surrounded President Obama's 2008 campaign for the presidency as a result of a sermon preached by his pastor, Dr. Jeremiah Wright. During that controversy the black church as well as black theology came under attack. Both were essentially accused of not being Christian mainly because they called into question the very narrative of America's exceptionalism. This was what put Dr. Wright under the microscope of white scrutiny in the first place.

We have now come full circle. It is with the construction of whiteness as cherished property that a stand-your-ground culture is finally born. From the Anglo-Saxon myth of America's exceptionalism to whiteness as cherished property comes a stand-your-ground culture. A stand-your-ground culture is nothing other than the enactment of whiteness as cherished property. It is the culture that protects the supremacy of whiteness, hence an inexorable cultural expression of whiteness as cherished property—that is, of white supremacy. Stand-your-ground culture spawns its own means, legal and extralegal, to insure that nothing nonwhite intrudes on white space. In other words, stand-your-ground culture protects the rights that come with cherished white property. With this understanding, we can now answer the following question: "Could Trayvon have stood his ground on that sidewalk?"

Stand-Your-Ground Rights

A Mother's Questions in a Stand-Your-Ground Culture

I remember it like it was yesterday. My son was seven or eight years old. He and his best friend, who was white (I will call him James), were sitting in the backseat of the car as I was driving them home from school. It was during black history month, so they were learning about "famous" black people. That day, Arthur Ashe was the focus of their black history lesson. As my son and James were discussing Ashe, James said, "Good thing we [meaning white people] decided to share our stuff with you guys [meaning black people] or Arthur Ashe would have never been a champion."

Already implanted within James's young consciousness was the awareness that with his white skin came certain rights that were not given to black people. The only way for black people to attain these things was for white people to decide to share them. Otherwise, these rights were off limits to black people. I knew James's parents well. I could not imagine that they had articulated these notions directly to James. But clearly, they did not do anything to prevent them from becoming a part of James's consciousness. James's comments were a reflection of the insidious and subtle way that America's narrative of exceptionalism is ingrained within America's collective consciousness, impacting even the children.

This narrative of exceptionalism simply has not gone away. It is stubborn. It continues to enact itself through the stand-your-ground culture it produced to reinforce its shield, whiteness. Again, exceptionalism's stand-your-ground culture is dynamic, in that it generates the legal and extralegal instruments required to protect America's most cherished property. These tools, like the Stand Your Ground law, are meant to enforce the fundamental rights of this property—rights accorded only to those who possess it. And for a mother of a black child this culture poses a special challenge.

When my son was born, I reimmersed myself in the writings of James Baldwin. I knew that he had written about negotiating the reality of being black and male in a world where blackness was not valued. I wanted to gain insight from his wisdom, in order to equip my son to be a proud and healthy black man in America. In reading Baldwin I rediscovered his "Letter to My Nephew." This letter asked the questions that plagued me from the moment my son was born.

How was I to raise my black child in a society in which his body is not cherished? How was I to raise him to cherish his black self in a society defined by a narrative that tells him he has no value? How was I to raise him to be proud of his blackness when a stand-your-ground culture "spell[s] out with brutal clarity, and in as many ways possible, that [he is] a worthless human being" because of his blackness?[90] How is he to be psychologically, spiritually, and emotionally whole when a culture has been "deliberately constructed to make [him] believe what white people say about [him] . . . ," that he is inferior?[91] These questions, ones that James Baldwin raised a half-century ago, are not just my questions. They are questions that haunt mothers of black children even today.

For me, the answers to these questions begin with constructing another narrative about who our children are. This is a narrative that starts not in the ancient woods of Germany but in the rich lands of the continent of Africa. This narrative comes not through the Church of England but through the invisible institution of slavery. This narrative tells the story of a proud and noble people whose fortitude, ingenuity, and genius allowed them to survive the Middle Passage crossing

---

90. Baldwin, "Fire Next Time: My Dungeon Shook," in *Price of the Ticket*, 335.
91. Ibid.

and to forge an affirming and empowering culture. This narrative tells the story of a faith that testifies to a God on their side as they struggle for their freedom. This is a narrative filled with the wisdom, wit, and witness of our black mothers that helped them, in the words of James Baldwin, "in the teeth of the most terrifying odds, achieve an unassailable and monumental dignity."[92] This is a narrative that contests the very narrative of America's grand narrative of Anglo-Saxon exceptionalism.

The first step in raising our black children to become proud and healthy human beings is to tell them their story, the story that our mothers told us, so that they can understand that the stand-your-ground culture that assaults their value is not a testament to their inferiority but an expression of the indecency of America's narrative of Anglo-Saxon exceptionalism.

From the moment he could listen, I read my son the stories of proud black people. On his fourteenth birthday, I gave him James Baldwin's letter to his nephew. And, from the moment that he was born I took him to church. I tried to show him the benefits of blackness that supersede the rights of whiteness—none more important than the faith of the black church.

The Question Answered

And so let us now answer President Obama's question, "If Trayvon was of age and armed, could he have stood his ground on that sidewalk?" The answer resounded in the black community way before the president asked it: No! Trayvon did not possess the property that would have afforded him that right.

In that same July 19, 2013, speech President Obama went on to say, "If a white male teen was involved in the same kind of scenario . . . from top to bottom, both the outcome and the aftermath might have been different." These words reflect a sad irony. For even though America has its first black president, the narrative of Anglo-Saxon exceptionalism is alive and well within American society, and even the black president knows this.

In the final analysis, what happened to Trayvon Martin did not start with an encounter on a sidewalk. It was set in motion through a

---

92. Ibid., 336.

book that extolled the virtues of ancient Germans. So what happened to Trayvon was not really about a Florida law. It was rather about a stand-your-ground culture that is intrinsic to America's identity. In the words of the old adage, this is a tradition that is "as American as apple pie." While it may manifest itself in different ways throughout history, it is a persistent part of the American social-cultural landscape. As long as America's sacred narrative of exceptionalism goes unchallenged, bodies like Trayvon's, which do not possess the cherished property of whiteness, will not have the right to stand their ground.

After his friend James got out of the car, I asked my son what he thought about what he had said. My son answered, "I didn't pay attention to it because I thought it was stupid." At that moment I smiled, but my anxiety did not go away. For even though my son was fortified against the rhetoric of America's narrative of Anglo-Saxon exceptionalism, there was more to fear than the rhetoric; there was the stand-your-ground culture it had spawned.

This is a culture that turns deadly in relation to the black body. The question is why? To answer that question, we must appreciate another construction that is a part of America's collective consciousness: the construction of the black body as a guilty body. We turn to this in Chapter 2.

2

The Black Body: A Guilty Body

"Why are black murder victims put on trial?" This is the question that CNN contributor L. Z. Granderson asked as more young black men and women fell victim to the violence of stand-your-ground culture.[1] This question was in response to the murder of nineteen-year-old Renisha McBride. She was shot in the face by a white man when, after a car accident, she knocked on his door to ask for help. Renisha's dead body was checked for alcohol and drugs. The toxicology report revealed that she had a blood alcohol level that exceeded the legal limit for driving. However, as Granderson points out, her alcohol intake explained her single-car accident, but it did not explain why a white man "shot an unarmed [black] girl in the face with his shotgun."[2] While her death was eventually ruled a homicide, this ruling came only after protests and the attention of national media.

The immediate legal response to Renisha's murder reflects a disturbing pattern within the country. Black victims of fatal violence are presumed guilty of bringing their deaths upon themselves. Their white killers are given the benefit of the doubt. It is readily assumed that the white killer "acted as a reasonable person would who is in fear for his life."[3] Such was the initial belief in the case of Jonathan Ferrell,

---

1. L. Z. Granderson commentary, "Why Are Black Victims Put on Trial?" CNN Opinion, http://www.cnn.com/2013/11/15/opinion/granderson-whites-shooting-blacks.
2. Ibid.
3. Cheryl Carpenter, lawyer for the alleged shooter of Renisha McBride, quoted in Granderson commentary, "Why Are Black Victims Put on Trial?"

an unarmed twenty-four-year-old black man who was killed when a white police officer fired ten bullets into his body. Toxicology reports found no drugs or alcohol in Jonathan's system. He, like Renisha, was victimized as a result of knocking on a door to ask for help after a car accident. While the officer was eventually charged with voluntary manslaughter, being charged does not equate to being found guilty—as made evident in the case of Trayvon's killer.

During the trial of Trayvon's killer, it was as if Trayvon was being charged for his own death. He was placed on trial. His character, not his killer's character, became the focus of the case. In a similar manner, seventeen-year-old Jordan Davis was in effect placed on trial for his own murder. Though his killer was convicted of attempted murder for firing into a fleeing vehicle, the jury hung on whether or not he actually murdered Jordan. It seemed plausible to some on the jury that a white man could feel threatened by a black boy playing loud music. After all, the killer thought Jordan had a gun. There was no gun, and Jordan "died with his back to his killer."[4] Nevertheless, a plea of self-defense was just enough to hang the jury.[5]

After the trial of Jordan's killer, the sentiment literally voiced throughout the black community was, "a dead black boy is always more guilty for his death than his white killer." The question is why? Why is it reasonable to believe, even in face of all evidence to the contrary, that a black murder victim is culpable in his or her own slaying? Why is she/he viewed as a threat even when asking for help? Why is self-defense so easily granted as a justification for killing an unarmed black person, especially when the killer is white? L. Z. Granderson says that there is "a subconscious element of our culture that looks at a black corpse and quietly puts it, instead of the perpetrator, on trial."[6]

Granderson is correct. That which practically convicts a black person for her or his own murder is an "element" of stand-your-ground culture. It is a deadly secretion, replete with religious legitimation, generated by America's surreptitious narrative of Anglo-Saxon exceptionalism.

---

4. Kim Lute, "Jordan Davis, Trayvon Martin and the American't Dream," February 21, 2014, Huffington Post, http://www.huffingtonpost.com.

5. The final adjudication of the case would come in a retrial, which will be discussed in the epilogue.

6. Granderson, "Why Are Black Victims Put on Trial?"

This chapter will not retry the perpetrators in the slayings of Renisha, Jonathan, Trayvon, Jordan, or any other black victims of stand-your-ground culture. Rather, this chapter will attempt to identify the social-cultural conceptions that coalesce to deem the black body—especially the black male body—as not just inferior to the white body but as a threat to it. These conceptions depict the black body as chattel, hypersexual, and dangerous. Validated with a sacred canopy, these conceptualizations interact to inscribe indelible guilt upon black bodies. This chapter deconstructs the inviolable perception of the black body as guilty in order to answer the question, "Why are black murder victims put on trial?" The answer to this question brings us closer to why stand-your-ground culture turns so deadly in relation to the black body. It raises its own challenges for black faith, as we will see throughout this discussion. That answer begins with the theo-ideological narrative that legitimates the Anglo-Saxonist characterizations of the black body.

Natural Law Theo-Ideology

Just as America's narrative of Anglo-Saxon exceptionalism produced an ideological framework, cherished white property/white supremacy, to sustain the super-ordination of the white body, it generated a theo-ideological framework to sustain the subordination of the black one. Both racialized paradigms provide a protective cover for the grand narrative of Anglo-Saxon exceptionalism that actually shapes American identity. As it pertains to the black body, America's grand narrative spawned its own theory of natural law. This Anglo-Saxonist version is the theo-ideological underpinning in the ultimate construction of the guilty black body. This theo-ideology serves to exonerate white people from their brutal and sometimes fatal assaults upon black bodies. If versions of civil religion and evangelical Protestantism provided sacred legitimation for America's narrative of exceptionalism, this racialized version of natural law bolsters that narrative by providing the sacred canopy for white mistreatment of black bodies. In other words, this theo-ideology makes it appear that the ideology of cherished white property is not an ethnocentric construct but instead reflects an ontological truth. A natural law theo-ideology provides sacred legitimation for the deadly enforcement of stand-your-ground culture.

There are various interpretations of natural law theory. While there was no doubt a combination of interpretations, such as Thomas Hobbes's or John Locke's, that influenced America's social political consciousness, most versions of natural law reflect aspects of St. Thomas Aquinas's natural law doctrine. St. Thomas's doctrine typically provides the foundation from which other natural law theories are derived. For that reason, we turn to him for our understanding of natural law, so to appreciate the nuanced use of natural law theory in the construction of the guilty black body.

St. Thomas's doctrine is grounded in the presupposition that law, a function of reason, is always "directed to the common good."[7] There is, he argues, an eternal law that is "a dictate of reason emanating from the ruler who governs a perfect community" (the ruler is, of course, presumed to be governed by reason).[8] Eternal law is the way in which God creates and orders the world. According to eternal law, God orders the world so the "common good" of the world is served. In doing this, God endows creatures with a particular essence into which they are to live. Natural law becomes the human response to eternal law. It is, St. Thomas explains, the way in which creatures "partake" of the eternal law. Creatures do this by aligning themselves with God's creative design and vision for the world. This is accomplished through living in accordance with the "inclinations" of the nature that God has "imprinted on them."[9] To do otherwise is an abrogation of eternal law. St. Thomas makes clear that "the good are perfectly subject to the eternal law, as always acting according to it."[10] The wicked, on the other hand, act contrary to eternal law. They are essentially embodiments of evil since they have turned away from good; hence living against their God-given essence. As we will see, the version of natural law generated by the narrative of Anglo-Saxon exceptionalism reflects key themes of St. Thomas's doctrine, even if they are distorted.

The notion of divine natural law saturated America's collective consciousness from America's earliest beginnings. A version of natural law theory certainly influenced the authors of the Declaration

---

7. Thomas Aquinas, *Summa Theologica*, First Part of the Second Part, Q9 1a1-2.

8. Ibid., Q9 1a1.

9. Ibid., Q9 1a2.

10. Ibid., Q9 3a6.

of Independence as they proclaimed, "all men are created equal . . . and are endowed by their creator with certain inalienable rights, . . . Life, Liberty and the pursuit of Happiness." Owing to the influence of the Anglo-Saxon myth upon natural law in America, black people were initially precluded from enjoying the "inalienable rights" that were accorded white people. As Charles Mills has aptly pointed out, the Declaration of Independence was a part of a "Racial Contract" that "restricts the possession of this natural freedom and equality to *white* men."[11] Just as the omnipotence of the Anglo-Saxon myth in the American consciousness distorted the meaning of romanticism, it did the same with natural law. The Anglo-Saxon myth is a corrupting and distorting influence. In the cases of romanticism and natural law, it took a universal ideal and particularized it. It racialized both perspectives. The co-mingling of the Anglo-Saxon myth with natural law theory created a theo-ideology that excluded black people not only from the category of citizens but also from the category of humans. America's exceptionalist version of natural law rendered black people effectively nonhuman, thereby disqualifying them from being holders of "inalienable rights." These presumably God-given rights were essentially declared "wages" of cherished white property. Mills puts it this way: "Nonwhites are appropriately relegated to a lower rung on the moral ladder (the Great Chain of Being). They are designated as born *unfree* and *unequal*."[12] As we will soon see, natural law theory, shaped by the Anglo-Saxon myth, suggested that black people had a natural "inclination" to be subjugated. It also equated white racist constructions of black character with the nature God "imprinted" upon black people.

Slavery provided the testing ground for the Anglo-Saxonist perversions of natural law. This racist perversion of natural law provided sacred justification for the enslavement of black bodies. It was a key factor in the sanctification of the black body as chattel.

The Black Body as Chattel

In America the principal conception of the black body is as chattel. This is the foundation on which all other racially stereotypical

---

11. Mills, *The Racial Contract*, 16 (emphasis in original).
12. Ibid.

perceptions of the black body are grafted. The black body as chattel is the core element in the construction of the inherently guilty black body. Its classification as chattel is also that which substantiates the fundamental distinction between the white body and the black body. This classification reinforces the protective line of whiteness with regard to America's Anglo-Saxon exceptionalism. It is, therefore, imperative to invest this conception with sacred legitimation. The Anglo-Saxon exceptionalist permutation of natural law theory did just that. Before looking at the way in which it did so, let us first carefully examine the black body as chattel. This will enable us to fully appreciate the necessity for a religious legitimation when it comes to this construct.

Commodified Body

A handbill printed on July 26, 1860, was distributed in and around Columbia County, Georgia. It announced sales to be held on August 14 and 16 of that same year. In bold print the handbill advertised the "Sale of Negroes, Mills, Mules, Hogs, Farming and Mining Tools, Wagons and Carts." The advertisement went on to specify the times and places of the sales along with some details of the items being sold. The Negroes' sale was to be held on the sixteenth; however, the handbill made clear that "a variety of articles useful to Mechanics, Miners, and Planters" would also be sold on that day. The names of the "Negroes" to be sold were given along with the names of their owners.[13]

To conceive of the black body as chattel literally renders it a commodity to be bought and sold on the open market, with all other commodities. The implications of this are vast, especially in relation to whiteness as cherished property.

First and foremost, to be chattel meant that black people did not have the rights to possess their bodies. They did not own them. Neither did they have the right to possess other black bodies, not even those of their children. In this regard, the chatteled black body is not cherished property. It is instead a valued commodity. To designate the black body as chattel makes clear the distinction between it and

---

13. Advertisement for Slave Sale, Georgia, 1860, Dr. Robert T. Vinson private collection, The Atlantic Slave Trade and Slave Life in the Americas, http://www.hitchcock.itc.virginia.edu/SlaveTrade/collection/large/NW0338.jpg.

the white body. It is as if they come from two very different creative stocks. If black people are by nature chattel then it is an ontological impossibility for them to ever become cherished property. The most that they can hope for is to be a valued commodity. As we will soon see, being such actually provided black people with a degree of protection that they did not have following emancipation.

On the other hand, as mentioned in Chapter 1, the fact that whiteness is cherished property precludes white bodies from being commodified. Cheryl Harris explains it this way: "The racial line between white and Black was extremely critical; it became a line of protection and demarcation from the potential threat of commodification."[14] To reiterate, whiteness is an attribute that gives those who possess it rights to ownership, in this instance ownership over their bodies as well as ownership over other nonwhite bodies, notably the black body.

The black body as chattel is essentially the valued commodity of whiteness. It is valued in a slave economy as a means of production. The role of chattel was to produce the labor needed to sustain a slavocracy: body work and potentially working bodies. The more labor that chattel can produce, then the more valued a commodity that chattel is. This is why healthy young black men and fertile young black women were sold for top dollar at slave auctions. According to an 1850s price table for slaves sold in the Forsythe County area of North Carolina, a black male between the ages of nineteen and twenty-five had the most value, selling for between $1,250 and $1,450. Women in that same age group were of second highest value, selling for between $1,050 and $1,225.[15] Prior to the sale, each human "commodity" was checked scrupulously to make sure it did not have a flaw that would hinder its production of labor. The female chattel was often taken to a separate area for gynecological inspection in an attempt to insure her ability to produce other laboring bodies. One former enslaved man described it this way:

> The slaves are made to shave and wash in greasy pot liquor, to make them look sleek and nice; their heads must be combed, and their best clothes put on; and when called out to be examined they are to stand in a row—the women and men apart—

---

14. Harris, *Whiteness as Property*, 1720-21.

15. South Carolina—African Americans—Buying and Selling Human Beings, http://www.sciway.net.

then they are picked out and taken into a room, and examined. See a large, rough slaveholder, take a poor female slave into a room, make her strip, then feel and examine her, as though she were a pig, or a hen, or merchandise.[16]

To guarantee the bodies that female chattel produced would become a part of the slave economy, laws were passed that stipulated that children follow in the condition of their mothers. Of course, this stipulation allowed for the fact that the white slave master fathered some of the children. Nevertheless, as Harris notes, the law "facilitated the reproduction of [slavery's] labor force."[17] Harris also explains that some slave owners, such as Thomas Jefferson, believed the production of female chattel more valuable than that of male chattel. He wrote to a friend, "I consider the labor of a breeding woman as no object, and that a child raised every 2 years is of more profit than the crop of the best laboring men."[18]

There is another significant aspect of being characterized as chattel related to this lack of ownership. To be chattel by definition means to belong to another. To characterize black people as chattel is to define them as quintessentially belonging to another. Blackness becomes virtually a synonym for enslavement. Freedom is not a right that black women and men are entitled to by their very chattel condition. That they do not have the right to be free is evident by the fact that they do not own their labor or their body. These two conditions reinforce each other when it comes to black people.

In John Locke's interpretation of natural rights, one that surely informed the framers of the Declaration of Independence, "every man has a property in his own Person. . . . The labour of his body and the work of his hands, we may say, are properly his."[19] That people had the right to own their bodies and labor was a signal of their freedom and

---

16. William J. Anderson, *Life and Narrative of William J. Anderson, Twenty-Four Years a Slave; Sold Eight Times! In Jail Sixty Times!! Whipped Three Hundred Times: or The Dark Deeds of American Slavery Revealed, Written by Himself* (Chicago: Daily Tribune Book and Job Printing Office, 1857), 14.

17. Harris, *Whiteness as Property*, 1719.

18. Quoted in Harris, *Whiteness as Property*, 1720.

19. John Locke, Second Treatise of Government, book II, chapter v, paragraph 27; www.gutenberg.org.

a sign that they were meant to be free. Clearly, as we have just seen, black women and men had the right neither to their body nor to their labor. Inasmuch as they did not possess these rights, it was presumed that they were not meant to be free. Of course, it was enslavement that prevented them from being free. Yet, this did not matter in the logic of the Anglo-Saxonist version of natural law. What mattered was that they were in fact not free. Their enslavement was held against them. It was considered a sign that God did not intend their freedom. Black people were trapped in a Catch-22 cycle of being perpetual chattel.

It is important to note that the cyclical logic that reifies the notion of black people as chattel points to a menacing vulnerability of natural law, at least when it is applied in a racially bigoted context. If God's eternal law is discerned through nature itself, in this instance through the way the world is, then the way things are can easily be construed as the way things are supposed to be. When explaining natural law theory, Mills says, "What is right and wrong, just and unjust, in society will largely be determined by what is right and wrong, just and unjust, in the state of nature."[20] At issue is the basis on which one determines "the state of nature." Natural law theory in the hands of subjugating power can become a dangerous tool. For it serves to justify unjust structures, and thus it sanctifies an oppressive status quo. We will see how this is the case with regard to the black body as chattel.

To repeat, this conception of the black body as chattel is vital. It lays the groundwork for the construction of the black body as irrevocably guilty. It is the precipitating agent for stand-your-ground culture's violent eruptions against the black body. An unimpeachable rationale for this construction is, therefore, imperative. Natural law provided that rationale.

Theo-Ideological Legitimation

Natural law theory, combined with the Anglo-Saxon myth, created an almost impregnable justification of the black body as chattel. It contributed to a formidable apologia for slavery. With the help of natural law, another sacred canopy was effectively contrived to validate America's narrative of Anglo-Saxon exceptionalism. No one articulated this Anglo-Saxonist version of natural law more effectively than

---

20. Mills, *The Racial Contract*, 15.

the vice-president of the Confederacy, Alexander H. Stephens. In his now infamous 1861 "Cornerstone Address," Stephens said that one of the cornerstones upon which the Confederacy rests is "that the negro is not equal to the white man; that slavery, subordination to the superior race, is his natural and moral condition." He went on to say,

> The negro by nature, or by the Curse against Canaan . . . is fitted for that condition which he occupies in our system. . . . It is best, not only for the superior but for the inferior race, that it should be so. It is, indeed, in conformity with the Creator. It is not for us to inquire into the wisdom of His ordinances or to question them. For His own purposes He has made one race to differ from another, as He has made "one star to differ from another in glory."[21]

Stephens perfectly illustrates the way in which natural law has been perverted to sanctify the conception of black people as chattel. In accordance with natural law theory, this Anglo-Saxonist theo-ideology argues that black people are created to be "ruled" by white people. Any other relationship is considered a violation of the Creator's intent, by implication a violation of eternal law. Indeed, Stephens says that black subordination is the "moral" condition of black people, thereby suggesting that equality with white people—and certainly not to speak of superiority over them—is immoral. Freedom from subjugation, in the word of St. Thomas, would be "wicked."

Other proslavery advocates were just as resourceful in their use of natural law. William Harper, one of the authors of the 1852 book *The Pro-Slavery Argument,* developed a theory of natural law in support of the slavocracy itself. He argues that slavery was a part of God's vision for the civilization of humankind. He wrote, "Will those who regard Slavery as immoral, or crime in itself, tell us that man was not intended for civilization. . . . Do they not blaspheme the providence of God who denounce its wickedness and outrage, that which is rendered indispensable to his purposes in the government of the world."[22]

---

21. Alexander H. Stephens, "Cornerstone Address, March 21, 1861," *Modern History Sourcebook.* http://www.legacy.fordham.edu/haslall/mod/1861stephens. asp.

22. William Harper, Governor Hammond, Dr. Simms, and Professor Dew,

Harper went on to explain that "Negroes" were essential to God's civilizing mission. It is for this reason that they are "peculiarly suited to the situation which they occupy."[23] In the same book, William Gilmore Simms also argued that slavery was a part of the divine plan to improve the overall condition of humanity. He claimed that slavery was the necessary step for people on their way to freedom. However, he seemed to abjure this argument when it came to black people. He said, "I do not believe that [the African] will ever be other than a slave, or that he was made to be otherwise; but that he is designed as an implement in the hands of civilization always."[24]

Dr. Samuel Cartwright authored an article entitled "Negro Freedom an Impossibility under Nature's Laws." The title itself promises a theo-ideology of Anglo-Saxon exceptionalism. In this article Cartwright wrote, "the negro must from necessity, be the slave of man or the slave of Satan."[25] That Cartwright proclaims a free "negro" to be evil again recalls St. Thomas's notion that it is the wicked who live contrary to their essence.

In the context of the black body as chattel, Cartwright, Simms, Harper, and others lay the theo-ideological foundation for understanding the free black body as a sinful black body. Freedom itself is seen as a sinful condition when held by certain races, namely, those who don't possess the property of whiteness. Proslavery proponents of natural law attempt to make clear that God did not make all humans equal, and God did not intend for all humans to be free. Proslavers are sure of this because black people are chattel.

This theo-ideology complements the ideology that emerged in collaboration with the construction of whiteness, that is, the ideology of whiteness as cherished property. The natural-law theo-ideology of course applies directly to the construction of black people as chattel. In the process, however, it provides a theological dimension to

---

The Pro-Slavery Argument; As Maintained by the Most Distinguished Writers of the Southern States Containing the Several Essays, on the Subject (Charleston, SC: Walker, Richards & Co. 1852), 4.

23. Harper, *Pro-Slavery Argument*, 5.

24. William Gilmore Simms, *Pro-Slavery Argument*, 270.

25. Quoted in George M. Frederickson, *The Black Image in the White Mind: The Debate on Afro-American Character and Destiny, 1817-1914* (Hanover, NH: Wesleyan University Press, 1971), 55.

the chattel/cherished property oppositional construction. It projects racial antagonism into the "heavens." The socially constructed white/black opposition becomes a divine construct. Instead of the white/black divide being a human production that can perhaps be overcome, it is a divine creation that must not be violated. The social order of an Anglo-Saxon–defined society becomes God's divine order. What one religious scholar calls an "ontocracy" develops. An ontocracy is a "situation in which the pattern of society is identified with the immemorial order of the cosmos."[26] In this instance, the status quo is regarded as the manifestation of eternal law.

This process by which a natural law theo-ideology provided a sacred canopy for the slavocracy, and thus the conception of chattel, illustrates Peter Berger's understanding of societal constructions. Berger says that "Man must *make* a world for himself . . . " in order to establish "a relationship with [the world]."[27] Humans do this by creating what Berger calls a "nomos," that is, a predictable social order. This nomos reflects the society's worldview as well as value structure. This, "as objective reality, provides a world for [humans] to inhabit."[28] This nomos is, however, inherently unstable by virtue of the fact that it is a human production. It is vulnerable to chaos, what Berger calls "anomy." To fend off anomy it is necessary to invest the nomos with stability and thus, to create an undetectable illusion that the social order is organic and not a human construction. Religion provides that illusion. "Religion is," Berger says, "the human enterprise by which a sacred cosmos is established."[29] With a religious sacred canopy the nomos is stabilized. It is effectively connected to the sacred cosmos. It is in this way that the constructed social order is presented as a reflection of God's eternal order. Projecting the nomos into the sacred cosmos invests the nomos with eternal stability. Berger explains, "The sacred cosmos, which transcends and includes [humans] in its ordering of reality, thus provides [humans] ultimate shield against the ter-

---

26. Arend T. van Leeuwen, quoted in Sydney Ahlstom, ed., *Theology in American: The Major Protestant Voices from Puritanism to Neo-Orthodoxy* (reprint, Indianapolis: Hackett Publishing Company, 2003), 89 n. 78.

27. Peter Berger, *The Sacred Canopy: Elements of a Sociological Theory of Religion* (New York: Doubleday, 1967), 5.

28. Ibid., 13.

29. Ibid., 11.

ror of anomy." Berger continues, "To be in 'right' relationship with
the sacred cosmos is to be protected against the nightmare threats of
chaos."[30] In the end, Berger's analysis explains the logic of America's
racialized version of natural law: the world, the way it is, is viewed as
the way God intends for it to be. As long as the status quo is maintained, stability is assured. A threat to the status quo is therefore
regarded as an affront to God. It is construed as a violation of the
sacred cosmos. In a slavocracy a free black person represents such a
threat. Within the framework of a racialized version of natural law, a
free black body is her-/himself a threat to God.

There is another troubling implication of Anglo-Saxonist natural
law theo-ideology. The logic of this sacred canopy suggests that not
only is God Anglo-Saxon, but God is also a white supremacist. For,
inasmuch as a social structure in which white people subjugate black
people is viewed as a reflection of eternal law, then God must be a
white supremacist. As will be addressed in Part II of this book, this
theo-ideology clearly challenges any black faith claim concerning
the blackness of God as well as any faith claim that suggests racial
reconciliation as a part of God's divine vision for humanity. Moreover,
this theo-ideology compels the need to determine a theological norm
for discerning God's vision. Black faith must be able to adjudicate
between competing claims concerning God's movement in history.

Just as this theo-ideology has implications regarding what it means
for black people to live in accordance with their nature, it implies
the proper behavior of white people. By legitimating black space as
an enslaved space, this theo-ideology validates white space as a free
space. For blacks to become free is both a violation of their nature as
chattel and an intrusion into white space. Hence, white people are
compelled by Anglo-Saxonist versions of natural law to resist this
intrusion. They are "morally" obligated to maintain the free space as
a white space. They are, therefore, required by their very nature to
continue their tyranny over black bodies. In the words of Mills, they
are required to patrol their space for "dark intruders."[31] To do otherwise is to be "wicked." Within this racialized conception, sacred legitimation is provided for stand-your-ground culture because it necessi-

---

30. Ibid., 26.
31. Mills, *The Racial Contract*, 48.

tates whiteness standing its free ground against blackness. Essentially, according to this Anglo-Saxonist version of natural law, white subjugation of black bodies is good because it is consistent with God's alleged plan for creation. In the words of St. Thomas, "the good are perfectly subject to the eternal law, as always acting according to it." To reiterate, any social-political agenda that grants freedom to black bodies is a sinful agenda within the Anglo-Saxonist version of natural law. In effect, by sanctioning the status of black people in a social-historical context defined by Anglo-Saxonist exceptionalism, natural law theo-ideology becomes the sacred canopy for white supremacy.

A Religio-Scientific Foundation

During the nineteenth century a religio-scientific discourse emerged that supported natural law theo-ideology. This discourse went beyond the suspect findings of phrenology and physiognomy. Though in some cases, scientists drew upon these areas of study.[32] The religious science of Anglo-Saxonist theo-ideology actually alleged religious and scientific evidence for a differentiated creation of whites and blacks. The most prominent advocates of this specious religious science promoted polygenesis theories as the basis for their claims. Polygenetic perspectives assert that there were multiple divine creations, thus, the creation of Adam and Eve is only one of many. Polygenetic scientists offered scientific and ethnological "proof" that whites and blacks originated from different creation moments, all in an effort to prove the profound differences between whites and blacks. There is no better representative of polygenetic religious science than Louis Agassiz.

Agassiz was a Swiss biologist whose work garnered wide international respect. Americans were perhaps the most receptive audience for his work. His writings were, in fact, published in both American scientific journals and in popular magazines. Agassiz's American appeal was no doubt due to the fact that his theories appeared to support the chattel status of black people. Despite his protest that he

---

32. One of the most prominent religio-scientific researchers, George Morton, did his own extensive study of human skulls. He actually had one of the largest collections of human skulls, which Agassiz examined to support his own religio-scientific theories. Morton published his findings in his 1839 book *Crania Americana*.

did not intend to enter a "moral" or "political" debate concerning the
"condition of negroes," his religio-scientific arguments landed him
right in the middle of that debate.[33]

When Agassiz arrived in the United States in 1845, the debate concerning the innate differences between white and black people was at
its height. This debate was fueled by the rising momentum of the abolitionist movement and the religious arguments against the morality
of slavery. Proslavery advocates were concerned to provide a scientific
and religious foundation for black inferiority, and hence, black peoples' necessary subjugation. The proslavery community essentially
needed to bolster their natural law theo-ideology with scientific and
biblical evidence. Agassiz's work seemed to do just that. His findings,
in fact, lent credibility to American scientists such as Samuel Morton
and Charles Caldwell who made scientific arguments for polygenesis
theories well before Agassiz's arrival in the United States. However,
prior to his arrival the arguments of these men attracted more controversy than respect. Biblical literalists consistently attacked their arguments. The "traditional" Christian vanguard eschewed Morton's and
Caldwell's religio-scientific perspective not because it contested the
biblical claim that "all humans are created in the image of God" but
because it disputed the notion of one human creation.

When Agassiz entered the debate, he confronted the biblical tra-
ditionalists head-on. He said, "this assertion of the common descent
of all races of men from a common stock is a mere human construction."[34] He challenged "those who maintain[ed] that mankind originated from a single pair [Adam and Eve] to quote a single passage in
the whole of Scripture" in support of such a claim.[35] Agassiz's original
support of monogenesis made his polygenetic position even more
impressive. His change of mind suggested a thoughtful consideration
of the facts before adopting a polygenetic view. He, in fact, claimed
that nature itself converted him to a polygenetic position.

Agassiz argued that monogenetic theory could not account for the
vast differences between races around the world. Even if one assumed

---

33. Louis Agassiz, "The Diversity of Origins of the Human Races," *Christian
Examiner* (July 1850): 30.

34. Ibid., 27.

35. Ibid., 26.

that the environment contributed to many of these differences, he said there was not enough time from the point of creation for humans to have migrated to different environmental contexts, let alone for the environment to create such radical racial variance. He explained, "We can see but one conclusion to be drawn . . . races cannot have assumed their peculiar features after they migrated into these countries from a supposed common centre."[36] Agassiz, therefore, concluded that the variation between races was "introduced into the human race by the Creator himself."[37]

Agassiz attributed these variations to multiple creations in distinct environmental settings. Such an understanding, Agassiz says, accounts for both the diversity of races and the unity of humankind. He argues that there is a "higher unity among men, making them all equal before God, because all of them have been created in his image."[38] Of importance, however, is the fact that this unity and equality before God, which Agassiz notes, obviously did not extend to an equality between races. For, as Agassiz later argued, "Negroes . . . were by nature, 'submissive, obsequious, and imitative' and that it was 'mock philosophy' to consider them as equal to whites"[39] (so much for Agassiz not entering into the debate about the status of black people). As for his polygenetic theory, Agassiz said that the creation of Adam and Eve, as well as the book of Genesis, applies "chiefly . . . to the history of the white race, with special reference to the history of the Jews."[40] Again, he contended that other races were the result of separate creations in environmental settings different from that of Adam and Eve. The belief in multiple creations, he concluded, was not only scientifically sound, but also gave the Creator "wider control over the origins of life" than did monogenetic theories.[41] In the end, with the alleged support of science and scripture, Agassiz provided the religio-scientific foundation for natural law theo-ideology. With religious and scientific evidence that black people

36. Ibid., 19.

37. Ibid., 26.

38. Ibid., 12.

39. Quoted in Edward Lurie, "Louis Agassiz and the Races of Man," *Isis* 45.3 (September 1954): 238.

40. Agassiz, "The Diversity of Origin of the Human Races," 29.

41. Agassiz, quoted in Edward Lurie, "Louis Agassiz and the Races of Man," 235.

were "genetically" and naturally inferior to white people, their status as chattel could be accepted as a "natural one" that did not controvert any "moral" codes.[42] In fact, any moral code that suggested otherwise was considered "blasphemous."[43]

What is interesting is that while biblical literalists were concerned about various polygenetic religio-scientific theories defying scripture, they seemingly overlooked the ways in which Anglo-Saxonist natural law theo-ideology itself challenged central Christian doctrines. For instance, this theo-ideology contests both the triunity of God and the goodness of God's creation. It implies that dualistic relationality reflects the image of God and that God actually constructed "wicked" creations. These theological implications will be discussed more fully later in this book. What such theological concessions point to, however, is the urgency to provide religious justification for the conception of black people as chattel. With religio-scientific support, natural law theo-ideology supplied this justification.

It cannot be stressed enough that the black body as chattel is a necessary foundation for constructing the guilty black body. It is the specter of slavery that perhaps has the greatest impact on black people's current social-cultural realities. It is infused into America's collective consciousness. It is an insidious aspect of America's exceptional identity. The construction of black people as chattel is unquestionably the construct that compels the aggressive assertion of stand-your-ground culture in response to the black body. In order to understand the violent force of this culture when it comes to the black body, we must explore two other conceptualizations that are required to complete the construction of the guilty black body. Both inexorably flow from the concept of black chattel.

Hypersexualized Black Body

The stereotype of black people as hypersexualized has been well documented in many places. I will, therefore, not spend much time examining the complexity of this stereotype in this discussion. What I will highlight is its crucial role in constructing the guilty

---

42. Lurie, "Louis Agassiz and the Races of Man," 234ff.
43. See William Harper quote above, n. 22.

black body. The hypersexualized stereotype is actually an indispensable precursor to the final cog in construction of the guilty black body, even as it insinuates the guilt. Let us briefly first review the sexualized caricature.

The primary reason for the construction of black people as hypersexualized was to support the sexual abuse of the black body during slavery. According to this stereotypic construction, black women are Jezebels, that is, sexual temptresses always thirsting for sex. Black men are sexually proficient, predatory bucks who are always on the prowl for their next sexual conquest. Both black women and men are endowed with an insatiable sexual appetite. This hypersexualized prescription served several purposes in protecting the narrative of Anglo-Saxon exceptionalism and thus in the construction of the guilty black body.

First, it further verified the profound difference between white and black people. They were now clearly as different as night and day. For, according to the Anglo-Saxon myth, white people are paragons of virtue who are ruled by their reason. According to the constructed discourse of Anglo-Saxon exceptionalism, black people are ruled by passion and hence without virtue. Correspondingly, this hypersexual characterization gives credence to the necessary subjugation of black people by white people. It is only fitting, as implied by natural law, that those endowed with reason should be the rulers of society.

Second, the hypersexualized black body provided a rationale for the sexual exploitation of black bodies during slavery and concomitantly inferred their enduring guilt. As earlier mentioned, black peoples' value as a commodity was initially dependent on their ability to produce other laboring bodies. Put simply, black men and women were expected to breed, and breed as much as possible. Forced "breeding" was not, therefore, unusual during slavery. One interview of a former slave revealed the following:

> On this plantation were more than 100 slaves who were mated indiscriminately and without regard for family unions. If their master thought that a certain man and woman might have strong, healthy offspring, he forced them to have sexual relation, even though they were married to other slaves. If there seemed to be any slight reluctance on the part of either of the

unfortunate ones, "Big Jim" would make them consummate this relationship in his presence. He enjoyed these orgies very much and often entertained his friends in this manner, quite often he and his guests would engage in these debaucheries, choosing for themselves the prettiest of the young women. Sometimes they forced the unhappy husbands and lovers of their victims to look on.[44]

This slave testimonial also reveals the other exploitative "benefit" of portraying the enslaved as hypersexual. This portrayal enabled white men to literally rape black women with moral and legal impunity. In the logic of "cherished whiteness" a black woman could never be raped since she was an unabashed temptress.

White women also used the stereotype of hypersexualized blackness for their own benefit. One former slave remembered:

In them times white men went with colored gals and women bold[ly]. Any time they saw one and wanted her, she had to go with him. . . . Not only the men, but the women went with colored men too. That's why so many women slave owners wouldn't marry, 'cause they was goin' with one of their slaves.[45]

As is well documented, the danger in these white women/black men liaisons was typically for the black males alone. Given the alleged predatory nature of the black man, his guilt was readily assumed. Regardless of the situation, he was viewed as a rapist. The logic of the hypersexualized caricature similarly held black women responsible for their rape at the hands of white men, especially in the antebellum and immediate postbellum context. The hypersexualized stereotype meant that the guilt of white men was projected onto black women,

---

44. Interviewer's summary, Sam and Louisa Everett, enslaved in Virginia, interviewed October 8, 1936, Mulberry, Florida, by Pearl Randolph, field worker, John A. Simms, ed., "Slave Narratives from the Federal Writers Project, 1936–1938: Florida Narratives," vol. 3, http://www.gutenberg.org.

45. Sylvia Watkins, enslaved in Tennessee, interviewed ca. 1937 [WPA Slave Narrative Project], "On Slaveholders' Sexual Abuse of Slaves: Selections from 19th–20th-Century Slave Narratives," National Humanities Center Resource Toolbox, The Making of African American Identity: vol. 1, 1500–1865, http://www.nationalhumanitiescenter.org.

and the guilt of white women was projected onto black men. This projection provides an early example of the concept of racialized guilt that ultimately ensnares the black body.

Guilt is not the only thing ascribed to the hypersexualized black body. So too is sin. This hypersexualized caricature further brands the black body as an intrinsically sinful body. Within the evangelical Protestant tradition that sanctions America's narrative of exceptionalism, chastity is esteemed and nonprocreative sex is deemed sinful. Within such a religious narrative, a body portrayed as lustful and libidinous is by definition a sinful body. Hence, the conception of the hypersexualized black body once again equates blackness with sin. The hypersexualized black body is always a blameworthy body. In this regard, the black body carries a double burden of guilt—social and religious. There is another implication of the hypersexualized black body that actually precipitates the decisive factor in the construction of the black body as an inexorably guilty body. The hypersexualized body is necessarily a violent body.

French anthropologist René Girard clarifies the interactive and inextricable relationship between sex and violence. He describes sex and violence as different sides of the same coin. He explains that sexual excitement and violent impulses elicit identical "bodily reactions."[46] "Like violence," he says, "repressed sexual desires" eventually erupt, "causing tremendous havoc."[47] He goes on to say, "Thwarted sexuality leads naturally to violence."[48] Perhaps the most troubling of his observations is that "the shift from violence to sexuality and from sexuality to violence is easily effected, even by the most 'normal' of individuals."[49] Girard's findings spell trouble for the black body in a context defined by cherished whiteness.

Given the intricate relationship between sexuality and violence, a hypersexualized body is by nature a hyperviolent black body. This means that the black body, according to the discursive productions of white exceptionalism, is a ticking time bomb. Because it is consistently sexually charged, it is an ever-present threat to the social order, specif-

---

46. René Girard, *Violence and the Sacred,* trans. Patrick Gregory (Baltimore: Johns Hopkins University Press, 1979), 35-36.

47. Ibid., 35.

48. Ibid.

49. Ibid.

ically to the white body. At any time, the sexually charged black body can erupt into a violent sexual rage. Already inscribed with predatory inclinations, the black male is seen as most threatening of all. If his predatory sexual desires are not fed, then he becomes like a wild animal in heat—roaming about to satiate these desires. Of course, as we will see, within the racialized narratives and constructs of America, this meant that he was a danger to white women. After all, given black women's sexual predilections there was nothing that the black male could do to them that would be a violation, at least in the logic of the racist discourse that fed America's sense of exceptionalism.

The hypersexualized stereotype of black people, for all intents and purposes, casts black women and men as wild beasts. Thomas Jefferson said as much when he offers in his *Notes on the State of Virginia* that the orangutan has more of a preference for black women than for "his own species." Jefferson goes on to say that black males "are more ardent after their female: but love seems to be more an eager desire, than a tender delicate mixture of sentiment and sensation."[50] The hypersexualized/hyperviolent black body brings us to the definitive concept in the construction of the guilty black body: the dangerous black body.

The Dangerous Black Body

As earlier mentioned, black people are viewed as more than just inferior to white people. They are perceived as a threat. They are viewed as a chronic danger to cherished white property. That which makes the black body most dangerous is when it betrays its created nature. Within the social-cultural context of Anglo-Saxon exceptionalism, that nature has been established as chattel. Thus, a free black body and a dangerous black body are practically equivalent, according to the theoretical logic of America's Anglo-Saxonist exceptionalism. This is the case for several reasons.

First, according to the logic of Anglo-Saxon exceptionalism, freedom is the right of cherished white property. Free black bodies thus possess something that does not belong to them. Free black bodies have essentially intruded upon the white space. The white supremacy

---

50. "Thomas Jefferson on the African Race 1781," excerpted from *Notes on the State of Virginia*, http://www.historytools.org/sources/Jefferson-Race.pdf.

ideology and natural law theo-ideology of the Anglo-Saxon exceptionalist narrative clearly demarcate space. The free space is a well-defined white space. When black people step into that social space, they do so as intruders, and thus they have created a dangerous situation because white people are compelled, by divine law nonetheless, to protect their space from intruders.

Second, a free black body is a dangerous body because it presumably threatens the very social order. It does this in several ways. By entering into the white space, and perhaps even thriving in it, a free black body contests the very notion of white supremacy. The ideology of white supremacy is maintained to the extent that white bodies continue their subjugating control over nonwhite bodies. The moment that this controlling relationship is subverted, the ideology of white supremacy is fractured. The body that is presumed most inferior to the white body subverts that relationship and truly calls the ideology of white supremacy into question. If white people cannot subdue the most inferior beings, than whom can they control? Perhaps, then, whiteness is not a mark of superiority, as suggested by America's grand narrative of Anglo-Saxon exceptionalism. Worse still, blackness may not be the radical inferior other to whiteness. Instead, it may actually be the "kryptonite" to whiteness. Whatever else the case may be, a free body invariably endangers narratives of white supremacy.

In addition, a free black body is living contrary to its presumed created nature, as constructed by the theo-ideology of America's exceptionalism. In so doing, it theoretically threatens the very stability of the nomos. Berger might call a free black in a context of white supremacy a "marginal situation." These situations imply "that the accepted definitions of reality may be fragile or even fraudulent."[51] Essentially, a free black person contests the notion that the world as it is is the way that God ordained it to be. A free black body literally points to the possibility of a different cosmic order. The free black person suggests that there is a different divine vision and punctures the sacred canopy of America's Anglo-Saxon exceptionalism. The very reality of a free black body serves as a counternarrative to the Anglo-Saxonist narrative that Anglo-Saxon America is "the city on the hill" showing forth the glory of God. A free black body implies that the Anglo-Saxon

---

51. Berger, *The Sacred Canopy*, 23.

narrative is in fact blasphemous. The sacred connection between the racialized American nomos and the sacred cosmos is disrupted by the advent of a free black body. In the end, a free black body poses an ontological danger to an Anglo-Saxon exceptionalist social order. It also presents an existential danger.

The very construction of the black body as an uncontrollable beast, given its hypersexualized nature, means this body must be controlled. Indeed, as natural law theo-ideology contends, control of this body is for the common good. A free black body is tantamount to a wild animal on the loose. So, once again, a free black body is, according to the productions of America's exceptionalist narrative, quintessentially a dangerous black body.

As chattel, the black body remains in its constructed space, lives into its created nature, does not disrupt the order of things, and is under the control of white people; therefore, it is not dangerous. The moment the black body is no longer chattel and thus free, it becomes dangerous. The equation of the free black body with a dangerous body was actually more than an abstract, theoretical notion. This construct became embedded into the collective consciousness of the nation following emancipation. The vast array of postemancipation "polemical literature" that emerged discussing the "black peril" is proof of this.[52]

In this literature, the free black male was perceived as the greatest peril. In light of the caricature of him as a hypersexualized predator, he was viewed as an imminent danger to white women. To drive that point home, in 1903 Dr. William Lee Howard, writing in *Medicine,* a respectable journal at the time, claimed the sexually violent behavior of the black man was genetic. He said that the "large size of his penis" lacked "sensitive fibers." He, therefore, concluded that this deficiency drives him to "sexual madness and excess."[53] Painting an even more ominous picture of the black male danger George T. Winston wrote in 1901:

> When a knock is heard at the door [a white woman] shudders with nameless horror. The black brute is lurking in the dark, a monstrous beast, crazed with lust. His ferocity is almost demon-

---

52. Friedrickson, *The Black Image in the White Mind,* 262.
53. Dr. William Lee Howard, quoted in George M. Fredrickson, *The Black Image in the White Mind,* 279.

ical. A mad bull or tiger could scarcely be more brutal. A whole community is frenzied with horror, with the blind and furious rage for vengeance.[54]

Clearly both these diatribes reverberate with the undertones of the natural law theo-ideology and the racist religio-science that said certain black behaviors were innate. With such portrayals, it is no surprise that most of the literature concerning the perils of a free black body centered on the alleged rape of white women by black men. There is perhaps no better representation of this literature than an article written by a bishop in the Methodist Episcopal Church, Atticus G. Haygood, in the October 1893 issue of *The Forum*.

In his article, "The Black Shadow in the South," Haygood seeks to understand the justification for lynching. He begins his article by calling lynching "a crime against society."[55] Nevertheless, in explaining the reason for lynching he paints the emancipated "negro" as a dangerous "negro." Accepting that the rape of white women is the crime that lynching attempts to address, Haygood says, "This particular crime was practically unknown before Emancipation."[56] He implies that with emancipation black men's "thwarted sexual desires" were violently unleashed on vulnerable white womanhood. Haygood puts it this way: "An ignorant race, that in and through the ministry of slavery had grown into all that made it better than naked Africans, were suddenly turned loose . . . into a freedom they did not understand. . . . The recoil was tremendous."[57] To bolster his claims that "negroes" were not suited to possess freedom, he blamed Reconstruction for fostering the criminal nature of "the negro." He explained that during Reconstruction "negroes" were granted rights they were innately unprepared for. Consequently, he said during the period of Reconstruction "the negro grew more dangerous."[58] As if to provide

---

54. George T. Winston, quoted in David Pilgrim, "The Brute Caricature," Jim Crow Museum of Racist Memorabilia, "Using Objects of Intolerance to Teach Tolerance and Promote Social Justice," http://www.ferris.edu/jimcrow/brute.

55. Atticus G. Haygood, "The Black Shadow in the South," *Forum* (October 1893): 167.

56. Haygood, "The Black Shadow in the South," 172.

57. Ibid.

58. Ibid., 173.

the definitive proof for the good of slavery and the danger of emancipation, Haygood points out that "all crimes of violence by the negroes are committed by those who were children in 1865 [end of Civil War] or who have been born since that time."[59] Haygood, like others who viewed the free black person as a dangerous black person, longed for the "old ones"—those who had accepted their status as chattel.

In the same *Forum* issue Charles H. Smith also stressed the dangers of the free "negro." The very title of his article, "Have American Negroes Too Much Liberty?," makes the problem as he sees it clear. Similar to Haygood, he considers lynching a consequence of the freedom granted to black people. He opens his article by saying, "The rapid increase of crime among the negroes of the South and the alarming frequency of the most brutal outrages upon white women and children have excited the most serious apprehension of every good citizen."[60] Implying that black people were suited to be slaves, he says that even considering their criminal behavior, "they are good servants."[61] He, like Haygood, longs for the "old negroes" because "those who have come after them are sadly degenerated."[62] As if there is a need to make clear just how dangerous a free black person is, Smith demonstratively asserts, "A bad negro is the most horrible human creature on earth, the most brutal and merciless."[63] Of course for Smith "a bad negro" is a free "negro." Alluding to the hypersexual nature of the "negro" male and hence emphasizing his danger to white women, Smith adds, "When a desire to indulge his bad passions comes over him, he seems to be utterly devoid of prudence or conscience."[64] Judging from the arguments of Haygood and Smith, it would seem that the caricature of the black body as a hypersexualized and thereby hyperviolent body had fully situated itself in the collective American conscience. So too had the notion that slavery was the most appropriate condition for blacks, given their created nature.

---

59. Ibid., 174.

60. Charles H. Smith, "Have American Negroes Too Much Liberty? *Forum* (October 1893): 176.

61. Ibid., 178.

62. Ibid., 179.

63. Ibid., 181.

64. Ibid., 181.

Haygood and Smith were not the only ones who believed that without slavery, black people were unquestionably dangerous.

In 1836 William Drayton, a U.S. representative from South Carolina, published a book in which he was intent on "unmasking the evils and dangers of Emancipation."[65] In making his case, he made the familiar argument that the "negro" is "happier . . . as a slave, than he could be as a freeman." Drayton claims that this is due to "the peculiarities of his character."[66] Of course, the "peculiar" character of the "negro" is that which designates her/him as chattel. Again revealing just how embedded the Anglo-Saxonist natural law theo-ideology had become in the national consciousness, Drayton further argues that slavery is consistent with the "will and desire of God." This was evident by the "happiness of the human family."[67] Drayton was clearly not referring to the enslaved in his description of the "human family." Even if he were, he had already established that the "negro" was happiest when enslaved. Drayton's strongest case against emancipation, however, was the danger that he said the free "negro" posed. He said that with emancipation the once-contented slave "becomes the midnight murderer to gain that fatal freedom whose blessings he does not comprehend."[68] In order to secure the freedom for which he/she is not suited, Drayton said insurrections would erupt. Citing as evidence insurrections from the time of Spartacus in 70 B.C. to Barbados in 1816, he said emancipation would unleash the "overpowering burst of long-buried passion—the wild frenzy of revenge, and the savage lust for blood" that slavery had managed to contain.[69] As Drayton argued against the merits of emancipation he was clearly suggesting that without slavery the "negro" would actually revert to kind, that is, to being a wild savage beast. Others said this more directly.

In offering a review of the 1851 book *Negro-Mania*, a book that summarized the data in support of black people's inferiority, the author also presented his own polemic against emancipation. He argued, "The Almighty has thought well to place certain of his creatures in

---

65. William Drayton, *The South Vindicated from the Treason and Fanaticism of the Northern Abolitionist* (Philadelphia: H. Manly, 1836).

66. Drayton, *The South Vindicated*, 81.

67. Ibid., 83.

68. Ibid., 245.

69. Ibid., 246.

certain fixed positions in this world," which no persons [abolitionists] should dare to change.[70] To change such a thing, he argued, would be "blasphemy." He says that where God has placed "my poor black brother . . . there thou must stay."[71] He goes on to say that "The white and black race can only exist together in present relations."[72] Quoting Dr. T. D. English, he says that even though the negro race has been "taught by a superior species, it soon retrogrades to hopeless barbarism."[73] The review comes to a close as the reviewer cites arguments that make clear emancipation makes a "negro" like a dog without a master. He says the free "negro" would return "to the untaught habits and instincts of nature." This means that the "brutish propensities of the negro" would be "unchecked . . . ," thereby permitting him to exercise "his native barbarity and savageism."[74]

Echoing the same theme of reverting to savage form if not enslaved, William Cabell Bruce, a Baltimore lawyer, wrote in an 1891 pamphlet, "as [the Negro] recedes further and further from under the direct influence of the whites, his port becomes more and more aggressive."[75]

The writings that have been cited are actually a small sampling of the literature that appears after emancipation to make the case for slavery. What this literature makes abundantly clear is the effectiveness of the discourse that had branded black people as hypersexualized chattel. Michel Foucault's analysis of power helps us to understand how this has become the case.

Foucault argues that unjust social relationality is not effectively sustained solely, if at all, through the use of brutal force. He stresses that power, particularly inequitable power, is not coercive or even repressive. Rather, it is productive. Power's productive character begins with a "will to knowledge." That is, power itself generates the kind of knowledge it needs to be sustained. It enlists various communities of authority, such as the scientific and religious commu-

---

70. L.S.M., Review of John Campbell's *Negro-Mania*, in *Debow's Review, Agricultural Commercial, Industrial Progress and Resources* (May 1852): 12:5, 510.

71. Ibid., 511.

72. Ibid., 512.

73. Ibid., 519.

74. Ibid., 521.

75. W. Cabell Bruce, *The Negro Problem* (Baltimore: John Murphy & Co., 1981), 24.

nities, to provide the knowledge base to legitimize the social, political, and institutional constructs of power itself. In this instance, as we have seen, the scientific and religious communities provided the objective knowledge needed to sustain the supremacy of whiteness, thereby supporting the notion of Anglo-Saxon exceptionalism. The knowledge "willed" by power, according to Foucault's analysis, is then carefully disseminated through public discourse and various social institutions, such as churches and schools. Discourse is critical to the actualization of power. In other words, discursive power fuels and sustains social, political, and even ecclesiastical power. It is through discourse that people learn to behave in a certain manner and are also socialized, almost seamlessly, into supporting the realities of unjust power. Foucault puts it simply, "Discourse transmits and produces power; it reinforces it. . . ."[76]

It is worth reiterating that religious discourse is an essential component of discursive power. It can provide, and has in fact provided, sacred legitimation for inequitable social relationships. As we have seen, religious thinkers supplied the knowledge "willed" by white power structures to support black peoples' inferior if not nonhuman status. They supplied the evidence to support the sacred canopy for the construct of black people as chattel.

Michel Foucault's analysis helps us to understand the subtle manner in which an image of the black body as chattel has been implanted within the collective psyche of American society. We have seen in the course of this discussion how the first Americans influenced an Anglo-Saxon myth, constructing a narrative of Anglo-Saxon exceptionalism. This narrative, to sustain itself, then produced the ideology of cherished white property, that is, white supremacy. Subsequently, in an effort to validate the reality of cherished white property—which expresses itself as subjugating power endowed with rights that only white bodies can enjoy—knowledge was "willed" to foster the ideology of an ontological difference between black people and white people. In fact, various discourses were generated that cast the black body as a kind of beastly creation, which expressed itself as chattel. The proliferation of discourse and knowledge to sustain unjust

---

76. Michel Foucault, *The History of Sexuality,* trans. Robert Hurley, 3 vols. (New York: Vintage Books, 1990), 1:101.

systems of power provides another dimension of meaning to discursive power. For discourse seems to have its own generative potential. It is as if there is an inertia that builds which then reflexively produces increased knowledge and the discourses needed to sustain the various discourses already in place. Thus, from its Puritan and Pilgrim beginnings, Anglo-Saxon power has formed an intricate web of interactive narratives and discourse to sustain itself, or at least to maintain the illusion of America's Anglo-Saxon identity. This web began with the grand narrative of Anglo-Saxon exceptionalism. The black body has become trapped in this web that ultimately paints it as utterly guilty. Before examining the guilty black body, we must return to the construct of the black body as chattel.

As mentioned earlier in the chapter, the black body as chattel is the specter from slavery that perhaps has the greatest impact on black people's current social-cultural realities. In fact it does. This construct has not disappeared. It was firmly established within America's collective consciousness during slavery, and it remains a pervasive part of that consciousness today. This construct is a valuable part of America's exceptionalist identity, thus one not easily disposed of. Just because chattel slavery no longer exists in America, and both the U.S. House of Representatives and Senate passed resolutions apologizing for it, does not mean that the racist constructs slavery produced do not continue to exist. As Michelle Alexander has aptly pointed out, "racism is highly adaptable."[77] So too are the constructs that have fostered it. They just take different forms, those that are appropriate to the social-historical context. It is what one legal scholar has called "preservation through transformation."[78] Oftentimes the transformations effectively mask the racialized character of the new construct. Such is the case with the transformation of the black body as chattel. The twenty-first-century version of this construct is the criminal black body. The black body that was once marked as chattel is now marked as criminal. This construct serves the same purpose as the construct of chattel. It relegates the black body to an "unfree" space. It preserves the free space as a white space. This transformation began shortly after emancipation.

---

77. Alexander, *The New Jim Crow*, 21.
78. Reva Siegel, quoted in Alexander, *The New Jim Crow*, 21.

The Criminal Black Body

W. E. B. Du Bois says that "The slave went free; stood a brief moment in the sun; and then moved back again toward slavery."[79] What Du Bois is referring to is the brief period of Reconstruction. During this period black people began to enjoy some of the rights that were considered "wages" of whiteness. For instance, they were able to vote and run for political office. In fact, black men were elected to the U.S. Senate and House of Representatives during that period. However, as pointed out in the earlier discussion, the image of the black person as chattel still lurked in the imagination of American society. The fear of black people that consumed white people after emancipation was, as pointed out, driven by the belief that black people no longer saw themselves as chattel. This is why there was a longing expressed for the "old negro." Essentially, there was an urgency to re-inscribe black people with the identity as chattel, hence to return them to the space for which they had been allegedly created. It is, of course, not by chance that the stand-your-ground culture that was fostered to protect cherished whiteness, and hence the white space, began to assert itself in a more aggressive manner after emancipation. Even Alexis de Tocqueville recognized during his nineteenth-century travels across United States that "the prejudice that repels Negroes seems to grow as Negroes cease to be slaves."[80] Michelle Alexander says that after emancipation, "the development of a new racial order became the consuming passion for most white Southerners."[81] The assertion of stand-your-ground culture effectively removed the black body from the white space by criminalizing it.

The aggressive and violent enactment of stand-your-ground culture that emerged during Reconstruction is the focus for discussion in Chapter 3. It is important to realize now that the various assertions of Reconstruction/post-Reconstruction stand-your-ground culture, such as Black Codes, Jim Crow laws, and lynching, served to transform the construct of chattel into criminal. The various Black

---

79. Du Bois, *Black Reconstruction*, 30.

80. Alexis de Tocqueville, *Democracy in America,* trans. and ed. with an introduction by Harvey C. Mansfield and Delba Winthrop (Chicago: University of Chicago Press, 2000), 330.

81. Alexander, *The New Jim Crow* 28.

Codes and Jim Crow laws in particular served to plant the image of the black body as a criminal body deep within America's collective consciousness. Essentially, these legal productions criminalized black people. Just as black people became trapped in the chattel cycle, they became trapped in the criminal cycle. This occurred through the judicious implementation of racially biased laws. The primary target of the criminalizing project was, of course, the black male, since he was caricatured as the most dangerous free black body. He was the one that most urgently needed to be returned to a chattel space. The vagrancy laws illustrate how the black body, especially the male, became trapped in the criminal cycle.

Du Bois pays particular attention to these laws in his previously mentioned *essay* on the black reconstruction. He calls these laws "the most important and oppressive laws" of that period, "designed to fit the Negro's condition and to be enforced particularly with regard to Negroes."[82] Georgia codified such a law. The Georgia law in part stipulated: "All persons wandering or strolling about in idleness, who are able to work, and who have no property to support them; all persons leading an idle, immoral, or profligate life, who have no property to support them and are able to work and do not work; all persons able to work having no visible and known means of a fair, honest, and respectable livelihood . . . shall be deemed and considered vagrants, and shall be indicted as such. . . ." The Mississippi law was more direct in naming its target. It read, "That all freedmen, free Negroes, and mulattoes in this state over the age of eighteen years, found on the second Monday in January, 1866, or thereafter, with no lawful employment or business, or found unlawfully assembling themselves together, either in the day or night time . . . shall be deemed vagrants." This Mississippi law also deemed as vagrant whites that associated with the persons mentioned above. South Carolina declared "all persons without fixed and known places of abode and lawful employment" as vagrant.[83] These are just three examples of the many vagrant laws that were passed across the southern United States following emancipation. Even though many of these laws, unlike the Missis-

---

82. Du Bois, *Black Reconstruction*, 173.
83. These texts of these laws are quoted in Du Bois, *Black Reconstruction*, 174-75.

sippi law, did not mention race, it is clear that black people were the target of them. The chance of a black person gaining steady employment was next to none. Again, the black body did not enjoy the right to his/her own labor. This did not significantly change after slavery, meaning they could not expect to acquire a paid job. If they managed to do so, the pay was certainly not sufficient to support them. Therefore it is clear, as Du Bois said, that the vagrant laws were written to fit the "Negroes' condition." They were meant to ensnare them in a criminal cycle. Consequently, a new chattel identity was constructed. This identity was effectively transformed and reinscribed in two interlocking ways.

The penalty for vagrancy typically involved jail time and some form of forced labor. Both forms of punishment literally placed the black body back into an unfree space. The penalty removed the black body from the white space and returned it to the space that America's exceptionalist narratives said was suited for it, again an unfree space.

Alexander also notes that laws such as these were clearly meant "to establish another system of forced labor," that is, a new form of slavery.[84] The criminal was literally made into chattel. Through the punishment of forced labor, they again were deprived of the right to own their laboring bodies. The chattel identity was subtly reconstructed as a criminal identity.

At the same time, these laws assured that the black body would be viewed as a criminal body within the collective imagination. They literally made a criminal of black people. All the black person had to do was be black. Essentially, these laws penalized black people for "living while black." As Alexander notes, "vagrancy laws and other laws defining activities such as 'mischief' and 'insulting gestures' as crimes were enforced vigorously against blacks."[85] Again, the very conditions of black living were made illegal. It is in this way that blackness became a marker for criminality. The black body was effectively criminalized. And like chattel, a criminal does not belong in free space.

The construct of chattel was seamlessly transformed into a criminal construct. Consequently, the chattel construct remains alive today albeit in a new form, one acceptable to a society in which legal

---

84. Alexander, *The New Jim Crow*, 28.
85. Ibid., 31.

racialized slavery presumably no longer exists. The construct of the criminal body has been sustained in the twentieth and twenty-first centuries the way it was sustained in postemancipation America: through the racially biased laws of stand-your-ground culture.[86] One researcher put it this way: "So ubiquitous is the pattern of discriminatory law enforcement that the effect has been to criminalize an entire [black] population."[87]

Michelle Alexander has called the Prison Industrial Complex the new Jim Crow. She is right in the sense that it functions as a "well-disguised system of racialized social control . . . in a manner strikingly similar to Jim Crow."[88] The laws that have been generated to insure a majority black imprisoned population certainly are updated versions of Jim Crow laws. They represent, again to be argued in Chapter 3, the aggressive assertion of stand-your-ground culture. Nevertheless, the Prison Industrial Complex is about more than the Jim Crow laws that make it work. This "Complex" attempts to reinstall, in a more acceptable twenty-first-century manner, the same system that Jim Crow was developed to reinstate. The Prison Industrial Complex harkens back to slavery. It maintains the narrative of slavery that the black body is not meant to be free. It returns the black body to its "proper" place. It virtually reenslaves the black body by putting it behind bars. If the black criminal is the new chattel, the Prison Industrial Complex is the new slavocracy. As we will see more fully in the next chapter, the Prison Industrial Complex is the institutional manifestation of stand-your-ground culture. To reiterate, this culture does its job when it removes the black body from the white space (a free space) and returns it to the black space (an unfree space) in a way that seems reasonable and unbiased. With jails and prisons serving as the new plantations, cherished white property is protected, and the most "dangerous" black body, that is, the black male body, is adequately patrolled.

What makes the transformation complete is the insinuation of the image of the black body as criminal into the American collective con-

---

86. Again, Chapter 3 will provided a detailed discussion of these laws and their impact on the black body.

87. William Chambliss, quoted in Melissa Hickman Barlow, "Race and the Problem of Crime in *Time* and *Newsweek* Cover Stories, 1946 to 1995," *Social Justice* 25.2 (Summer 1998): 149-83.

88. Alexander, *The New Jim Crow*, 4.

sciousness. When this is done, the black body and the criminal body become virtually synonymous. To see a black male body is to see a criminal body. While the scientific and religious community provided the "evidence" to sustain the notion of the black body as chattel during the nineteenth century, today the mass news media has provided the evidence to sustain the black male body as criminal. The news media have all but taken up the mantle of phrenology, physiognomy, and other "alleged" evidentiary science. They have become the progenitor of scientific racism. They have subtly but firmly implanted within the American mind the notion that criminals are blacks and blacks are criminals. Many scholars and researchers have reached a similar conclusion after studying the news media's coverage of crime. They have variously concluded, "As a result of the overwhelming media focus on crime, drug use, gang violence, and other forms of anti-social behavior among African Americans, the media have fostered a distorted and pernicious public perception of African Americans."[89]

In a study on the cover stories "about crime in *Time and Newsweek* magazines from 1946-1995," Melissa Hickman found that even though the later cover stories studied tried to "avoid direct references to race . . . the abiding image in the cover stories is one of dark and dangerous street criminals from whom our only protection is the thin blue line." For instance, she points to a 1993 *Time* cover story entitled "America the Violent." Although "the article never mentioned race," Hickman points out that the cover "was a distorted and monstrous cartoon image of a Black male criminal, whose clenched fists were restrained by handcuffs." She goes on to say, "Public consent for the extreme levels of coercive control applied to a substantial proportion of the African American population is tied to the ideological linkages forged between 'young black males' and crime. . . ."[90] As her study

---

89. Stephen Balkaran, "Mass Media and Racism," *The Yale Political Quarterly* 2.1 (October 1999); see also Dennis Rome, *Black Demons: Mass Media's Depiction of the African American Criminal Stereotype* (Westport, CT: Praeger Publishers, 2004).

90. Barlow, "Race and the Problem of Crime in *Time and Newsweek* Cover Stories, 1946-1995." This article also provides an extensive bibliography for research on the topic of the news media's role in the criminalization of the black body.

revealed, the news media have played a significant role in forging this ideological link.

There was perhaps no more controversial magazine cover than *Time* magazine's picture of O. J. Simpson after his arrest for allegedly killing his wife and one of her male friends. The June 27, 1994, *Time* cover had been digitally altered to darken Simpson's skin. That it had been was made even more evident by the fact that *Newsweek* placed the same mug shot on its cover without alteration. The black community was generally outraged by the *Time* cover. Once again, a link was being forged between blackness and criminality. Moreover, given the fact that Simpson's wife was white, it subtly reinforced the postemancipation diatribe that black men posed a particular threat to white women. As one commentator put it, "The photo manipulation of Simpson rendered his blackness both unequivocal and menacing, in a murder case already infused with race—with Simpson, the black defendant, accused of murdering his blonde white wife."[91]

In a wide-ranging interview on crime and race, James Miller, the former executive director of the National Center for Institutions and Alternatives, offered his insights on the role the media plays in the criminalization of the black body. Recognizing that it was no longer socially acceptable to "mention race" when speaking of crime, he said, "There are certain code words that allow you to never have to say race, but everybody knows *that's* what you mean. . . . So when we talk about locking up more and more people, what we're really talking about is locking up more and more black men." He went on to discuss emerging literature that suggests "crime may, in fact, be genetic." Continuing his argument concerning media coverage of crime, he asserted, "when we talk about throwing away the keys, when we talk about cracking down on violent offenders, everyone knows that we're talking about blacks." The interview ended with Miller saying, "We want to prove a point with blacks, and we're going to do it with the criminal-justice system."[92] The point to be proven is that the black male body is a criminal body.

---

91. Ben Arogundade, "Black History 1994: The O. J. Simpson Criminal Murder Case Trial—'Time' Cover Deliberately Darkened Mugshot," http://www.arogundade.com.

92. Rick Szykowny, "No Justice, No Peace: An Interview with Jerome Miller," *Humanist* (January-February 1994): 9-19.

Miller's interview, as well as the aforementioned studies, also indicate that the "link" between blackness and criminality has indeed been successfully forged within the public mind and imagination. Numerous studies show this to be the case. They reveal that when white people, in particular, see a black body, they see a criminal. In one study to investigate the impact that the perception of a black person as criminal might have on police officers, a video game was used to present a series of young men. Some of the men were armed, and some were unarmed. Half of each category of men were white, the other half black. The object of the game was to shoot the armed targets. The study found that the participants were more likely to shoot an unarmed black target, and rarely missed shooting the armed black target. At the same time, they were least likely to shoot the white target, whether or not armed.[93] There are numerous other studies that reveal almost "automatic, unconscious" responses to black bodies as if those bodies are threatening or criminal in and of themselves. Alexander concludes that "blackness and crime, especially drug crime [has become so] conflated in the public consciousness" that the construct of the "criminalblackman" is an inevitable reality.[94]

It should be noted that the black female body has been criminalized as well, perhaps in a more gender-specific way. While not regularly portrayed as particularly predatory, she is often portrayed as criminally immoral and most times mean and angry. The Jezebel has morphed into the "welfare queen." Various studies have shown that the image of the black female welfare offender is just as implanted within the public consciousness as the criminal black male.[95] More-

---

93. Joshua Correll et al., "The Police Officer's Dilemma: Using Ethnicity to Disambiguate Potentially Threatening Individuals," *Journal of Personality and Social Psychology* 83 (2001), discussed in "Across the Thin Blue Line: Police Officers and Racial Bias in the Decision to Shoot," http://www.fairandimpartialpolicing.com.

94. Alexander, *The New Jim Crow*, 107. In speaking of the "criminalblackman" Alexander quotes legal scholar Kathryn Russel who coined the term in her book cited by Alexander, *The Color of Crime* (New York: New York University Press, 1988). Alexander also provides extensive references to studies concerning how people have consciously or subconsciously made the link between blackness and criminality.

95. See, for instance, Mark Peffley, Jon Hurwitz, Paul M. Sniderman, "Racial

over, the portrait that Daniel P. Moynihan painted of black women fifty years ago still lingers: breeders of the tangle of black criminal pathology.[96] Black mothers are viewed as responsible for raising the "criminalblackman."

A recent *Essence* magazine survey found that the media in general continue to forge negative images of black women, specifically as modern Jezebels, baby mamas, mean girls, and uneducated sisters.[97] In this regard, there is no cover that stirred more controversy than the July 28, 2008, *New Yorker* cover of then-presidential candidate Barack Obama and his wife, Michelle Obama. This cover played into perhaps the most prominent racialized caricature of the black woman, and that is as violently "angry."

The *New Yorker* cover was a cartoonish drawing that was presumably meant to satirize the lies that had swirled about the Obamas during the presidential campaign. However, perhaps confusing stereotype with satire, the cartoon seemed for many to have crossed the line. Most notably, it featured an angry looking Michelle Obama with an afro, dressed in military fatigues, with a machine gun flung across her back held up by a holster filled with serious ammunition. Satire aside, the image certainly played into the stereotype of the mean, angry black woman: another free black body to fear.

The commentary and news media coverage of the testimony from a key witness in the trial of Trayvon's killer are also telling with regard to the way black women are perceived. The witness was nineteen-year-old Rachel Jeantel. In pointing to the way Jeantel's phenotype became a source for scrutiny, implying to some a lack of credibility, one writer noted, "She is not thin or blond or demure."[98] During her testimony it was as if she was not a witness, but the defendant. Her diction was mocked throughout the trial. One newspaper reportedly described it as "difficult-to-understand," "cringe-worthy," and

Stereotypes and Whites' Political Views of Blacks in the Context of Welfare and Crime," *American Journal of Political Science* 41.1 (January 1997), 30-60.

96. See Daniel P. Moynihan, "The Case for National Action," Washington, DC: Office of Policy and Planning and Research, US Dept. of Labor (March 1965).

97. Dawnie Walton, "Essence's Images Study: Bonus Insights," www.essence.com.

98. Mary Elizabeth Williams, "The Smearing of Rachel Jeantel," *Salon* (June 27, 2013) http://www.salon.com.

"humiliating."[99] At one point in the trial the prosecutor asked her if she understood English. She was further ridiculed for not being able to read cursive writing. By the end of her testimony the prosecutor with support from the media had successfully painted her as an uneducated black woman. That, however, was not the worst of it.

Because of her defiant way of responding to the prosecutor's badgering and her display of rightful indignation for the insults that were hurled at her by the prosecutor, she was portrayed in the media as an "Angry Black Woman." One online site, *Smoking Gun*, combed through her social media history and then proclaimed her "not just a 'thug,' but proof the gene pool NEEDS more chlorine!"[100] In his commentary on the media treatment of Jeantel, *Orlando Sentinel* reporter Darryl Owens spoke to the racialized construct that was being reinforced. He said, "Today, the Angry Black Woman is stitched into our racial fabric. In movies. On TV. In the media. She's mad as hell about everything, and she isn't going to take it anymore. And she's quick to lash offenders with her sharp tongue, finger-wagging, and eye rolling."[101]

This portrayal of black women as angry is the female version of the dangerous black man. Both are portrayed as hostile and as a threat to the wider society, namely, white. Both need to be controlled. David Pilgrim, sociologist and museum curator, says of this caricature, "It is a social control mechanism that is employed to punish black women who violate the societal norms that encourage them to be passive, servile, non-threatening, and unseen."[102] In other words, black women have stepped out of their space as chattel where they are to submit to white subjugation. At the end of his commentary on Rachel Jeantel's treatment at the trial and by the media, Owens said, "in the court of public opinion, the verdict on black women already is in: Angry as charged."[103]

---

99. Quoted in Mary Elizabeth Williams, "The Smearing of Rachel Jeantel."
100. Ibid.
101. Darryl E. Owens, "Zimmerman's defense succeeded in portraying Rachel Jeantel as the Angry Black Woman" (July 1, 2013), *Orlando Sentinel,* http://www.articles.orlandosentinel.com.
102. David Pilgrim, quoted in Darryl E. Owens, "Zimmerman's defense."
103. Owens, "Zimmerman's defense."

The transformation from chattel to criminal is complete. The free black body is viewed as a "clear and present danger" to cherished white property. It is a body that needs to be kept from roaming freely about society. It needs to be controlled. This is a criminal body. It is an unalterably guilty body.

Guilty of Something

Free black bodies have to be guilty of something. In fact, according to the web of discourse and knowledge spun by America's grand narrative of Anglo-Saxon exceptionalism, they are. They are guilty of trespassing into the white space. They are guilty of betraying their divine creation. Free black bodies transgress both natural law and eternal law. Unless controlled, as the discourse of Anglo-Saxon exceptionalism has asserted, free black bodies are bound to revert to their more "savage" nature and commit a crime.

America's exceptionalist identity is sustained by the construction of racialized guilt. It is a foil for the transgressions of whiteness. As long as there is a black body, then the white body can maintain its essential innocence. Practically speaking, a free black body does not enjoy the presumption of innocence. It must always be guilty of something. With this understanding, we can now answer the question, "Why are black murder victims put on trial?"

A Mother's Fear

My son was about two years old. I had taken him to the park to play in a "Flintstones"-like car that was in the park's playground. This particular park was next door to an elementary school. After being in the park for about fifteen minutes, what appeared to be a class of first graders recessed into the park. Two little boys, one blond-haired, the other red-headed, ran down to the car where my son was playing. Seeing them coming, my son immediately jumped out. Soon the two little boys began fighting over who was going to play in the car. My son looked on with the fascination of a two year old. The little red-headed boy, who seemed to be winning the battle for the car, saw my son looking on. He suddenly stopped fighting for the car and turned toward my son. With all the venom that a seven- or eight-year-old boy could muster, he pointed his finger at my son and said, "You better stop looking at us, before I put you in jail where you belong." This little boy was angry. My son had intruded into his space. My son was guilty of being black, in the park, and looking.

I was horrified. Before I could say anything to the offending boy the white teacher, who was in earshot, approached. She clearly heard what the little boy said to my son. I expected her to admonish the little boy and to make him apologize. Instead, she looked at my two-year-old son as if he were the perpetrator of some crime and said to the little boys, "Come on with me, before there is trouble." At that moment, I was seething with anger. I took my son and left the park.

As I was driving home, tears flowed from my eyes. I felt an unspeakable sadness and pain. At two years old my son was already viewed as a criminal. At seven or eight years old the link between a black body and a criminal had already been forged in the mind of a little white boy. If at two years old my son was regarded as guilty of something by the white teacher, I feared what his future would bring as he got older. If at two, looking like a guilty criminal got a finger pointed in his face, and a teacher hustling kids off to safety, what will the response be to him now that he is a proud, six-foot, twenty-one-year-old man? Unfortunately, I know that response.

The Question Answered

"Why are black murder victims put on trial?" Because they are black and free; they must be guilty of something. Renisha, Jonathan, Jordan, and Trayvon were victims of American exceptionalism's constructed reality of black guilt. They were free black bodies in a white space; they were surely guilty of a crime. It was a white space because white people occupied it. They had to be doing something other than asking for help, or walking home, or playing loud music. The discursive productions of America's narrative of exceptionalism had done their job. It seemed reasonable that Jordan's murderer thought there was a gun. Jordan was a black male; of course he had a gun.

In another instance when a person was denied the right to use a stand-your-ground defense, the notion of the guilty black body also prevailed. This was the case of Marissa Alexander. Marissa was sentenced to a twenty-year prison term after she fired a warning shot during an incident with her estranged husband. In fact, Marissa argued convincingly that she was a victim of domestic violence, being chased and abused by her husband at the time of the incident. She, in other words, believed her life to be threatened. She did not kill anyone; she did not even aim the gun at her husband. Yet, she was denied a stand-your-ground defense. She was convicted of assault with a deadly weapon. Marissa was trapped in the construct of America's narrative of Anglo-Saxon exceptionalism. She had to be guilty of something. In this instance, the guilt was perhaps easy to determine. She was guilty of being an "Angry Black Woman."

In a 2008 speech on race, in response to the media firestorm created by a sermon given by Jeremiah Wright, his former pastor, then-presidential candidate Barack Obama said, "The past isn't dead and buried. In fact, it isn't even past." He is right. Slavery's past of the black body as chattel has been so seared into the American psyche that it continues to cheapen black life. The apologies for slavery can never be enough as long as America's narrative of Anglo-Saxon exceptionalism continues to generate new constructions of the black body as chattel. To be chattel is for the black body never to be free from the fatal mark of being guilty of something.

Ironically, as I am writing this book, I can hear an ESPN commentator talking about O. J. Simpson. ESPN is doing a feature story on O. J. Simpson, twenty years after his trial for murdering two people. Other news outlets are doing the same. I sit thinking, when is it going to stop? Why, when we have a black president, is the media still fixated on O. J. Simpson? Maybe it is because we have a black president that the media must reinforce the image of the black male body as a criminal body. The past is truly not past.

I watched and listened intently as Jordan Davis's mother, Lucia McBath, spoke at a press conference after the trial of her son's murderer. She asked that people pray for her son's killer, given the torment that would plague him the rest of his life. She was happy that some of the jurors saw the "truth" of what happened when Jordan was killed. Yet, she said that she "would continue to stand and continue to wait for justice for Jordan." Jordan's father, Ron Davis, followed by saying that "it didn't come out in the trial, but Jordan was a good kid."

As I watched the press conference, tears once again came to my eyes. I recalled the day in the park with my son. I remembered how he, at two, was invested with guilt. It cost him a day of play in the park. It cost Jordan his life. After their son had been virtually put on trial for his own murder, Jordan's parents were testifying to his innocence. After the press conference, I called my son, who was at college, and I told him about it. I repeated to him the words I had spoken to him after the trial for Trayvon's killer. I said, "I am your mother, and like Trayvon's and Jordan's mother I will defend you until my death. But, I don't want to have to defend you in death. So, be safe because the world is not safe for a black male body."

Jordan's mother said she prays for her son's killer. I pray that those like Jordan's killer will be able to see our black sons and daughters as the children of God that they are. I pray that those that would see our children as "criminals" will be able to see that they are a part of God's *good* creation. I pray to God that God's justice will be done, so that Jordan's mother will have justice for her son.

In bringing his remarks to a close Jordan's father said his son did not deserve to be "collateral damage." He went on to say that none of our children deserve to be collateral damage, as if Jordan and young black bodies are in the middle of war. In fact, our black children are in a war. But Jordan, Renisha, Jonathan, and Trayvon are not the collateral damage of that war. Our black children are the targets of the "stand-your-ground war" that America's narrative of Anglo-Saxon exceptionalism has incited. This is the topic for discussion in Chapter 3.

3

Manifest Destiny War

During an interview following the trial of Trayvon's killer, one of the jurors (B37) attempted to explain the jury's not-guilty verdict. She said, "Oh, I believe [Trayvon] played a huge role in his death. . . . He could have walked away and gone home."[1] The juror's comment raises many issues. Her response reflects a culmination of the complex discursive productions of America's narrative of exceptionalism. In the end, it was impossible for her, and apparently other jurors as well, to view Trayvon as an innocent victim. He had to be guilty of something. If he was guilty of nothing else, he was guilty of not walking away. Her comment points to the conclusions of the previous chapter: it is virtually impossible to see the black body as an innocent body, even when it is a murdered body. The juror's comment also suggests something more. It was acceptable for Trayvon's killer to pursue him. Even though she acknowledged the situation had gotten out of hand that Florida evening, and that perhaps the killer had gotten in over his head, she was insistent that he had a right to pursue Trayvon and to do so with a gun. He was justified, she believed, in his actions.

While many of the details of that evening likely will never be more than speculation, three facts are undisputed. First, Trayvon's killer got out of his car and pursued the teenager, even after being told by a 911 dispatcher not to do so. Second, the pursuer had a gun. Third, Trayvon Martin is dead.

---

1. Anderson Cooper, 360 Degrees, "Interview of Zimmerman Juror B-37"; Aired July 16, 2013, http://transcripts.cnn.com/TRANSCRIPTS/1307/15/acd.01.html.

While black bodies have not been the only victims of Stand Your Ground laws, now enacted in at least twenty-three states, these laws have disproportionately victimized black people.[2] A study conducted by the Urban Institute found "substantial racial disparities exist in the outcomes of cross-race homicides." It further concludes that Stand Your Ground laws "worsen the disparity."[3] More specifically, this study found that in cases with a "fact pattern" similar to Trayvon's, "the rate of justifiable homicide is almost six times higher." It also showed that "Racial disparities are much larger, as white-on-black homicides have justifiable findings 33 percentage points more often than black-on-white homicides. Stand Your Ground laws appear to exacerbate those differences."[4]

Though Stand Your Ground laws are the most visible, and perhaps most deadly, assertions of stand-your-ground culture in the current historical context, they are not the only expressions of this culture. Stand-your-ground culture has generated other laws within the twenty-first-century context, as it has done in other historical periods, that disadvantage black bodies. We will explore some of these laws later in this chapter. What is important to remember at the outset is the fact that black bodies are meant to be the most victimized of stand-your-ground culture. As we have seen, this is a culture that emerged to protect cherished white property. Given the fact that America's narrative of Anglo-Saxon exceptionalism has constructed the white body in extreme opposition to the black body, it is predictable that black bodies are disproportionately assaulted by this culture. What perhaps is not so predictable is the deadly force of this culture in relation to the black body. What has allowed this culture to become so acceptably deadly when it comes to the black body? Why does this culture seemingly pursue black bodies with murderous intent?

While a stand-your-ground defense was not used in the case of Trayvon's killer, it was referred to in the instructions read to the jury.

---

2. For a list of states with precise Stand Your Ground laws at the time of this writing, see http://criminal.findlaw.com/criminal-law-basics/states-that-have-stand-your-ground-laws.html.

3. John K. Roman, "Race, Justifiable Homicide, and Stand Your Ground Laws: Analysis of FBI Supplementary Homicide Report Data," July 2013, p. 11, http://www.urban.org/uploadedpdf/412873-stand-your-ground.pdf.

4. Ibid., 8-9.

The judge instructed the jury that if the perpetrator "was not engaged in an unlawful activity and was attacked in any place where he had a right to be, he had no duty to retreat and had the right to stand his ground and meet force with force, including deadly force."[5] For whatever reason, it was important to the judge that stand-your-ground be mentioned as a plausible rationale for acquittal, even if the defense did not mention it. It is also clear from the comments of juror B37 that the six-person jury, perhaps influenced by the judge's instructions, had the stand-your-ground culture in mind when reaching their verdict. When asked why the jury did not find the killer guilty of one of the two options before them, second-degree murder or manslaughter, she responded, "because of the heat of the moment and the stand your ground."[6] Perhaps Stand Your Ground laws serve as a cover for justifying murderous violence against black bodies. Whatever the case, it is obvious that in the context of a stand-your-ground culture, juror B37 believed that Trayvon's killer was right to pursue Trayvon with a gun, and then to kill him.[7] Such circumstances suggest enemy combatants at war. How does this happen? Why does stand-your-ground culture so often assert itself not simply aggressively but with violent disregard when it comes to the black body? Why does it seem not just reasonable, but right and even urgently so, for a man to pursue, with a gun, a black teenager? How is it that in this stand-your-ground culture guns become the weapon of choice against black bodies? Why is retreat considered the right thing for the black body to do, but not the white body?

Again, this chapter will not attempt to readjudicate the facts of the Trayvon Martin case, the propriety of the judge's instructions, or even explore the many questions raised by the comments of juror B37. Rather, this chapter will examine the way in which America's grand narrative of Anglo-Saxon exceptionalism has generated a divinely sanctioned war against black bodies. It will demonstrate that the deadly force of stand-your-ground culture is an expression of that

---

5. Instructions read to jury by The Honorable Debra S. Nelson, Judicial Circuit Court, http://www.scribd.com/mobile/doc/153354467.

6. Cooper, "Interview with Zimmerman Juror B-37."

7. It should be noted that four other jurors (B51, B76, E6, E40) released a statement after the interview distancing themselves from the statements of B37. See the statement at Anderson Cooper, 360 Degrees, http://ac360.blogs.cnn.com.

war. In the end, this chapter will address the options available to the black body in a stand-your-ground war. It will answer whether "going home" was a viable recourse for Trayvon. The answer to this question begins with America's sense of Manifest Destiny. In many respects the various discourses and constructs of America's narrative of Anglo-Saxon exceptionalism come together in the ideology of Manifest Destiny. It is fitting, therefore, that it is the particular ideology that results in the most violent enactments of stand-your-ground culture.

Manifest Destiny

There is perhaps no book that better articulates the early American's sense of Manifest Destiny, as well as revealing the troubling implications of such a divine calling, than Protestant clergyman Josiah Strong's 1885 publication *Our Country: Its Possible Future and Its Present Crisis.* Strong makes his case for America's divine calling by first recognizing that "Every race which has deeply impressed itself on the human family has been the representative of some great idea." As he quickly points out, however, "The Anglo-Saxon is representative of two great ideas."[8] Making clear that the best of the Anglo-Saxon race was in the United States, Strong said those "closely related" ideas are "civil liberty" and "a pure *spiritual* Christianity."[9] Having established the "exceptional" nature of the Anglo-Saxon, Strong then makes his case for the Manifest Destiny of the race. He says, "It follows . . . that the Anglo-Saxon, as the great representative of these two ideas, the depository of these two great blessings, sustains peculiar relations to the world's future, is divinely commissioned to be, in a peculiar sense, his brother's keeper."[10] While the phrase "brother's keeper" might suggest a certain charitable benevolence toward other races, this was not what Strong had in mind. This becomes clear as he develops his case for the special Anglo-Saxon mission.

Strong develops his case by first scrupulously projecting the likely increase of Anglo-Saxons in various parts of the world over

---

8. Josiah Strong, *Our Country: Its Possible Future and Its Present Crisis,* with an introduction by Prof. Austin Phelps, D.D. (New York: Baker & Taylor Co., 1885), 159-60.

9. Ibid., 159-60.

10. Ibid., 161.

the course of several decades. He goes so far as to suggest that in 1980 the United States would have the largest population of Anglo-Saxons anywhere. He, therefore, concludes, "There can be no reasonable doubt that North America is to be the great home of the Anglo-Saxon, the principle seat of his power, the center of his life and influence."[11] As if to give his claims more credence, Strong draws on Charles Darwin's theory of natural selection. He says that when "the world enter[s] upon a new stage of its history—*the final competition of races for which the Anglo-Saxon is being schooled*," the Anglo-Saxon race will be the last race standing.[12] It is, he argues, a matter of "survival of the fittest." It is at this point in his argument that what it means to be the "brother's keeper" becomes clear. Strong says, "Nothing can save the inferior race but a ready and pliant assimilation," even though he admits their "extinction . . . appears probable."[13] He does concede, however, that some of the "stronger [non–Anglo-Saxon] races may be able to preserve their integrity, but in order to compete with the Anglo-Saxon, they will be forced to adopt his methods, his civilization and his religion."[14] Even with that concession, Strong concludes that given the "*centrifugal* tendency, inherent in this [Anglo-Saxon] stock and strengthened in the United States . . . this race of unequaled energy and with all the majesty of numbers . . . having developed peculiarly aggressive traits calculated to impress its institutions upon mankind, will spread itself over the earth."[15] It seems that to be a "brother's keeper" is to do one's best to help other races to survive by impressing upon them Anglo-Saxon ways and culture. If they are unable to adapt to those ways, then their extinction is certain.

Strong's book engaged more than just an elite community of academicians and fellow clergy. It quickly sold more than 200,000 copies. The popularity of the book indicated that it strongly resonated with America's collective Anglo-Saxon identity. It spoke to Anglo-Saxon America's sense of what it meant to be a people chosen by God for a special mission to the world. In so doing, it revealed the underside

---

11. Ibid., 165.
12. Ibid., 175.
13. Ibid., 175-77.
14. Ibid., 177.
15. Ibid., 175.

of this identity and this mission. With his emphasis on race and the fact that certain races are destined not to survive, Strong sounded the prevailing themes of America's notion of Manifest Destiny that culminate in a declaration of war against black bodies. This becomes clear as we explore the implications of Anglo-Saxon Manifest Destiny more closely.

An Anglo-Saxon Mission

As Protestants began to develop an identity shaped by the new reality of separation of church and state, Martin Marty says a "strong sense of place was fused with their sense of mission and destiny."[16] The same can be said for Americans who were less evangelically oriented and more civil sectarians. With America's independence from the British, these Americans also had a renewed sense of place as it related to mission and destiny. Whether influenced by evangelicals or the civil sacred canopy, Americans believed they were on a mission for God. For the evangelical sectarians it was about spreading the great Anglo-Saxon idea of "a pure spiritual Christianity." For the civil sectarians, the primary focus was spreading the great Anglo-Saxon idea of "civil liberty." For both it was a manifest destiny. This was a mission destined to be launched from the place that was "the great home of the Anglo-Saxon," the United States.

Before continuing our discussion, it is important to point out that while there were clearly two different religious canopies that legitimated and drove America's sense of self and Manifest Destiny, these canopies were not always so distinct. They overlapped, and so, as Marty explains, the claim to "cultural superiority" was always related to a claim of "spiritual superiority."[17]

One thing immediately becomes clear in both Manifest Destiny narratives, whether civil or evangelical. The place from which these divine missions were to begin was an Anglo-Saxon place. America considered itself a bastion of Anglo-Saxonism, as we have demonstrated throughout this discussion. This made America exceptional. Inasmuch as it was this bastion, it had a special mission. The narrative of Manifest Destiny, in other words, was a product of Ameri-

---

16. Marty, *Righteous Empire*, 46.
17. Ibid., 50.

ca's Anglo-Saxon narrative of exceptionalism. These two narratives are intricately and inextricably related. They are perhaps a different side of the same coin of America's Anglo-Saxon identity. This will become even clearer as we go further in our examination of Manifest Destiny.

The phrase "Manifest Destiny" was first used, at least publically, in an 1845 editorial written by John O'Sullivan. O' Sullivan coined the phrase as he argued for the annexation of Texas to the United States. He said that those nations who injected themselves into the debate concerning Texas's entrance into the Union were "thwarting our policy and hampering our power, limiting our greatness and checking the fulfillment of our Manifest Destiny to overspread the continent allotted by Providence for the free development of our yearly multiplying millions."[18] O'Sullivan sounded themes already embedded in America's sense of self. He even echoed the belief in Anglo-Saxon exceptionalism when later in his editorial he discussed the plight of California. He said, "The Anglo-Saxon foot is already on its borders. Already the advance guard of the irresistible army of Anglo-Saxon emigration has begun to pour down upon it. . . ."[19] From the Pilgrims forward, the idea of Manifest Destiny, even if the precise phrase was not used, was the driving force behind the founding, building, and expansion of the nation. Again, it was integral to America's Anglo-Saxon exceptionalist identity. If people believe themselves to be chosen by God because they and their way of life are superior to others, then the idea of acting as "their brothers' keeper" is inevitable. As Marty explains, "the [chosen] mission *to* America from colonial days had now become the mission *of* America to the world."[20]

What must not be lost in the "charitable" rhetoric of Manifest Destiny, however, is that this narrative is about land. It is, from its inception, an aggressive narrative. It was, in this regard, always more than rhetoric. It was the rationale for acting on the implications of being "chosen" for the mission of God, if not a rationalization for America's

---

18. John O'Sullivan, "Annexation," *United States Magazine and Democratic Review* 17.1 (July–August 1845): 5-10.

19. Ibid.

20. Marty, *Pilgrims in Their Own Land*, 186.

program of imperialistic expansion. Either way, the two go together. The important factor for appreciating the relationship between the narrative of Manifest Destiny and stand-your-ground culture is recognizing the belligerent nature of Manifest Destiny policy. It is telling, therefore, that the phrase "Manifest Destiny" emerged in a debate about acquiring land. The underlying question was, who had the right to land, to place? Within America's narrative of Manifest Destiny, that right belonged to God's chosen, those who had been called to carry forth God's mission of virtue and liberty across the globe. Those chosen were, of course, Anglo-Saxons. Within the Manifest Destiny narrative, land and race are connected. One's right to land was dependent on being of the right race. We will see the implications of this for non–Anglo-Saxons as we examine the narrative of Manifest Destiny even further.

An Urgent Mission

There was urgency with regard to America's Manifest Destiny project that was about more than acquisition of new land. In fact, the cause of that urgency was almost the requirement for America's expansion, at least within the narrative of Manifest Destiny. It was urgent for the Manifest Destiny mission to be successful at home.

Americans believed, and perhaps rightly so, that the eyes of the world were upon them. The leitmotif still lingering in the American imagination, at least during nineteenth-century expansion, was that American Anglo-Saxons were the remnant of those Urfolk from the east moving westward to civilize the world. Even non-Americans held the belief that it was from the United States that the "civilizing movement toward the sun" would continue. In 1752 bishop of the Church of England George Berkeley published a poem titled "America, or the Muse's Refuge: A Prophecy." In this poem he speaks of America's destiny to spread an empire across the world. He concluded his poem with what some have called the most famous lines he ever wrote. In these lines, he captures the idea of America's westward Manifest Destiny. He writes;

> Westward the Course of Empire takes its Way;
> The four first Acts already past,

A fifth shall close the Drama with the Day;
Time's noblest Offspring is the last.[21]

Americans were quick to take up the westward mantle. After all, they firmly believed they were the elite descendants of those Urfolk from the east. For evangelical sectarians, taking up this mantle meant spreading the gospel of Jesus. There was no better spokesman for the evangelical Manifest Destiny project than one of the most prominent ministers of the nineteenth century, Lyman Beecher. Beecher was clear that America was in fact going to be that "city on a hill" leading the way in bringing "glory to God."

In an 1827 sermon delivered at Plymouth, Massachusetts, Beecher began by saying that the world was in dire need of moral restoration. He went on to assert that America had "been raised up by Providence to exert an efficient instrumentality in this work of moral renovation."[22] This was not an easy position for Beecher to come to. For in a later speech, he admitted to scoffing at his predecessor Jonathan Edwards's belief that "the millennium would commence in America."[23] However, providential evidence convinced Beecher that Edwards was right. "Look now at the history of our fathers," he said, "and behold what God hath wrought. . . . And now, behold their institutions; such as the world needs, and, attended as they have been able by the power of God, able to enlighten and renovate the world."[24]

In the speech in which he admitted to once doubting Edwards, Beecher reiterated his belief in America's special mission. He argued, "There is not a nation upon earth which, in fifty years, can by all possible reformation, place itself in circumstances so favorable" as America with the "moral power to evangelize the world."[25] For him, that evangelizing project of moral renovation was to begin in the nation's West. Not only was America a part of the westward civilizing mission,

---

21. George Berkeley, "America or the Muse's Refuge: A Prophecy," http://tigger.uic.edu/~hilbert/Images%20of%20Berkeley/Berk_life.htm.

22. Lyman Beecher, *The Memory of Our Fathers: A Sermon Delivered at Plymouth, on the Twenty-Second of December, 1827* (1828), 7.

23. Lyman Beecher, *Plea for the West*, 2nd ed. (Cincinnati: Truman & Smith; New York: Leavitt, Lord & Co., 1835), 9-10.

24. Beecher, *Memory of our Fathers*, 13-14.

25. Beecher, *Plea For the West*, 10.

but it was from America's West that Beecher believed this mission would continue. He said, "It is equally plain that the religious and political destiny of our nation is to be decided in the West . . . the West is destined to be the great central power of the nation and under heaven, must affect powerfully the cause of free institutions and the liberty of the world."[26]

On the more sectarian side of America's Manifest Destiny idea, a person no less than John Adams expressed the same belief that America was continuing the march of civilization westward. In an 1807 letter to Benjamin Rush, after discussing whether the line "And the empire rises where the sun descends" was from Bishop Berkeley, Adams says, "There is nothing, in my little reading, more ancient in my memory than the observation that arts, sciences, and empire had travelled westward; and in conversation it was always added since I was a child, that their next leap would be over the Atlantic into America."[27]

John Quincy Adams, the son of John Adams, went further than his father in articulating America's divine mission, and thus taking up the mantel of westward movement. He said, not only must the nation continue its expansion toward the Pacific, but it needed to be culturally and politically unified. Such unity, he thought, was all a part of God's plan. In an August 1811 letter to his father he wrote, "The whole continent of North America appears to be destined by Divine Providence to be peopled by one *nation*, speaking one language, professing one general system of religious and political principles, and accustomed to one general tenor of social usages and customs."[28]

In these testaments to America's divine mission another crucial part of that mission becomes clear, and it is that which creates the urgency. Inasmuch as the focus of America's project of Manifest Destiny was about land, and it was, this project began with a racialized mission at home. In accepting the mantel of the providential movement westward, America truly positioned itself as the city on the hill. If the eyes of the world were not on the nation before, they surely

---

26. Ibid., 11-12.

27. John Adams, May 23, 1807, "To Benjamin Rush," *The Works of John Adams,* vol. IX: *Letters and State Papers 1799–1811,* http://oll.libertyfund.org/titles/2107.

28. John Quincy Adams, *Writings of John Quincy Adams,* vol. IV, *1811-1813,* ed. Worthington Chauncey Ford (New York: Macmillan, 1914), 209.

were after such vociferous and public claims to be, as one senator proclaimed from the Senate floor, "the chosen land of liberty—vineyard of the God of peace . . . [who] feed[s] the famished nations with the food of independence"[29] Given the chauvinistic hubris, failure was not an option for America. America's religious and civil project had to succeed. America thus carried an extra burden, albeit one that Americans brought upon themselves, but a burden nonetheless. Thomas Jefferson spoke of it in an 1811 letter to his friend John Hollins. He said, "the eyes of the virtuous, all over the earth are turned with anxiety on us, as the only depositories of the sacred fire of liberty, and that our falling into anarchy would decide forever the destinies of mankind. . . ."[30] Essentially, America's language of Manifest Destiny meant that they were to be "moral examples to the whole world."[31] Given the racialized way in which America's mission of Manifest Destiny was defined, the possibility for failure was real. It was in its own land.

An Ignoble Mission

To repeat, the Anglo-Saxon myth is the underlying presupposition that has shaped virtually every aspect of American identity. As we have seen, it was no different when it came to the narrative of Manifest Destiny. This providential calling was an Anglo-Saxon calling. America perceived its mission as one of expanding Anglo-Saxon virtue and liberty across the world. America's sense of Manifest Destiny was about the destiny of Anglo-Saxons. The civilizing project was an Anglo-Saxon project. To be civilized was synonymous with assimilation to Anglo-Saxon social, political, and religious culture. Would America succeed or fail in its civilizing mission? Would Anglo-Saxonism reign supreme in the world or not? This depended upon what took place in America itself. As John Quincy Adams alluded to, America was not a culturally unified nation. If the mission was to go forward, as John Quincy Adams also said, the nation would have to be "peopled" with those "accustomed" to the

---

29. David Trimble, quoted in Horsman, *Race and Manifest Destiny*, 88.

30. Thomas Jefferson to John Hollins, May 5, 1811, http://www.founders. archives.gov.

31. Marty, *Pilgrims in Their Own Land*, 186.

"same social usages and customs." Essentially, the mission to spread Anglo-Saxonism across the globe had to start at home. The Manifest Destiny project had to be carried on American soil first. The Anglo-Saxon destiny in the world began with the destiny of Anglo-Saxons in America. If America was the North American cradle of Anglo-Saxon social, political, and religious culture, then it had to be so not just rhetorically but in fact. According to the discursive productions of America's narrative of exceptionalism, this meant that America had to be white.

The "mission to the world" had to begin with "a mission in America." This domestic mission required the advocates of Manifest Destiny to decide what to do with those nonwhite persons in their very midst, those who were in dire need of being civilized by means of Anglo-Saxon customs and practices. How was the presence of Native Americans and former black chattel to be reconciled with the narrative of Manifest Destiny? Would these bodies that threatened America's project of Manifest Destiny be assimilated or exterminated? It is here that the dark underside of the Manifest Destiny narrative fully comes to light. This underside was presaged in Josiah Strong's previously highlighted remarks.

No one better articulates the ignoble side of Manifest Destiny than Missouri senator Thomas Hart Benton. Echoing the themes of America's divine westward mission, he proclaimed in an 1846 speech before Congress:

> It would seem that the White race alone received the divine command, to subdue and replenish the earth! For it is the only race that has obeyed it, the only one that hunts out new and distant lands, and even a New World, to subdue and replenish. Starting from western Asia, taking Europe for their field, and the Sun for their guide, and leaving Mongolians behind, they arrived, after many ages, on the shores of the Atlantic, which they lit up with the lights of science and religion, and adorned with the useful and elegant arts. Three and half centuries ago, this race, in obedience to the great command, arrived in the New World, and found new lands to subdue and replenish. . . . Civilisation, or extinction, has been the fate of all people who have found themselves in the track of the advancing Whites, and civilisation, always the preference of the Whites, has been

pressed as an object, while extinction has followed as a consequence of its resistance. The black and the Red race have often felt their ameliorating influence.[32]

Benton's remarks make clear the other defining feature of Manifest Destiny. It was not just about land and race. It was also about life. These three constructs of land, life, and race are intricately interwoven in the narrative of Manifest Destiny. Those who had the right to land were also those who had a right to live. Manifest Destiny was about more than who was destined to occupy a certain land, it was also about who was destined to live. If the manifest vision was the expansion of Anglo-Saxonism from east to west, than those who did not capitulate to Anglo-Saxon ways were destined to become extinct. Benton was clear: it was whites who had the right to land and life; others were eligible for extinction. Given the aggressive nature of the Manifest Destiny narrative, "extinction" was certainly a euphemism for a more forceful elimination. Historian Reginald Horsman explains the underlying assumptions of America's mission of Manifest Destiny this way, "By 1850 the emphasis was on the American Anglo-Saxons as a separate, innately superior people who were destined to bring good government, commercial prosperity, and Christianity to the American continents and to the world. This was a superior race, and inferior races were doomed to subordinate status or extinction."[33] There was in fact a religio-science to support the "extinction" presumption of Manifest Destiny.

The Religio-Science of Manifest Destiny

In 1854 J. C. Nott and George Gliddon published *Types of Mankind*. In this book, Nott and Gliddon attempted to put forth the preponderance of dubious research, such as Agassiz's, which suggested the creation of superior and inferior races. This book was in fact dedicated to the memory of Nott's one-time collaborator in the racist science of phrenology, the aforementioned Samuel Morton. Morton

---

32. Senator Thomas Hart Benton, speech to Congress, 1846, justifying white supremacy, http://www.ucl.ac.uk/USHistory/Building/docs/Manifest%20Destiny.htm.

33. Horsman, *Race and Manifest Destiny,* 1-2.

died three years before the book's release. Despite its length of nearly eight hundred pages, *Types of Mankind* proved to be a popular book, going through ten editions by 1871. It was doubtlessly popular for the reason that other books of its kind were popular at that time; it upheld America's grand narrative of Anglo-Saxon exceptionalism. It resonated with America's collective identity. Within this book, Nott and Gliddon practically set forth a religio-science of Manifest Destiny.

Nott and Gliddon based their arguments on the claim that history has shown, tracing all the way back to Tacitus, that distinct characteristics of races are "fixed and unalterable."[34] This claim was a part of a larger argument that suggested more than one divine human creation. Their polygenetic argument provided the foundation for the contention that races were created with distinct destinies. Nott and Gliddon's position of distinct created destinies becomes clear in their discussion of Native Americans.

In describing Native Americans, Nott and Gliddon say, "In America, the aboriginal barbarous tribes cannot be forced to change their habits, or even persuaded to successful emigration; they are melting away from year to year. . . . It is as clear as the sun at noon-day, that in a few generations more the last of these Red men will be numbered with the dead." Nott and Gliddon's use of the phrase "melting away" was prescient. For while the phrase "melting pot" would become a metaphor for the expectation that all immigrants would be assimilated and thus transformed into "Americans," until the early twentieth century, the usage of "melting away" suggested the expectation for the nonwhite bodies. If America was to become an Anglo-Saxon melting pot, then certain people would have to "melt away." Nott and Gliddon continue by saying that although missionaries claim to have been successful in civilizing them, "it is in vain to talk about civilizing [the American Indian]. You might as well attempt to change the nature of the buffalo."[35]

Nott and Gliddon's portrayal of the "American Indians" as stubborn to change lends support to the Manifest Destiny presuppo-

---

34. J. C. Nott and G. R. Gliddon, *Types of Mankind or Ethnological Research Based upon the Ancient Monuments, Paintings, Sculptures and Crania of Races, and upon Their Natural, Geographical, Philological, and Biblical History* (Philadelphia: Lippincott, Rambo & Co., 1854), 54-56.

35. Ibid., 69.

sition that refusal to assimilate to Anglo-Saxon ways can lead to extinction. According to Nott and Gliddon, extinction is a certainty when it comes to American Indians. Their resistance to change is not simply a "habit"; it is a "fixed and unalterable" characteristic. Their created nature, in other words, does not permit them to change. This of course suggests their ultimate destiny. They are doomed for extinction.

As for "those groups of races heretofore comprehended under the generic term of Caucasians," Nott and Gliddon say they "have in all ages been rulers." The men continue, "It requires no prophet's eye to see that they are destined to conquer and hold every foot of the globe . . . it is written in man's nature by the hand of his Creator."[36] While Nott and Gliddon argue that "American Indians" acquiesce to their nature, they contend that it is in spite of themselves that Caucasians carry out the mission for which they were created. They explain, "The Creator has implanted in this group of races an instinct that, in spite of themselves, drives them through all difficulties, to carry out their great missions of civilizing the earth . . . it is destiny . . . is it not reasonable to conclude that they are fulfilling a law of nature?"[37]

Nott and Gliddon make clear that there are certain races that are destined to rule the earth, and others that are destined to disappear from the earth. They assert, "Nations and races, like individuals, have each an especial destiny: some are born to rule and others are to be ruled. . . . No two distinctly-marked races can dwell together on equal terms. Some races, moreover, appear destined to live and prosper for a time, until the destroying race comes, which is to exterminate and supplant them."[38]

In the final analysis, Nott and Gliddon provide, through their own arguments and those put forth in their book, the religio-scientific knowledge needed to sustain Manifest Destiny's chauvinistic presumption that extinction is a part of a natural cycle of human history, as opposed to being a result of deadly human power. This religio-science also implies that God creates races to be ruled and destroyed. There appears to be a scriptural basis for making such a claim.

---

36. Ibid., 79.
37. Ibid., 77.
38. Ibid., 79.

A God of Manifest Destiny

The relationship between land, life, and race that characterizes the narrative of Manifest Destiny is not without biblical precedence. Indeed, Manifest Destiny itself is supported by the very biblical story that provides America's quintessential identity as the new Israelites. This is the exodus story.

The exodus story does not just chronicle the Israelites' divinely orchestrated escape from slavery into freedom. It is also an account of the Israelites entering into a land promised to them by God. This promised land, however, was not uninhabited. Canaanites and other tribes already occupied the land. Yet, God sent the Israelites there anyway, knowing that other peoples had already made a home there. God said to Moses, "And I promise that I will bring you up out of the affliction of Egypt to the land of the Canaanites, the Hittites, the Amorites, the Perizzites, the Hivites, and the Jebusites, a land flowing with milk and honey" (Exodus 3:17 ESV). The chosen people of God thus enter the land with the understanding that they are not to become like the Canaanites or any of the other tribes living on the land, if there are any remaining at the time of their arrival. For God had promised that these tribes would be destroyed. Moses told the Israelites, "The Lord your God himself will go over before you. He will destroy these nations before you, so that you shall disposses them and Joshua will go over at your head, as the Lord has spoken. And the Lord will do to them as he did to Sihon and Og, the kings of the Amorites, and to their land, when he destroyed them. And the Lord will give them over to you, and you shall do to them according to the whole commandment that I have commanded you" (Deuteronomy 31:3-6 ESV). With the entrance into an already occupied "promised land," the God who was once a liberator of the Israelites was now an exterminator, destroying people and despoiling their land for the sake of a people's Manifest Destiny.

As much as this exodus story is a story of moving out of bondage into freedom, it is also a story of invading an occupied land. The exodus provides a theological paradigm for Manifest Destiny just as much as it does for liberation. It is in this way that the Anglo-Saxonist narrative of Manifest Destiny has biblical precedence. That it did was not lost on the stewards of America's sense of Manifest Destiny. Marty says this of them: "In the colonial era the image of the wilderness prevailed. Now the familiar term was 'the Promised Land' and they were the Israelites who were called to conquer it."[39]

Once again the black faith tradition is challenged by America's narrative of exceptionalism. However, this particular challenge is even more pointed. The exodus story has traditionally provided the primary scriptural foundation for black people's understanding of God's movement in their own history. This story is central to black faith. It is the story that stirred the imagination of the enslaved and allowed them to affirm, even as their enslavers said otherwise, that God did not choose them be chattel but rather to be free. However, with the narrative of Manifest Destiny, the theological paradigm of black people as the Israelites is contested.

The narrative of Manifest Destiny compels one to engage the exodus story beyond the escape of the Israelites from Egyptian bondage. When one engages the exodus beyond the Red Sea, the wilderness journey, and across the Jordan into the land of Canaan, black people's identification with the Israelites cannot be sustained. This identification does not fit the reality of the black historical journey. In the context of Anglo-Saxon Manifest Destiny, the black body is not the chosen Israelite body. Rather, it is more like the scorned Canaanite body. This is not a body that God frees. It is instead a body that God allows to be destroyed. Again, the God of the exodus becomes a God of Manifest Destiny. Such a God sanctions the "extinction" of a people. At the least, this God subjects people to conquering violence.

What the exodus story does unquestionably affirm is, "The world is not without God, and God is not without the world."[40] The pressing challenge for black faith is to discern what the exodus story tells us concerning what God is doing in the world. In so doing, it is imperative to understand the meaning of God's violence within the exodus/ promised land story. Within this story, the non-Israelite bodies were unsuspecting victims of divine murderous violence. They were not the collateral damage of the Israelites' manifest destiny; they were the

---

39. Marty, *Righteous Empire* 46.

40. Gerhard Spiegler, quoted in Claude Welch, *Protestant Thought in the Nineteenth Century*, vol. 1: *1799–1870* (New Haven: Yale University Press, 1972), 64.

targets. The theological challenge to black faith becomes especially urgent as the narrative of Manifest Destiny takes an even more decisive and deadly turn. In order to appreciate the magnitude as well as inevitable nature of this turn, let us review this narrative of Manifest Destiny.

The narrative of Manifest Destiny inevitably flows from America's exceptionalist identity. As earlier mentioned, if a race of people believes itself to be chosen by God because it and its way of life is superior to others, then a sense of Manifest Destiny becomes inevitable. It is only right, in other words, to make the world "better" by investing it with a superior way of living, especially if that way is considered a reflection of eternal law. This is what is in the "best interest" of the world. Manifest destiny presumes to be a way to "serve the common good." In many respects, then, the narrative of Manifest Destiny is the culmination of the numerous discourses and productions of knowledge generated by America's grand narrative of exceptionalism. It reflects the Anglo-Saxon natural law theo-ideology that sanctions white supremacy. In fact, Manifest Destiny is an expression of that ideology as it assumes both the supremacy of whiteness, the shelter for Anglo-Saxon exceptionalism, and the inferiority of non-whiteness, a threat to Anglo-Saxon exceptionalism. This narrative further exonerates white people from taking moral responsibility for certain immoral, dehumanizing, and even deadly actions they might perpetrate against nonwhite bodies, all in the name of Manifest Destiny. Extermination, for instance, is read as a natural process of extinction, rather than the result of a violent imposition upon a people's life. True to the constructions of the narrative of Anglo-Saxon exceptionalism, the nonwhite body becomes responsible for its own fate, even when it is a deadly fate. In effect, the narrative of Manifest Destiny is that which ultimately legitimates the deadly use of subjugating power. The narrative of Manifest Destiny *is* a declaration of war. And this is a war that begins at home. The deadly and violent enactment of stand-your-ground culture is nothing less than a response to the Manifest Destiny declaration of war. In order to appreciate how this is the case, we must first understand how the narrative of Manifest Destiny represents a declaration of war. Foucault helps us to understand how this is the case.

Manifest Destiny: A Declaration of War

Foucault argues that historically "one of the characteristic privileges of sovereign power [has been] the right to decide life and death." He explains that this privilege was probably a carry-over from the Roman family law *patria potestas*.[41] This law gave the male head of household, presumably the father, power over the life of his children and slaves. He had the right, Foucault says, to "dispose" of their lives. Over time, this sovereign right over life and death, namely, the prerogative to end another's life, was no longer unconditional. It could only be "exercised" if "the sovereign's very existence was in jeopardy." Foucault explains, "If he were threatened by external enemies who sought to overthrow him or contest rights, he could then legitimately wage war."[42] In modern times, Foucault says this sovereign right expresses itself in a dissymmetrical fashion. "The sovereign exercise[s] his right of life only by exercising the right to kill, or by refraining from killing." Foucault says to be in power means that one has the "right of seizure: of things, time, bodies, and ultimately life itself."[43] In the final analysis, Foucault says, the "underside" of power is its ability "to expose a whole population to death . . . to guarantee [its] continued existence." Power, he says, "has to be capable of killing in order to go on living."[44]

Foucault is describing the dynamics of Anglo-Saxon exceptionalism and its concomitant narrative of Manifest Destiny. As has been shown, cherished white property, that is, white supremacy, is the expression of Anglo-Saxon exceptionalism. In reality it is about the power of white bodies. In order to maintain this power, a war was waged against those bodies that threatened this exceptionalist narrative. This war was the Manifest Destiny mission. If Anglo-Saxons were the chosen race, exceptional in virtue and liberty, and if America was the seat of that exceptionalism, then this had to be demonstrated through the ability to rule the world. Exceptionalism authenticates itself in the form of dominating and deadly power. Moreover, while the rhetoric of Manifest Destiny claimed that control over life and

---

41. Michel Foucault, *History of Sexuality*, trans. Robert Hurley, vol. 1 (New York: Vintage Books, 1990), 135.

42. Ibid., 135.

43. Ibid., 136.

44. Ibid., 137.

death was in the hands of the non–Anglo-Saxon body, it actually was not. This control was a right of Anglo-Saxon power. In the context of Manifest Destiny this was the right to determine if another was assimilated enough to Anglo-Saxon "social usages and customs" to be eliminated as a threat to the narrative of Anglo-Saxon exceptionalism. For resistance to assimilation implied that Anglo-Saxonism was not that exceptional after all. Such resistance was a stumbling block to the Manifest Destiny mission to rule the world. If one was deemed not assimilated, then one's extermination was likely to follow. It is in this way that the narrative of Manifest Destiny amounts to a declaration of war. If it is to be implemented, it calls for nothing less than the aggressive assault on non–Anglo-Saxon peoples' rights to live peaceably according to their own "social usages and customs." It compels an encroachment upon the land and life of those who are deemed not compatible or compliant with the narrative of America's Anglo-Saxon exceptionalism. Even the progenitor of the phrase manifest destiny spoke of it in terms of war. When O'Sullivan described the Anglo-Saxon incursion into California, as the "advance guard of the irresistible army of Anglo-Saxon emigration," he certainly created an image of war.

Even more telling that Manifest Destiny is a declaration of war, this narrative actually provided the ideological underpinning for America's militaristic expansion ventures during the nineteenth and early twentieth centuries. Some have argued that the policy of Manifest Destiny was "a logical extension of the Monroe Doctrine."[45] President James Monroe issued this doctrine in his 1823 State of the Union address. The Monroe Doctrine declared that the Western Hemisphere, particularly Latin American countries, was off-limits to European nations. In return, the United States promised not to interfere with nations in the Western Hemisphere that Europe had already colonized. This doctrine basically provided the United States with free reign to expand into the rest of the Western Hemisphere. It was of no small consequence that John Quincy Adams, who would become

---

45. Keith T. Ressa, "U.S. vs. the World: America's Color Coded War Plans and The Evolution of Rainbow Five: A Thesis in History," p. 42, http://www. digitalcommons.liberty.edu. This thesis provides a good discussion of the military planning necessitated by the narrative of Manifest Destiny.

one of the most vocal supporters of Manifest Destiny, actually crafted the Monroe Doctrine. He was, at the time, the secretary of state for President Monroe. The point to be noted for this discussion is that many considered Manifest Destiny itself a policy for war. If Manifest Destiny was to be pursued, war plans were necessary. In the end, the narrative of Manifest Destiny is not passive. The implementation and success of the narrative is what validates its claims. It is in this way that the narrative itself serves as a declaration of war. This is a war that must be fought and won.

A Religious War

The stakes in the Manifest Destiny war are high. For this war is ostensibly for the purpose of fulfilling God's call for "good, hard-working white English-speaking Protestant Americans to occupy all of the North American Continent. . . ."[46] To fail in the mission of Manifest Destiny was to fail the call of God.

It is important to remember, when considering the narrative of Manifest Destiny as a declaration of war, that this narrative is by definition a religious narrative. It presumes that it has divine authority. So again, to contest the fulfillment of the Manifest Destiny mission is to actually contest the rule and authority of God. Therefore, inasmuch as it is a declaration of war, the narrative of Manifest Destiny is a call for a religious war. Whether or not this war is "just" is perhaps debatable.

The origins of just-war theory are most likely found in a synthesis of classical Greco-Roman and Christian values. The thought of Cicero, Aristotle, and Augustine contributes most to what is now known as "just-war theory." While just-war theory was initially seen, especially in the early church, as a way to limit war, it actually provided a means to legitimate war. It created the possibility for "ethical" warfare. It prescribed the criterion for "initiating" a just war (*jus ad bello*), for "conducting" a just war (*jus in bello*), and for "terminating" a just war (*jus post bellum*). Doubtless, the arbitrators of Manifest Destiny would think of the pursuit of the Manifest-Destiny mission in terms of just war. For to believe otherwise would contest the very notion that Americans were chosen to implement, essentially, God's eternal law. Hence, to submit to the narrative of Manifest Destiny is

---

46. Ibid., 43-44.

to believe that it at least complies with the fundamental requirements for initiating a just war. For instance, just-war theory stipulates that there must be a just cause for going to war. Within the logic of the Manifest Destiny narrative, the pursuit of its mission is waged for a just cause—to fulfill the vision of God for a moral and free world. The second just-war criterion says that a legitimate authority must call the war. According to the rhetoric of Manifest Destiny, that authority is God. Third, a just war must be an action of last resort. It could be argued that the mission of Manifest Destiny is only actively pursued when others fail to assimilate to the ways of God, which of course in the narrative are Anglo-Saxon ways. The three remaining criteria for just war require a public declaration before the war is fought, probability for success, and a proportional response to the offense. Again, it is reasonable to believe that the arbitrators of Manifest Destiny would consider the pursuit of this mission compliant. To be sure, as pointed out earlier, America's intention to spread the values of Anglo-Saxon morality and freedom was never hidden. Moreover, the stewards of Manifest Destiny believed the response proportional—if assimilated, one lives; if not, one becomes the cause of one's own extinction. As for the probability for success, that depended particularly on the afore-mentioned "problem" at home, to which we will soon return.

Understanding the pursuit of Manifest Destiny within the frame of a just war affirms the aggressive and warring nature of this narrative. Again, it is a narrative that demands action against those who are considered "others." Such action cannot, therefore, help but be bellicose. In the end, interpreting Manifest Destiny through the lens of just-war theory makes one thing abundantly clear: Manifest Destiny is about a religious war. The narrative itself is a declaration of a war for God. How precisely that war is to be carried out depends on the historical context and most significantly on the way the targets for that war respond. Nevertheless, that Manifest Destiny amounts to the declaration of a religious war is significant. For it is generally under-stood that "religious wars are the bloodiest conflicts. When men invoke the name of God on their side and against the enemy, they tend to license outrage and atrocity."[47] We will soon see the reality of that as we examine the enactment of stand-your-ground culture. For

---

47. Marty, *Righteous Empire*, 35.

the stand-your-ground culture is the religious war of Manifest Destiny being pursued at home. In this regard, what O'Sullivan said about
the nations who attempted to block America's expansion can be said
of those races on America's own land that refuse to bow to the ways of
Anglo-Saxonism: "they are hampering [the nation's] power, limiting
[its] greatness and checking the fulfillment of [its] manifest destiny."
They, therefore, have to be dealt with in a manner proportional to the
degree of their threat to America's destiny. The stage is set, therefore,
for the most violent assertion of stand-your-ground culture on the
black body, especially the black male body.

The Warring Violence of Stand-Your-Ground Culture

Let us remember that stand-your-ground culture is the culture that
protects cherished whiteness. This protection is vital because, as has
been argued, whiteness shelters America's narrative of Anglo-Saxon
exceptionalism. It is the barrier between America's exceptionalist
identity and anything that would threaten it. It is for this reason that
certain rights are accorded to whiteness. They are fundamentally the
right to occupy land and space and the right to exclude others from
land and space. Foucault calls these the rights of power to "seize," in
this instance, land and space. These rights are consistent with the
agenda of Manifest Destiny. Inasmuch as the rights of cherished white
property are preserved as in fact "wages of whiteness," then the war of
Manifest Destiny has been won at home. Stand-your-ground culture
is meant to protect and defend the rights of whiteness. In this respect
it is carrying out the war declared by the Manifest Destiny narrative.

It does not matter that the narrative of Manifest Destiny is no
longer explicitly articulated. This narrative, like that of America's
Anglo-Saxon exceptionalism, is deeply embedded within the collective psyche and consciousness of America. Both narratives are a palpable part of American culture. And, if the Manifest Destiny mission
is to reify America's narrative of exceptionalism, then stand-your-
ground culture is the pursuit of that mission within America's own
societal context. As its "domestic" arm, stand-your-ground culture
is true to the defining principles of Manifest Destiny: land, life, and
race. Within stand-your-ground culture one's right to occupy certain
land/space and even to live depends on one's race. It is in this way
that stand-your-ground culture must be understood as nothing less

than the war declared by the narrative of Manifest Destiny against those bodies that most threaten America's Anglo-Saxon exceptionalist identity at home.

Native Americans and Stand Your Ground

While the focus of this book is the enactment of stand-your-ground culture against the black body, it would be remiss not to recognize this culture's devastating impact on Native American bodies. Native Americans were viewed to be as much of a threat to America's narrative of Anglo-Saxon exceptionalism as were African Americans. Even Alexis de Tocqueville recognized that "the white man" relegated Native and African Americans to a similar subjugated status. He argued, "These two unfortunate races have neither birth, nor face, nor language, nor mores in common; only their misfortunes look alike. Both occupy an equally inferior position in the country they inhabit; both experience the effects of tyranny; and if their miseries are different, they can accuse the same authors for them."[48] Indeed, the rhetoric concerning the potential for civilizing the "red" body was just as virulent and violent as the rhetoric concerning the black body. Using language similar to that found in *Types of Mankind,* John Quincy Adams said then-Secretary of State Henry Clay believed "it was impossible to civilize Indians; that there never was a full-blooded Indian who took to civilization. It was not in their nature." He further said, "[Clay] believed they were destined to extinction, and, although, he would never use or countenance inhumanity towards them, he did not think them as a race worth preserving."[49] History shows us that the Anglo-Saxon mission of Manifest Destiny considered Native Americans unworthy candidates for assimilation. They, therefore, became targets for extinction. There is no better example of this than the Indian Removal Act, which President Andrew Jackson signed into law May 28, 1830. While this law was presumably a "benevolent policy" to remove "Indians beyond the white settlements," it resulted in the forced removal of many Native Americans. Reportedly four thousand Cherokees died on a forced march later known as the "Trail of

---

48. De Tocqueville, *Democracy in America,* 303.
49. Quoted in Horsman, *Race and Manifest Destiny,* 197.

Tears."[50] The Anglo-Saxon Manifest Destiny mission of land, race, and life intruded on Native American bodies first. In many respects, the brutal treatment of Native Americans provided the blueprint for the treatment of other nonwhite bodies.

The impact of stand-your-ground culture on Native American peoples is a story that deserves much more attention than is given to it here. Still, it is important to recognize that while the black body is perhaps the most visible target of a stand-your-ground war, at least in the current context, black bodies have not been the only targets of this war. Nevertheless, it is because the black body presents such a threat to America's notion of exceptionalism that it has consistently been a primary target of stand-your-ground war. Before examining how this is the case, it is important to recognize an indicator in the current historical context that stand-your-culture is indeed warfare.

Guns and Stand Your Ground

The signature law for what is being identified as stand-your-ground culture, "Stand Your Ground law," was apparently precipitated after an incident in the aftermath of Hurricane Ivan in 2004. The incident involved an elderly Florida homeowner, John Workman, and a volunteer Federal Emergency Management Agency worker (FEMA), Rodney Cox. The worker was in Florida to help in the hurricane recovery efforts. For some reason, Cox became confused late one night and, as a consequence, tried to get into the damaged home of Workman, which at the time was unoccupied. Workman, who was staying in an RV on the property, mistook Cox for an intruder. In response, he grabbed his .38 caliber handgun, left his RV, shot, and killed Rodney Cox. Though no criminal charges were filed against John Workman, a period of three months passed before the decision not to file charges was made. The National Rifle Association lobby (NRA) seized upon this incident. They suggested that Workman was left too long wondering if he would be charged. They asserted that it should have been obvious that he killed Cox in self-defense. This was the way the NRA told the story as they lobbied for what is now the Stand Your Ground law.

---

50. Indian Removal Act of May 28, 1830, http://www.loc.gov/rr/program/bib/ourdocs/Indian.html.

This law extended the "castle doctrine" to include defense of one's space as well as one's home. The castle doctrine was now applied to public space. It, in effect, allowed for the protection of white space, which is whatever space white bodies inhabit. The white body becomes essentially a mobile castle. The significant connection being made now, however, is between the NRA and the Stand Your Ground law—which initially was called a "Shoot First law." That the gun lobby introduced a law that in effect made an existing stand-your-ground culture more deadly suggests the violent and bellicose nature of this culture. Whether or not actual weapons are used, stand-your-ground culture is violent. Inasmuch as violence is understood as the exertion of unjust power over another, then stand-your-ground culture is inherently violent. Even more telling of the NRA's role in enacting "Stand Your Ground law is the fact that the NRA is the most powerful lobby for the right to bear arms in public places. To think of the NRA is to think of guns. Guns are weapons for war. The stand-your-ground culture is nothing less than the enactment of war. The NRA's support of the Stand Your Ground law symbolizes this fact.

Also telling are beliefs of the organization that joined with the NRA to insure the passage of Stand Your Ground laws in various states across the country. That organization is the American Legislative Exchange Council (ALEC). ALEC is a right-wing, corporate-backed group that crafts "model legislation" that they then lobby for to implement as law. In fact, the NRA was once one of ALEC's funders. The laws that ALEC has successfully lobbied for include voter suppression laws, three-strike laws, and mass-incarceration laws. These are laws that tend to have a disproportionate negative impact on nonwhite bodies. They are as much a reflection of a stand-your-ground culture as the Stand Your Ground law itself. The relationship between the NRA, ALEC, and various Stand Your Ground laws is consistent with the identification of stand-your-ground culture as a war enacted against nonwhite bodies, in this instance, the black body. This triple alliance again symbolizes the reality of stand-your-ground culture as a Manifest Destiny war.

Stand-Your-Ground War and the Black Body

"[B]lacks and whites will sooner or later end by entering into conflict."[51] This is the conclusion de Tocqueville reached as he contemplated the significance of slavery in determining the limits of a relationship between white and black people. He says that slavery marked
the "Negro" as inferior and essentially the "property" of the white
man. Using the experience of "free" blacks in the North as an example, he says the "abolition of slavery, therefore does not allow the slave
to arrive at freedom. . . ."[52] Even though in this particular comment he
was referring to the reality of free Northern blacks ultimately being
passed over into the hands of Southern masters, he later broadens its
reference. He says, "As for freed Negroes . . . they remain half-civilized
and deprived of rights . . . they come up against the tyranny of laws
and the intolerance of mores."[53] To emphasize the dire predicament of
"freed Negroes," he compares their situation to that of Native Americans. He says, "More unfortunate in a certain respect than the Indians, they have the remembrance of slavery [working] against them,
and they cannot claim the possession of a single spot on the soil . . .
they lead a precarious and miserable existence."[54] De Tocqueville goes
on to describe the white "fear" of free blacks. He suggests that the
greatest fear is that of sexual "intermingling," resulting in a mulatto
population. He said what a white person fears most is "resembling
the Negro, his former slave, and descending below his white neigh-
bor."[55] He says that as the separation between whites and Negroes are
lessened legally there is a sense of "danger" that overcomes whites in
both the South and the North. The fear is so great, he suggests that
"the abolition of slavery . . . will increase the repugnance for blacks felt
by the white population."[56] It is because of this understanding that de
Tocqueville concludes conflict is inevitable.

De Tocqueville's observations are incredibly prescient. He accu-
rately described the reality of a free black body. The moment the black

---

51. De Tocqueville, *Democracy in America*, 343.
52. Ibid., 336.
53. Ibid., 336.
54. Ibid., 336-37.
55. Ibid., 342-43.
56. Ibid., 343.

body steps out of its chattel space, it is an imminent threat to cherished white property. While de Tocqueville described the fear of "intermingling" in terms of sexual interaction (and as we noted in Chapter 2 this was an expressed fear, even if imaginary), he could have just as well been describing the fear of blacks "intermingling" into the free space of white people. To do such a thing suggested an equality that was intolerable. Indeed, as we have argued, it is a threat to Anglo-Saxon exceptionalism. De Tocqueville essentially describes an inveterate fear of free black bodies that consumes the "white population." The "tyranny of laws" and eventual "conflict" that de Tocqueville describes is nothing less than the enactment of stand-your-ground culture. In essence, de Tocqueville describes the war that is declared on the black body the moment it experiences any form of social-political freedom.

It is no accident that stand-your-ground culture has been most aggressively if not fatally executed after every period in which certain "rights" are extended to black people, ostensibly bringing them closer to enjoying the "inalienable rights of life, liberty, and the pursuit of happiness." This pattern of "white backlash" began with the emancipation. After emancipation, Black Codes, Jim Crow laws, and the heinous "punishment" of lynching was enforced. The "law and order" mandates of the post–civil rights era continued this pattern. White backlash surely is reflected in the virulent stand-your-ground reality that has followed the election of the first black president. In each instance, stand-your-ground culture has asserted itself in an effort to "seize" the rights of whiteness and to return the black body to its chattel space. Essentially, the more the black body is free, the more intense the war against its body. We will now look to see how this is the case.

Black Codes, Jim Crow, and Lynching

The period following emancipation gave way to one of the most violent periods that the black body was to experience. Historian Jean Baker said that during that period, "the typical 'free' Black had . . . a single accepted public role: that of the victim of rioters."[57] This makes sense in light of the fact that this was the first time white society, particularly in the South, had to deal with a population of free

---

57. Quoted in Roediger, *Wages of Whiteness* 56.

black bodies. The only way in which white society could even tolerate black people in their midst was as chattel. Du Bois describes the emancipation of black people as something "the [white] world at first neither saw nor understood. Of all that most [white] Americans wanted, this freeing of slaves was the last."[58] A white panic shaped the ethos of the postbellum South. "The very joy in the shout of emancipated Negroes," Du Bois said, "was a threat" to white people. "Who were these people," they wondered. "Were we not loosing a sort of gorilla into American freedom."[59] The bottom line for white people was that black people had encroached upon the space reserved for cherished white property, the space of freedom. There was an urgency to return the free black body to a chattel state, and to do so by any means necessary. In a report to President Andrew Johnson about conditions in the South after emancipation, Charles Schultz described the black predicament. In so doing he captures the ideology of cherished white property that led to the post-Reconstruction assertion of stand-your-ground culture. It is, therefore, worth quoting at length. Schultz reports as follows:

> The emancipation of the slaves is submitted to only in so far as chattel slavery in the old form could not be kept up. But although the freedman is no longer considered the property of the individual master, he is considered the slave of society, and all independent state legislation will share the tendency to make him such. The ordinances abolishing slavery passed by conventions under the pressure of circumstances will not be looked upon as barring the establishment of a new form of servitude.
>
> The people boast then when they get freedman's affairs in their own hands . . . "the niggers will catch hell."
>
> The reason for all of this is simple and manifest. The whites esteem the blacks their property by natural right, and however much they admit that the individual relations of masters and slaves have been destroyed by war and by the President's emancipation proclamation, they still have an ingrained feeling that the blacks at large belong to the whites at large.[60]

---

58. Du Bois, *Black Reconstruction*, 125.
59. Ibid., 132.
60. Quoted in ibid., 136.

After the war that freed them, black people found themselves engaged in a war to take away that freedom. A stand-your-ground-culture war was launched against the black body.

The insidious intent of this war was actually articulated by the highest court in the land. In the now infamous March 6, 1857, Dred Scott decision, writing the majority opinion, Chief Justice Roger B. Taney said, "when the Constitution of the United States was framed and adopted . . . [black people] had for more than a century before been regarded as beings of an inferior order, and altogether unfit to associate with the white race, either in social or political relations; and so far inferior, that they had no rights which the white man was bound to respect; and that the negro might justly and lawfully be reduced to slavery. . . ."[61] The postemancipation stand-your-ground-culture war tried to make good on the Dred Scott decision and return black people to slavery. Neither their rights nor their bodies were respected.

This war took many forms. As mentioned in the previous chapter, Stand Your Ground laws were instituted to make chattel of black people by criminalizing them. Black Codes, such as the aforementioned vagrancy laws, were established. Some Black Codes, such as those in South Carolina, were defined so that there would be no mistake for whom they were intended. Thus, it was specified that they applied to anyone with more than "one-eighth Negro blood."[62] The South Carolina Black Codes included the proviso that "No person of color" could come into the state and "reside" there "unless within twenty days after his arrival he shall enter into a bond with two freeholders." The Kentucky Black Codes prohibited blacks from consuming alcohol on the same premises as whites. The Louisiana Black Codes required that "Negroes" had to "be in the regular service of some white person." They even went so far as to say, "No negro shall be permitted to preach, exhort, or otherwise declaim to congregations of colored people, without a special permission in writing from the president of the police jury."[63] Clearly, this particular code suggests that the theology

---

61. The Dred Scott Decision: Opinion of Chief Justice Taney, p. 19, http://www.memory.loc.gov.

62. See "The Southern 'Black Codes' of 1865–66," Southern Black Codes–Constitutional Rights Foundation, http://www.crf-usa.org/bill-of-rights-in-action/bria-15-2-c-the-southern-black-codes-of-1865-66.

63. Black Codes cited from "Black Codes and Jim Crow," Central Piedmont

of the black faith tradition was not compatible with the narrative of Anglo-Saxon exceptionalism (we will return to this in Part II of this book). As indicated in the previous chapter, the penalties for breaking these laws typically involved jail time and forced labor. The purpose of these codes was clear. As Du Bois says, "The Codes spoke for themselves. . . . No open-minded student can read them without being convinced that they meant nothing more or less than slavery in daily toil."[64] At the same time, these codes reinforced the image of black people as criminal, the postemancipation version of chattel.

As Black Codes were overturned in federal courts, Jim Crow laws emerged to take their place. In this respect, stand-your-ground culture is persistent and adaptive. Again, there is much at stake: the success of the Manifest Destiny mission at home. Jim Crow laws, therefore, were instituted to accomplish the same thing as the Black Codes. They attempted to remove black bodies from the white space. These laws created segregated spaces. These were the laws that would not ultimately be struck down until the 1960s civil rights movement. In general, stand-your-ground culture expressed itself through laws that did precisely what Charles Schultz reported white people intended postemancipation legislation to do: return black people to "a new form of servitude."

The most vicious and violently gruesome weapon of the postemancipation stand-your-ground culture was, of course, lynching. As earlier mentioned, lynching was fueled by the construction of the black male as a hypersexual predator. The black male body represented the most dangerous threat to cherished white property, so he had to be destroyed. Despite the fact that lynching was primarily a Southern phenomenon, its message was universal: no longer the legal property of white people, black life had little or no value apart from providing "strange fruit to swing from Southern trees." Lynching, especially spectacle lynching, made clear that there was no "protected space" for a free black body. All space was white space.

For all intents and purposes, lynching is the extralegal, postemancipation version of the NRA- and ALEC-sponsored Stand Your

---

Community College, http://www.sciway.net/afam/reconstruction/blackcodes.html.

64. W. E. B. Du Bois, "Reconstruction and Its Benefits," (July 1, 1910), p. 784.

Ground law. Lynching gave white people the right to end black life with impunity, especially black male life. (It seems as though the current Stand Your Ground law does the same.) While the lynchers were most often protected from prosecution for their deadly assaults by being regarded as "persons unknown," such anonymity was only a legal ruse. The lynchers—those who had an actual hand in the crime and those who were part of the mob of spectators—were generally known, if not specifically, at least in the main. Du Bois observed that the "mob" lynchings were often carried out by a "nucleus of ordinary men."[65] The lynch crowds were often made up of so-called good men and women of white society. As we have seen from our earlier discussion, the only justification needed for lynching was that a white woman felt threatened or insulted by a black male.

While the height of lynching was during the late nineteenth and early twentieth centuries, various forms of lynching continue into the twenty-first century. All one needs to remember is the 1998 lynching of forty-nine-year-old James Byrd to know that lynching is not a crime solely of the past. Again, many in the black community suggest that stand-your-ground murders are the twentieth-century adaptation of lynching. To be sure, both are weapons of stand-your-ground culture. In fact, implicitly recognizing the tenacious and adaptable nature of stand-your-ground culture, many within the black as well as the community at large made direct comparisons between the 2012 murder of seventeen-year-old Trayvon Martin and the 1955 murder of fourteen-year-old Emmett Till.

It is easy to make comparisons between the two murders. There are similarities that warrant comparison of the two deadly crimes, including the fact that the perpetrators in both cases were acquitted. However, the connection between what happened to Emmett and Trayvon goes beyond the surface comparisons. To stop there, in fact, misses what these murders say about the American social-cultural context. Both slayings point to the ingrained fear in America's collective consciousness of the black male body. As we have seen, this fear is a by-product of America's narrative of Anglo-Saxon exceptionalism. This is a fear that just does not go away. In this regard, the slayings

---

65. W. E. B. Du Bois, "The Shape of Fear" *North American Review* (June 1926), 295.

of Emmett and Trayvon are a message writ large for the black community. It is the same message that spectacle lynching was sending: a free black body is not a safe black body the moment it has intruded into white space. One commentator put it well when he said, "the sequence of events that led to Till's and Martin's deaths began with the two teenage boys failing to accept their 'assigned' social place without realizing what a threat that posed. After that line was crossed, everything else followed."[66] To be sure, both teenagers were victims of the Manifest Destiny war that is the stand-your-ground culture.

Before leaving the Emmett–Trayvon connection, there is a comparison that presents another theological challenge to the black faith tradition. Both Emmett's and Trayvon's murders became a catalyst for a national conversation on race. Notwithstanding the futility of the conversation, there were those who argued that at least these two deaths were not in vain. The issue of redemptive suffering comes into full view. Many within the black faith community tried to find meaning in Trayvon's murder. To be sure, these senseless stand-your-ground murders raise issues of theodicy. How are we to understand the justice of God in relation to the slaying of young innocent black people? How are we to understand the goodness of God in light of such evil? What is the nature of God's power in the face of a stand-your-ground culture? What is God saying to us as our children are targets of war?

In telling his poignant story of life in a concentration camp during the Jewish holocaust, Elie Wiesel recalls a "most horrible day, even among all of those other bad days," when he witnessed the hanging of a child. As he watched the little boy die a slow and agonizing death, not even being granted a quick end to the hanging torture, Wiesel heard a man cry out, "For God's sake, where is God?" To that question, Wiesel said a voice inside of him answered, "hanging from this gallows."[67] This is a question that black faith must ask in the midst of stand-your-ground culture. Where is God? Where was God when Emmett and Trayvon were slain? If God was with them, what does

---

66. Nicolaus Mills, "A Longer Look at the Emmett Till–Trayvon Martin Comparison," http://www.huffingtonpost.com.

67. Elie Wiesel, *Night*, trans. Marion Wiesel (New York: Hill & Wang, 1958, 2006), 64-65.

that mean? If nothing else, the "lynchings" of Emmett and Trayvon raise questions about the compassion of God.

Lynching, whatever form it takes, is one of the most blatantly violent weapons of stand-your-ground culture. There have been, however, other less violent weapons that were effective in protecting cherished white culture. Restrictive housing policies were one of these weapons.

Restrictive Covenants and Redlining

These are two stanzas from Langston Hughes's 1948 poem "Restrictive Covenants."

> *The moon doesn't run.*
> *Neither does the sun*
>
> In Chicago
> They've got covenants
> Restricting me—
> Hemmed in
> On the South Side,
> Can't breathe free.

In this poem, Hughes speaks to the way in which stand-your-ground culture limited where black people could live. Restrictive covenants were deliberate and flagrant attempts to control housing patterns and thus to protect white space. In the 1917 Buchanan v. Warley case, the Supreme Court ruled against racial zoning laws that had been adopted in various cities across the country. The court held that these laws violated the Fourteenth Amendment. In response, "realtors, developers, and private citizens" found a new way to circumvent the Constitution to protect the white space. That way was restrictive covenants.[68] In the 1926 Corrigan v. Buckley case the Supreme Court basically upheld these covenants because they were privately, not publicly, established.[69] "Restrictive covenants were made to order for enforcing segregation in

---

68. Roediger, *Working toward Whiteness*, 170.

69. This discussion is informed by Wendy Plotkin, "'Hemmed In': The Struggle against Racial Restrictive Covenants and Deed Restrictions in Post-WWII Chicago," *Journal of the Illinois State Historical Society* 94.1 (Spring 2001).

established neighborhoods."[70] These covenants were codicils on deeds. They specified that a particular property could not be sold to certain ethnic groups. While some restrictive covenants referred to new-stock immigrants, they were notoriously designed to keep blacks out of white communities.

Government housing agencies soon developed their own brand of restrictive covenants. The New Deal housing policies implemented under President Franklin Roosevelt were unabashedly discriminatory. If black people were able to get housing under the New Deal programs, it was substandard at best. It was also most notably not near white neighborhoods. With the 1933 creation of the Home Owners Loan Corporation (HOLC), the government's practice of protecting white space was even more notorious. The HOLC developed the redlining system. In this system, a red line literally was drawn around areas on a map where black bodies were permitted to go. Loans were given to black people only in those restricted areas. Even after HOLC was abolished, the Federal Housing Administrative (FHA) continued the redlining practice. The FHA published "underwriting manuals" that essentially encouraged redlining and supported restrictive covenants. One manual stated that restrictive covenants were the "surest possible protection against undesirable encroachment and inharmonious use."[71] In 1948 an NAACP official said that the redlining policies of the FHA had done "more than any other single instrumentality to force nonwhite citizens into substandard housing and neighborhoods."[72]

Though restrictive covenants and redlining were not fatal attacks upon the black body, they were as much a reflection of Manifest Destiny war as lynching. Restrictive covenants and redlining maintained the Manifest Destiny connection between land and race. They made clear that only cherished white property had the right to certain land, in this instance, neighborhoods. The government-based housing policies served to protect white space. More particularly, they served to protect "white houses." Roediger explains, "it was the

---

70. Roediger, *Working toward Whiteness*, 172.

71. Quoted in ibid., 229.

72. Ibid., 227. See Roediger's detailed discussion of discriminatory housing policies in the same book, 157-234.

existing and potential value of the white house that was being protected and that value lay in large part in its whiteness."[73] Stand-your-
ground culture was doing its job. It was protecting cherished white
property at the same time that it was proscribing the space that a
free black body could enter.

In the post–civil rights age, Jim Crow laws were ruled unconsti-
tutional. Restrictive covenants and redlining nominally ended. This
did not mean, however, that the practice of restrictive covenants and
redlining was over. It remains a weapon of stand-your-ground culture. It has simply reappeared in a new form. Renisha, Jonathan, and
Trayvon were victims of it. They were in neighborhoods where they
were not meant to be. Renisha and Jonathan were killed because they
knocked on a house and in a neighborhood that was not meant for
them. Trayvon stood out to his killer because he was a black body
in the wrong neighborhood. These three young black people had
crossed the red-line boundaries. In a stand-your-ground-culture war,
it cost them their lives.

Nevertheless, after the 1960s civil rights struggles, black people
enjoyed more freedom than any time in their history. This meant,
however, that black bodies were encroaching more and more upon
white space, and hence were more of a threat. Once again, therefore, stand-your-ground culture was asserted in an aggressive manner. There was as great an urgency to return the black body back to
his chattel state as there was after emancipation. This time, however,
there was no masking the warring intent. A deliberate war was being
declared on the black body. It was called the War on Drugs.

The War on Drugs

By all accounts the black body, especially the black male body, was
the target of the War on Drugs. President Ronald Reagan's declaration of a War on Drugs was a continuation of President Nixon's "law
and order" agenda, an agenda that actually got underway with the
emergence of the civil rights movement in the late 1950s. It was a part
of the "white backlash" to put black people back into the place most
befitting their "nature." In doing so, the law-and-order expression of
stand-your-ground culture went back to tactics that had worked the

---

73. Ibid., 174.

last time white space was grossly violated, after emancipation. The law-and-order version of stand your ground again tried to trap the black body in a criminal cycle.

Michelle Alexander provides a detailed and compelling argument that unambiguously links the law-and-order agenda with efforts to not simply forestall but to "turn back the clock on racial progress."[74] There is no need to repeat that argument here. It is important to understand in the context of stand-your-ground culture that the law-and-order agenda was just another sign that the stand-your-ground-culture war was still being fought.

Paying special attention to the tactics of the Republican leadership, led by Richard Nixon, Alexander shows how the rhetoric of law and order was actually a way to advance a racist agenda without talking about race. Through campaign rhetoric and with the help of the mass media, Republicans cleverly linked the black body with crime. The aforementioned images of the black female "welfare queen" and the black male criminal predator were implanted within the public imagination. Moreover, Alexander argues, the law-and-order advocates reframed the civil rights movement. It became a lawless movement to destroy the social fabric of the United States as opposed to a movement to extend the democratic principles that presumably made the country exceptional. Congressman John Bell Williams explicitly linked black freedoms to the increase in crime. He said, "This exodus of Negroes from the South, and their influx into the great metropolitan centers of other areas of the Nation, has been accompanied by a wave of crime. . . . What has civil rights accomplished for these areas?"[75] In general, as Alexander explains, "The shift to a general attitude of 'toughness' toward problems associated with communities of color began in the 1960s when the gains and goals of the civil rights movement began to require real sacrifices on the part of white Americans, and conservative politicians found they could mobilize white racial resentment by vowing to crack down on crime."[76]

---

74. Alexander, *The New Jim Crow*, 42. It is in this book that one can find a detailed argument on the "law and order" agenda as well as on the "war on drugs."
75. Quoted in ibid., 41.
76. Ibid,. 55.

The mandates of Manifest Destiny were palpable in this "crack down on crime" program. The issues of land/space, race, and even life were linked. Even if the law-and-order agenda did not lead to the actual loss of life, it destroyed many black lives by trapping them in an unforgiving criminal justice system. To the stewards of America's Manifest Destiny, this seemed proportionate to the crime black people were committing. They were not simply unfit to be citizens, they were actually "anti-citizens."[77] Black people were viewed as threatening the core of America's exceptionalist identity. During the civil rights era, they were doing this in at least two ways. First, they were demanding rights that were meant only for cherished white property. These were rights to nonsegregated space. Second, as images of the protests and the violence that was perpetrated against the black protestors were broadcast around the world, America's image of exceptionalism was directly challenged. The America shown across television screens was not that bastion of Anglo-Saxon virtue and freedom it claimed to be. The civil rights movement seriously damaged America's self-proclaimed status as "the city on the hill" exemplifying Anglo-Saxon virtue and freedom. Of course, it was black people who were blamed for destroying America's reputation, not those who violently resisted black inclusion in America's democracy. The point of the matter is, America's project of Manifest Destiny was being threatened, and so it was necessary for the Manifest Destiny war to take a more aggressive form. It was left for stand-your-ground culture to carry forth that war, which it did through a law-and-order agenda.

An aspect of this law-and-order agenda that was not noted by Alexander actually reinforces the fact that it was the continuation of the Manifest Destiny war. In 1968 the military put into effect "Operation Garden Plot." This operation permitted "deadly force to be used against any extremist or dissident perpetrating any and all forms of civil disorder."[78] Operation Garden Plot nullified the 1878 Posse Comitatus Act that prohibited military involvement in domestic law-enforcement matters. However, this operation was actually a reenact-

---

77. David Roediger uses this term to describe the way black people were viewed in American society in comparison with the way white immigrants were viewed. See *Working toward Whiteness*.

78. "Operation Garden Plot," http://www.uhuh.com/control/garden.htm.

ment of the military's 1920 War Plan White. The War PlanWhite was developed for the same purpose as Operation Garden Plot, to crack down on dissidents. In 1920 that meant communists as well as blacks. What is most telling is that the White Plan was a part of a series of color-coded military plans generally initiated to further America's Manifest Destiny mission.[79] So once again, while the language of Manifest Destiny is no longer a part of public discourse, it remains a part of America's exceptionalist identity. Stand-your-ground culture helps to carry forth its mission.

This mission continued as the law-and-order program gave way to the War on Drugs. Alexander points out that although President Nixon called for a war on drugs, it was not until President Reagan that the war became official. Two aspects of this war made it clear that it was about incarcerating black bodies and not stopping drugs. First, very few Americans believed drugs to be a major problem when President Reagan called for the war. In fact, the drug that he targeted, crack cocaine, had yet to infiltrate the urban landscape as it later would. Alexander says, "President Ronald Reagan officially announced the current drug war in 1982, before crack became an issue in the media or a crisis in poor black neighborhoods."[80] The presence of crack in the poor black community did not reach crisis proportions until at least three years later, an occurrence that the Reagan administration took full advantage of in terms of criminalizing black people. As a part of this drug war, the Posse Comitatus Act was again violated. Military teams joined SWAT teams in drug raids. These raids have disproportionately targeted black persons.

A second indicator that the War on Drugs was actually a war on black bodies was the drug the Reagan administration targeted, crack cocaine. Even before it became a crisis in poor black communities, it was the drug most likely to be used by black users for the simple reason that it was cheap. It was notable that the administration did not target the powder form of crack cocaine, which was more likely to be used by white drug users. With its accompanying racially biased mandatory sentencing guidelines, the War on Drugs has served its purpose. It has

---

79. For more on the color-coded military plans and their relationship to Manifest Destiny, see Ressa, "U.S. vs. the World."

80. Alexander, *The New Jim Crow*, 5.

returned unprecedented numbers of black bodies to a chattel space—the new plantation of jails and prisons. A 2000 Human Rights Watch report said that in seven states black people accounted for 80 to 90 percent of all drug offenders sent to prison, which is grossly disproportionate to the percentage of black drug users.[81] In large part because of the War on Drugs, the United States imprisons more of its "racial or ethnic minorities" than any other country in the world.[82]

The stand-your-ground-culture war on drugs worked. The white space of freedom is protected. The narrative of Anglo-Saxon exceptionalism is maintained. Black bodies have once again been returned to an unfree space. The mission of Manifest Destiny is being executed.

In the end, the narrative of Manifest Destiny is the policy side of America's narrative of Anglo-Saxon exceptionalism. It is a mission to make good on the exceptionalist claim. With war strategies and weapons, it has moved to create a world in the image of Anglo-Saxon social usages and customs. Stand-your-ground culture is the war of Manifest Destiny that is fought at home. This is a war, thereby a culture, that is malleable. It engages the tools and weapons that are appropriate to secure its goal, which again is to defend and protect white space. To protect this space is to safeguard America's exceptionalist identity.

It should be no surprise that stand-your-ground culture has at times employed deadly force. For one must remember that the war it is carrying out is a religious war. Whether legitimated by the civil or evangelical canopy, it is a war being fought for God. As history has shown, and as stand-your-ground culture affirms, religious wars are some of the most violent and deadly of all. It should also not be surprising that stand-your-ground culture becomes most deadly in relation to the black body. This is the body that has been constructed in stark opposition to cherished white property. It is the most threatening body to America's narrative of exceptionalism and, thus, to the success of its Manifest Destiny mission. The black body, in this regard, is an enemy of Anglo-Saxon America. So it is that black bodies are the targets of the Manifest Destiny war that is stand-your-ground culture. This brings us to the question of whether "going home" was a viable option for Trayvon.

---

81. Cited in ibid., 98.
82. Ibid., 6.

Going Home

A Mother's Nightmare

There has been no story in the news that has disturbed me more than the murder of Trayvon. When I first heard about it, my mind went back to Emmett Till, another young black man who had traveled from his mother's home to visit relatives. I became acutely aware that perhaps the only place my black male child was safe was in my home. Every time he leaves the house I pray, "God please be my eyes, and be my hands, watch over my son and bring him safely home." I am sure that I am not the only black mother who prays such a prayer when her black child, especially black male child, leaves home. The faith of Trayvon's and Jordan's mothers suggest that they probably prayed such a prayer when their sons left home. So I tremble at the thought that the world is not safe for our sons, because if God cannot protect them who can?

It happened one night on an isolated road. As they were headed back to college, my son and two of his black male friends were stopped by white police officers. By all accounts, even that of my son's white lawyer, they were stopped for the crime of driving while black. From putting them up against the car, frisking them, and searching their car numerous times, the officers did all that they could to let my son and his friends know that being college students did not exempt them from being criminals. As if to ensure that they recognized this, my son and his friends were made to appear in court. At the end of the day, no crime was committed so the case was eventually resolved.

This incident reminded me of how close my worst nightmare was to becoming reality. The wrong word spoken, the wrong move made, and my son could have become a stand-your-ground-culture war casualty. Without parents who were aware of the criminal justice system, my son could have become another black male trapped in the stand-your-ground-culture cycle of criminality. I think of all of those sons of black mothers that become trapped in the cycle, simply because they are black.

The Question Answered

Today, the Manifest Destiny stand-your-ground-culture war is fueled by the presence of a black man living in the White House. There is no greater challenge to America's grand narrative of Anglo-Saxon exceptionalism than a black president. This represents a complete encroachment upon the space reserved for cherished white property. It is no surprise, therefore, that stand-your-ground culture has asserted itself in an aggressive and unrelenting manner. All of the weapons that have been used over time have been brought to bear in the current climate of stand-your-ground culture. The "Stop and Frisk laws," which are disproportionately applied to black and brown bodies, harken back to the Black Code vagrancy laws. Once again, you can be stopped and arrested for living black. The dismantling of the 1965 Voter's Rights Act, as well as racialized gerrymandering, is reminiscent of the white backlash that followed Reconstruction, the first time that black people ascended into white political space. And most troubling of all, the Stand Your Ground laws, in conjunction with the Conceal and Carry gun laws, have made legal a murderous act that was extralegal, that is, lynching. Our black children are falling victims to the twenty-first-century version of stand-your-ground-culture lynching. It is in this context that we must determine if going home was a viable option for Trayvon.

Home is a "safe space." It is a space where a person is able to live and grow into the fullness of her or his created identity. Home is a free space. It is a space where people are free to love and be loved, and to be whoever it is that God has created them to be. The purpose of stand-your-ground culture is to deprive black bodies of homes. Juror B37 said that Trayvon could have gone home. If only he had that opportunity. In expressing her disappointment after the nonguilty verdict of her son's killer, Trayvon's mother said, "I just knew that [the jury] would see that this was a teenager just trying to get home. . . . This was no burglar, this was somebody's son that was trying to get home."[83] Stand-your-ground culture does its job when it deprives black bodies of the safe space that is home. No matter where he is, I do not rest at night until my son lets me know that he is home. Our stand-your-ground-culture society is not a home for black bodies.

A mantra of black faith comes from Psalm 121. It is, "I lift my eyes to the hills. From where does my help come? My help comes from the

---

83. Sybrina Fulton, "Trayvon Martin's Parents Speak Out on Not Guilty Verdict," *Time,* http://newsfeed.time.com.

Lord who made heaven and earth." What is the meaning of God's help in the context of a stand-your-ground culture that would deprive the black body of a home? This is the question to be explored in Part II of this book.

From Tacitus to Trayvon

"The notion that Stand Your Ground laws are some form of veiled racism may be a convenient political attack, but is not borne out by the facts remotely." This is what Senator Ted Cruz said during an October 29, 2013, Senate Judiciary Hearing on the Stand Your Ground law. Trayvon Martin's mother was present at the hearing. She was there to urge the Senate to do something about the law that resulted in her son's death. As if to emphasize the point he was trying to make, Senator Cruz addressed Ms. Fulton directly. He said, "It is always a tragedy when a child loses his life, and please know that we are all feeling your loss. . . . Sadly, we know that some in our political process have a desire to exploit that tragic violent incident for agendas that have nothing to do with that young man who lost his life. . . . We have seen efforts to undermine the verdict of the jury and more broadly to inflame racial tensions that I think are sad and irresponsible."[1]

It is often said that if you tell a big enough lie, then perhaps people will believe it. One of the tactics of stand-your-ground culture is to foster unabashed lies about the reality of white racism in America. The media-supported rhetoric that we are now living in a postracial America serves to mystify the reality of the narrative of Anglo-Saxon exceptionalism that continues to shape race relations in this country. The claims of a postracial society put those who are victims of the discourses and constructs of America's exceptionalist narrative on the defense. How is one to prove the presence of racism when its stewards have proclaimed that it has been successfully eradicated? It is even

---

1. Comments reported by Morgan Whitaker, "Cruz: Stand your ground laws good for African Americans," http://www.msnbc.com/msnbc/cruz-condemns-exploiting-trayvon.

more difficult to prove when the very laws and tactics that fuel racism carefully avoid the language of race. Once again, stand-your-ground culture employs language as a tool to protect cherished white property. It is the language of exclusion in a new form. In this instance, racially sterilized language reveals another right of cherished white property—it has the right to determine what is racist and what is not. Indeed, when black people make such a claim they are the ones "guilty" of racism.

Stand-your-ground culture and the narratives and laws that it generates are all about race. They are about the Anglo-Saxon race. Part I of this book has shown that stand-your-ground culture is an integral part of the American story. When the Pilgrims and Puritans fled England to come to America, they brought with them the seeds of this deadly culture. Those seeds were in a people's claim to be the chosen Anglo-Saxon remnant of Tacitus's Germans. The Anglo-Saxon myth, which emerged from Tacitus's *Germania,* has shaped and continues to shape America's sense of self. This myth is the unspoken, but pervasive, narrative that determines who is and who is not entitled to the rights of "life, liberty, and the pursuit of happiness."

This book has thus far shown that what happened to Trayvon, Jordan, Renisha, Jonathan, and unfortunately many others whose names have not entered into the public conversation was not about events that unfolded on any particular night. Their murders were the result of events that have unfolded over a number of centuries. The deaths of these young black people are about more than a Stand Your Ground law. They are about a culture that is bound and determined to protect the Anglo-Saxon "white country" that both Thomas Jefferson and Benjamin Franklin imagined and worked to build. As noted earlier, Tacitus's *Germania* has been called "one of the most dangerous books ever written." Our discussion thus far has sustained that observation. *Germania* has certainly provided the foundation for a culture that has, over the centuries, robbed countless black bodies of their lives.

After Trayvon's killer was acquitted, one of my church members, with tears in her eyes, despaired, "There is no hope; our black children will never be safe." I said to her, "As long as there is a God, there is hope." Part Two of this book will explore the meaning of that hope as we consider the freedom, the justice, and the time of God.

PART TWO

4

A Father's Faith: The Freedom of God

After his son's killer was acquitted Tracy Martin said, "My heart is broken, but my faith is unshattered." The stand-your-ground-culture war is a story of two faiths. There is the faith of a father whose son was not the "collateral damage" of the war but actually the target. There is also the faith of a nation whose very identity created the war that targeted Trayvon. Stand-your-ground-culture war reveals two different faith claims, presumably about the same God. Each claim, in effect, reflects a different side of the same story, the story of the Israelites' exodus. The father's faith claim points to the story of the God who liberated the Israelites from a land where their bodies were being devalued and destroyed. The faith of the nation tells the story of that same God who called the Israelites to a land where unsuspecting bodies were crushed and conquered. The faith of a father points to an exodus God who is with a people through a wilderness journey to forge a new life. The faith of a nation signals an exodus God who is with a people through a wilderness journey to bring unexpected death to many others. The faith of a nation gives way to a culture that negates black life. The faith of a father affirms black life in the midst of a culture of death.

This would not be the first time that a war, with black bodies at the center, would also be a battle of faith claims. Abraham Lincoln recognized that even as the Civil War was a conflict between the North and the South concerning slavery, it was also a conflict about God. He said of the two sides, "Both read the same Bible and pray to the same God, and each invokes His aid against the other. . . . The prayers of both could not be answered. That of neither has been answered fully. The Almighty has His own purposes."[1] These words echoed Lincoln's thoughts from a private meditation in which he wrote, "In great contests each party claims to act in accordance with the will of God. Both *may* be, and one *must* be wrong. God cannot be *for* and *against* the same thing. In the present civil war it is quite possible that God's purpose is something different from the purpose of either party...."[2]

This saga of two conflicting faith claims actually tells the story of black faith.

Black faith took root in the same soil as the faith of those who enslaved black bodies, and did so in the name of God. Black faith was born in the crucible of slavery. From the very beginning, black faith had to confront the absurdities of black life and the conflicting claims about God. Howard Thurman says, "This faith has had to fight against disillusionment, despair, and the vicissitudes of American history."[3]

Black faith was forged in the midst of the perverse and tragic paradoxes of black life. It is a faith, therefore, that does not ignore the unthinkable and irrational terror of black living. It takes it seriously. It does not belittle or romanticize the pains and sufferings of black bodies. It does not revel in illusions and false hope. Neither does it allow black bodies to give in to the hardship and to be overcome with despair. Indeed, the faith born in slavery provided a weapon to resist and to fight against the religiously legitimated tyranny of America's Anglo-Saxon exceptionalism. From its inception, black faith provided a counternarrative to those who would say that God created black bodies to be chattel.

Some have suggested that black faith "doesn't necessarily respect reason but instead favors fiction."[4] This criticism is born from the fact that black bodies still are not free from the tyrannical and sly grip of Anglo-Saxon exceptionalism; yet black faith continues to witness to a

---

1. Abraham Lincoln, "Second Inaugural Address of Abraham Lincoln" (Saturday, March 4, 1865), http://avalon.law.yale.edu.

2. Abraham Lincoln, "Meditation on the Divine Will" (Washington, DC, September 1862), http://www.abrahamlincolnonline.org.

3. Howard Thurman, *Deep River and the Negro Spiritual Speaks of Life and Death* (Richmond, IN: Friends United Press, 1975), 13.

4. Anthony B. Pinn, *Writing God's Obituary: How a Good Methodist Became a Better Atheist* (Amherst, NY: Prometheus Books, 2014), 218.

God who liberates the oppressed. A faith such as this is seen by some as a weakness, not a strength, in a stand-your-ground-culture war. Yet, the very strength of black faith is revealed in this very contradiction. It emerged at a time when black bodies were legal chattel. Yet, black people were still able to affirm the liberating presence of God in their lives. Even more significant, their faith grew in the cauldron of their enslaved oppression. It continued to have meaning for them, even for the generations that did not see freedom. This is the faith that black church people continue to affirm. This faith, therefore, continues to hold meaning for a black people in the middle of a stand-your-ground war. In this chapter I will attempt to understand the tenacity of black faith through trying to appreciate its meaning in black lives.

Even as we explore the meaning of black faith, this chapter and those that follow in Part II of this book are less a theological analysis and more an attempt to let black faith speak for itself. "Theology," as Karen Armstrong reminds us, "is a very wordy discipline." Theologians "have written reams and talked unstoppably about God."[5] In doing so, we claim that we are helping the faithful better understand their faith. And sometimes, maybe most times, we are. However, there are times, and maybe too many times, when we subvert the very faith that we seek to understand. We replace faith claims with doctrines. We replace the testimony of the faithful with words that are bound to confuse. We get lost in our narratives about God and perhaps lose God in the process. And to be sure, we sometimes lose sight of the faith that we seek to understand.

Faith is a response to God. Faith is possible only if God has acted and has initiated a relationship with human beings. Faith is the human response to God's invitation to be in a relationship. Black faith represents a resounding yes to God's offer. This yes signals black people's belief in the power of God to right what is wrong in the world, even though they find themselves in the midst of the harsh absurdity of black life in Anglo-Saxon America. Black faith is, therefore, a testimonial of the divine/human interaction between God and black people. As such it is a witness to black reality and black hope.

Inasmuch as theology is about God, it is a response to faith. It seeks to understand the relationship between God and the people of God.

---

5. Karen Armstrong, *The Case for God* (New York: Alfred A. Knopf, 2009), x.

This does not always mean that what the faithful say and believe about that relationship is true, or even that they are speaking about God at all, as Lincoln alluded to in the conflicting faith claims surrounding the Civil War. And so the theological task is not just about affirmation. It is also a critical task. But, before it can be that, it must at least listen to what the faithful are saying, seek to understand it, and then place the testimonial of faith in dialogue with the Bible. The point is, any theological reflection must begin with a respect for the faith it seeks to understand.

This chapter attempts to do just that. It attempts to listen to and respect a father's "unshattered" faith. In order to do so, we must begin where this faith began, which is in the cauldron of slavery. By beginning there, we will be able to understand the God about whom this faith speaks and, thus, to appreciate the strength and tenacity of this faith tradition as it negotiates the contradiction between black life and black hope. As we explore this faith we will address the various challenges that were raised in the previous chapters concerning the movement of God in human history. This chapter pays particular attention to the exodus story and its implications for the faith claims of those on both sides of the stand-your-ground-culture war. In the end, we will be able to understand a father's ability to stand in the contradiction of "a broken heart and an unshattered faith," and perhaps in the process come closer to understanding "the purposes of God." Let us thus begin with the faith testimonies of enslaved black bodies. These testimonies are expressed in song.

The Freedom of God

The Songs of Faith

> Oh freedom!
> Oh freedom!
> Oh freedom over me!
> And before I'd be a slave
> I'll be buried in my grave
> And go home to my Lord and be free.[6]

---

6. Unless otherwise indicated all spiritual lyrics are from http://www.negro spirituals.com.

It is well documented that music has been essential to black people as they have navigated a society that has seen them as chattel. Whether it is the spirituals or the blues, music has provided a way for black people to communicate about the contradictions and hardships as well as the joys and triumphs of black living. Practically speaking, music allowed the captured and enslaved Africans to speak to one another across the barriers of their indigenous languages and dialects that their enslavers did not respect. Music was also a dynamic cultural/historical/theological reservoir, allowing various traditions to be passed down to generations of enslaved blacks, most importantly to those who were born in and died in an unfree American space. Music was the medium through which the enslaved Africans spoke about their gods, and through which their gods spoke to them. Within African traditions the sounds and rhythms of music were one of the primary vehicles through which the divine presence entered the lives of African people. In this respect, the gods traveled across the Middle Passage through the music of the people and thus continued to be present in their people's lives—even in a strange land.

For the enslaved, music was a "safe space," not only to express their faith, but also to talk honestly about their life circumstances and to share their deepest aspirations for freedom, even when white ears were listening. Because the narratives of Anglo-Saxon exceptionalism had implanted in the white mind that black bodies were ignorant and dumb, and certainly not creative enough to outwit white people, through the sounds of music the enslaved were able to outwit their unsuspecting enslavers. The same music in which the white masters and mistresses found confirmation that their "chattel" were "happy-go-lucky darkeys" with an instinct for singing was used by the enslaved to exchange valuable information about survival, escape, and the "ways of white folks."[7] The significance of music in the enslaved space was the same as it was in the free African space. It was a means "to translate the experiences of life and of the spiritual world."[8]

The spirituals exemplify the role of music in the life and culture of the enslaved. Through the spirituals, life was navigated and faith

---

7. I am revisiting an argument that I made in *Black Bodies and the Black Church: A Blues Slant* (New York: Palgrave Macmillan 2012), 6-7.

8. Samuel A. Floyd Jr., *The Power of Black Music: Interpreting Its History from Africa to the United States* (New York: Oxford University Press, 1995), 32.

was proclaimed. In spirituals, black people spoke about their gods, and perhaps their gods spoke to them. Spirituals were one of the primary tools that black people crafted to help them resist the narratives of Anglo-Saxon exceptionalism. The spirituals were discourses of protest and resistance. They were a way to say no to Americas' grand narrative about black people and about God. In this respect, spirituals provide some of the earliest forms of protest against the way in which America's Anglo-Saxon identity tried to construct and circumscribe the identity of black people. Through the spirituals the black enslaved actually contested the Anglo-Saxon myth. And so we see, from one of the earliest testimonies of black faith, that black faith was always connected to the historical conditions of black life. In the midst of absurd realities, the spirituals sounded forth black people's core understandings of God's relationship with them, and theirs with God. Spirituals held together the "trouble that bore [the enslaved] down" with their faith in a liberating God.[9] Thus, they could sing, "Nobody knows de trouble I've seen/ Glory Hallelujah." Howard Thurman explains that through the spirituals the black enslaved "express[ed] the profound conviction that God was not done with them, that God was not done with life."[10] Spirituals, essentially, reveal the foundation for a faith that will sustain black people through the paradox of being faithful in a society defined by the Anglo-Saxon myth. James Weldon Johnson says it best:

> In the Spirituals the Negro did express his religious hopes and fears, his faith and his doubts. In them he expressed his theological and ethical views, and sounded his exhortations and warnings. . . . Indeed, the Spirituals taken as a whole contain a record and a revelation of the deeper thoughts and experiences of the Negro in this country for a period beginning three hundred years ago and covering two and a half centuries.[11]

It is with this appreciation for the role of music, and the significance of the spirituals, that we turn to the spiritual, "Oh, Freedom" to begin our exploration of black faith.

---

9. This phrase is a paraphrase of the spiritual "Trouble done bore me down."

10. Thurman, *Deep River,* 126.

11. James Weldon Johnson and J. Rosamond Johnson, *The Book of American Negro Spirituals* (New York: Da Capo Press, 1973; orig., 1926), 12-13 (preface to Book 2).

This spiritual, thought to date back to the Civil War era, expresses the very hub of black faith. By linking their hope for freedom to the "Lord," the black men and women who created this spiritual were not just expressing their own desires for freedom, they were also conveying their understanding of God's very nature. Essentially, they were proclaiming that their desire to be free was not only something God supported but something consistent with who God was. They were testifying to the very freedom of God.

For the enslaved an experience of freedom would mean being liberated from the constraints and constructs of cherished white property. This required freedom both from the chains of slavery and from the narratives that defined them as chattel. Freedom for them had ontological meaning, in that it spoke to the reality of their very being. It also had existential meaning, in that it spoke to the reality of their lives. Spirituals such as "Oh, Freedom" suggested that freedom held a similar meaning for God. The significance of black faith hinges upon the freedom of God. It is indeed the freedom of God, as the enslaved understood it, that gives black faith its enduring significance, even in a stand-your-ground culture.

According to the enslaved authors of the spirituals, the freedom of God concerned the nature of God's presence in their lives as well as God's very nature. Theologically speaking, the freedom of God as expressed in the spirituals bore witness both to the economy of God (God's movement in human history) and the aseity of God (who God is in God's self). The spiritual's testimony concerning the freedom of God suggested at least two interrelated things. First, God was by nature free, therefore, complete in God's self and dependent on no other being or power for existence. Second, God's movement in human history reflected God's freedom. We will first look at what it means for God by nature to be free, for this becomes the basis for all other understanding of God in black faith.

God's Own Freedom

> He's got the whole world in His hands
> He's got the big round world in His hands
> He's got the whole world in His hands.

This spiritual testifies not simply to the fact that God cares about God's creation but also to God's relationship with the world. It suggests that the world is in God's hands, not the other way around.

To proclaim God free by nature is in fact to attest to God's transcendence. The transcendence of God indicates that God is not bound by the world. God is free from all finite, limiting, human-constructed realities. The freedom of God *is* the transcendence of God. A transcendent God is one who is free from being boxed in by any human projections. And so the enslaved sang, God "can ride upon the air."[12] Again, the implication is that God is above all earthly/human constructs. The transcendence of God is what black church people testify to when they say, "God can be God all by Himself."

The transcendent freedom of God is essential for a black faith born on the soil of the oppressor's faith, directed presumably to the same God. It was an awareness of God's transcendent freedom that enabled enslaved men and women to know that the God their enslavers spoke of was not truly God. They recognized that their enslaver's God was as bound to the whips and chains of slavery as were their own black bodies. The enslaver's God was for all intents and purposes a white slave master sitting on a throne in heaven keeping black people in their place as chattel. The black enslaved knew that this was not the God who encountered them in their free African lives. They were certain, furthermore, that this was not the God they encountered in the Bible. The God of their enslavers simply was not free. The God of the enslaved, which they soon understood to be the God of the Bible, *was* free. Doubtless, it was the African religious heritage of the enslaved that facilitated their profound understanding of God's freedom and transcendence. We will look at this more closely, for it helps us to fully appreciate the significance of the freedom of God for an enslaved people, and subsequently black bodies, in a stand-your-ground-culture war of conflicting faith claims.

The Great High God

The enslaved Africans' first experience with God was not in slavery. They knew God before they were taken from their African homes and made chattel in America. As we will soon see, this African experience

---

12. See "He's the Lily of the Valley" (http://www.negrospirituals.com).

of God was crucial to their understanding of who they were, and who God created them to be. For now it is important to recognize that it was not through their European and American captors that they met God. They met God in Africa, before they were captured and enslaved. This prior divine/human encounter was significant. This was not the Anglo-Saxon God who came with the first Americans from England. They knew a God who was free from whiteness. Indeed, the God they met in Africa was free from all human limitations and finite realities. This God truly "rode in the air." This God was the Great High God of their West African culture.[13]

Unquestionably, the African theological heritage of those who crafted the black faith tradition was rich and diverse. This heritage consisted of various religious and theological systems. Despite this rich diversity, however, certain understandings of God were generally affirmed across the various West African religious traditions. One such affirmation is the reality of a Great High God.

The Great High God has been widely studied in the works of black religious scholars and theologians. In many respects, the Great High God provided the theological paradigm through which enslaved Africans appropriated the Christian faith and interpreted their experiences in the unfree American space. It was also the experience of a Great High God that fostered their identification with the exodus story and shaped their understanding of God's presence in that story. For, if nothing else, the belief in a Great High God represents a faith affirmation of God's utter freedom. To reiterate, the freedom of God is crucial if black faith is to be more than an illusion or false hope, and thus maintain its relevance in the time of stand your ground. Let us look more closely at the role of this Great High God in African understandings of the cosmos to further appreciate this fact.

While West African religious traditions bear witness to a pantheon of divine realities, these traditions are foundationally monotheistic. They maintain a core belief in the existence of a supreme deity. This deity, known as the Great High God, does not directly interact with the human realm. Some have suggested that "by maintaining distance

---

13. From this point forward when I speak of African it can be assumed that I am speaking of West Africa unless otherwise noted. West Africa was the cultural origin for most of the enslaved Africans.

from nature and humanity the [Great High God] manifests divine care."[14] Otherwise, human beings as well as nature would be overwhelmed and possibly destroyed by the sheer power and presence of this supreme deity. The remoteness of the Great High God is perceived as an act of divine kindness. Even as this divine remoteness protects the integrity of humans, it also protects the integrity of the Great High God. This God is so high that it is wholly independent of human beings. It is free from whatever it is human beings may want God to be. Instead, God is who God is, completely in God's self. This God does not need the intervention of humans to be fully God. The Great High God is perfect. This does not mean, however, that human beings have no access to this God. God provides the access through the creation of lesser gods and divinities. Through the creation of these beings God initiates a relationship with humans. Once again, the freedom of God is enunciated. For the relationship between God and human beings is not something that humans control; rather, it is in the control of God. Put another way, humans do not make God real in their lives. Rather, it is God who makes Godself known in the lives of humans.

This act of creation suggests another significant aspect of the Great High God. This God is the Great Creator. It creates all that is, again without the help of humans. This belief corresponds to the Christian testimony of *creatio ex nihilo*, that God creates out of nothing. This means that God is the source of all that is and that nothing exists apart from God. This is the God who "got the whole world in his hands." Dwight Hopkins explains, "Like Christianity, religions of the west coast of Africa held in highest esteem God the Supreme Being, comprised of absolute creating powers, unique in that nothing existed prior to this all powerful Spirit."[15] This belief in the God that brings all things into existence again serves to clarify the distance between humans and God. It does so by affirming God as creator and human being as creatures. The creator/creature relationship signals that humans are dependent on God for their existence, not the reverse.

---

14. See Peter J. Paris, *The Spirituality of African Peoples: The Search for a Common Moral Discourse* (Minneapolis: Augsburg Fortress Press, 1995), 30.

15. Dwight N. Hopkins, *Down, Up, and Over: Slave Religion and Black Theology* (Minneapolis: Augsburg Fortress Press, 2000), 110.

This theological principle of creation *ex nihilo* by the Great High God also confirms God's freedom. For if God is the beginning of all that is, then the divine creative act is an absolutely free act. There was nothing prior to God that constrained God to create. Within West African religious understandings this is even more profound when one considers that God brought the pantheon of other beings into existence. The creation of other divine powers punctuates the fact that there is no being or power in the earth, above earth, or under the earth that exists apart from God's free creative act. The enslaved Africans expressed it this way:

> Mah God is high, you can't git over Him (refrain)
> He's so low, yuh can't git under Him
> He's so wide, yuh can't git aroun' Him
> Yuh mus' come in by and through de Lam.[16]

It is interesting to note that the enslaved say that Jesus, referred to as 'de Lam' in the spiritual, is the way to get to God. Even as this is an indication of their Christian faith, some have suggested that one of the reasons the enslaved Africans were able to integrate Jesus into their religious worldview was because they saw him as one of the lesser gods. Perhaps this was the case. What is certain is that they saw similarities between their understanding of the Christian God and the God(s) they knew in Africa. What they did not find compatible with either the Christian or African God(s) was the God of their slaveholders, and thus the God that legitimates America's notion of exceptionalism.

As for creation, it witnesses to the freedom of God. As it does this it suggests something about the manifestation of divine freedom. One of the ways the freedom of God expresses itself is through fostering and nurturing life. At least in relationship to human beings, the first demonstration of God's freedom is a creative act; it is one that brings forth life. Hence, the freedom of God is effectively a life-giving force. The freedom of God is that which stands in opposition to death. We will see this even more in the next chapter in our discussion of the cross-resurrection event. What is clear now is the absolute relationship between the freedom of God and life. This again is vital for the faith of a people victimized by a stand-your-ground culture.

---

16. J. Cleveland, *Songs of Zion* (Nashville: Abingdon Press, 1981), 105.

The enslaved Africans carried across the Middle Passage to America their experientially derived understanding of the Great High God. This was an experience of a sovereign God, that is, a God who transcends and is distinct from all that God has created, including humans. It is this experience of a free God that allowed the enslaved Africans to recognize that whatever power their enslavers were talking about, it was not the God they knew, and it was certainly not the God they came to know from the Bible. For the God of the Bible, the one who "in the beginning created the heavens and the earth," sounded like nothing other than their Great High God. Moreover, the God the enslaved knew in Africa appeared to be the same one that spoke to Isaiah saying, "For my thoughts are not your thoughts, neither are your ways my ways. . . . As the heavens are higher than the earth, so are my ways higher than your ways and my thoughts than your thoughts." It did not take much to recognize that the thoughts and the ways of the enslaver's God were identical to the thoughts and ways of the enslavers themselves. And so it was that the slaveholders' God was not free, but bound to the constructs of slavery. While slavery may have stripped the Africans of their physical freedom, they knew that it could not take away the freedom of God. And so they testified in spirituals:

> God is a God!
> God don't never change!
> God is a God
> An' He always will be God.[17]

To hear this song with an appreciation of the Great High God, is to recognize that it is a protest against a God who would support enslavement. For the enslaved Africans it is not a matter of two views of the same God. To them, the slaveholders were not talking about God at all. Thus, as Thurman recognizes, the enslaved "undertook the redemption of a religion that their master had profaned in [their] midst."[18]

According to a faith informed by an African theological paradigm, for God to be God, God must be free. Freedom is what makes God God. The enslaved could "Go home to their Lord and be free," because

---

17. Quoted in James H. Cone, *The Spirituals and the Blues* (Maryknoll, NY: Orbis Books, 1992; orig., Seabury, 1972), 38.

18. Thurman, *Deep River*, 40.

their Lord was free. God meant freedom from the intricate fetters of Anglo-Saxon exceptionalism. To listen to a faith that was born during the ordeal of slavery is to hear a people's testimony that God is not one with those who consider them chattel.

Within the black faith tradition forged in the invisible institution of slavery, the freedom of God means that there is a profound difference between God and those who would make chattel of black bodies. God was not with the slaveholders. Their ways and thoughts were not God's. God was not the property of white people. Put simply, God was not Anglo-Saxon and God was not white. God was not cherished white property. The strength of black faith is grounded in the theological affirmation that God is free and, thus, that the "Almighty God has its own purposes." These purposes are distinct from those that would destroy black life. For a black father grieving the loss of a son to a stand-your-ground war, this affirmation is monumental. For it confirms that there is a power that is distinct from and greater than the racist power that took the life of his child. The freedom of God, in fact, suggests that God actually opposes stand-your-ground culture, which is nothing less than a culture of death. Coming to light is a fundamental contradiction of faith that we will discuss later—belief in a God who fosters life, even in the midst of death. What is clear even in this contradiction is that the freedom of God means life. This leads to a further examination of God's movement in history. Before looking at this, however, there is another significant implication of divine freedom that is important to establish when it comes to the black body.

Created to Be Free

"No more auction block for me/No more, no more/No more auction block for me/Many thousand gone." Inasmuch as this song was about actually being liberated from slavery, and it was, it was also about more than that. In the context of the singers' actual enslavement, this song had profound ontological meaning. It meant that the enslaved had not acquiesced to any notion that they were by nature chattel. This spiritual reflects the self-constitution of these enslaved men and women.[19] This self-constitution was born from their experience of God and an appreciation for God's own freedom.

---

19. This notion of self-constitution is informed by Dwight Hopkins's

The enslaved Africans knew God when they were free. Thus, God knew them as free beings. Therefore, the enslaved Africans were confident that they were not created to be chattel. They knew a life of freedom, and in that life they knew God. These two facts could only mean one thing: black bodies were not created to be enslaved bodies. More to the point, black bodies were not meant to be targets of a stand-your-ground-culture war. This affirmation speaks to a fundamental African theological principle that further suggests the meaning and continuing relevance of black faith.

This African principle maintains that everything the Great High God creates has sacred value because it is intrinsically connected to God. It is this belief that undergirds an African worldview that all reality is sacred. A prevailing African understanding maintains that everything that exists is sacred. There is no sacred/secular division within the traditional West African perception of the world. As has been well documented, "secularity has no reality" in the worldviews that informed the enslaved Africans.[20] The implications for black people are profound. For to hold all created reality as sacred means black people are themselves sacred. The whole of their beings has sacred value, including their bodies. Instead of being commodified bodies they are divine bodies. In short, the faith claim that all of creation is sacred means that "God is no despiser of Blackness."[21] God intends for black bodies to be cherished and respected, not abused and sold. They are divine creations. They are not chattel. They are not criminals. They are not anti-God. And again, they are not targets for Manifest Destiny missions.

The African affirmation of the sacredness of creation is consistent with the biblical teaching that as God looked out at all that God had created, "God saw that it was good." In the end, the knowledge of their sacred creation allowed the enslaved to resist their enslavers' attempts

---

recognition that even as the white enslavers were constituting an identity for the enslaved, the enslaved were constituting their own self-identity. Hopkins says that the enslaved "co-constitutes" the black self. I refer to it as "self-constitution" because it is done independently of and prior to their enslavers. See Hopkins, *Down, Up, and Over*, chap. 3.

20. Paris, *The Spirituality of African Peoples*, 27.

21. Kortright Davis, *Compassionate Love and Ebony Grace: Christian Altruism and People of Color* (New York: Hamilton Books, 2012), x.

to make chattel of them mentally, spiritually, and psychologically. In her narrative, once-enslaved Harriet Jacobs witnesses to this, as she comments, "[Slaveholders] seem to satisfy their conscience with the doctrine that God created the Africans to be slaves. What a libel upon the heavenly Father, who 'made one blood of all nations of men!'"[22] The enslaved's self-perception was, essentially, a divine self-perception. Hence, it was one that contested a chattel reality. Though their bodies may have been enchained, their minds and spirits remained free, and so they could sing, even in the midst of slavery, "No more auction block for me." Hopkins explains it this way: "If sunup to sundown (time claimed by the slave system) marked the multiplicity of assaults to turn black workers from their divine created origin and intent (being created freely and created to be free), then from sundown to sunup (time claimed by the enslaved) indicated the black chattels' turn from the evil creation of the master to the original divine origin and intent."[23] There was yet another theological understanding, indeed a Christian understanding, that confirmed that black bodies were meant to be free bodies.

To be created in the image of a God that is free means that the human person is meant to be free. That is, like God, free from all human constraints and constructs that prevent one from being fully who one is and that threaten one's very life. Because humans are created in the image of God, and not the other way around, black life has meaning beyond the images constructed by narratives of a stand-your-ground culture. Hopkins reaches this same conclusion concerning the importance of the *imago dei*. He explains, "As an act of grace, God creates through divine freedom women and men by giving them the freedom and liberation inherent in God's own self. . . . Because God was the Spirit of total liberation and freedom for humanity, God imparted this in humanity. The *imago dei*, therefore, is the Spirit of total liberation in all humanity"[24]

For black people, bearing the image of God not only means that black people are in themselves free, but it also necessitates being

---

22. Harriet Ann Jacobs, *Incidents in the Life of a Slave Girl Written by Herself*, ed. Lydia Maria Francis Child, p. 69, http://www.docsouth.unc.edu.
23. Hopkins, *Down, Up, and Over.*
24. Ibid.

free from the oppressive social usages and customs of Anglo-Saxon exceptionalism. Indeed, living into this image of freedom is the moral mandate of creation. Any rejection of freedom—as implied, for black people, by any acceptance of their status as chattel—is essentially a rejection of who they are as God's creatures; it means to turn away from God. If the Christian testimony that humans are created in the image of God means anything, it means that to live contrary to freedom is to sin. For black people the mandate is clear: living according to their created nature means living as free beings. This is the existential implication of God's freedom. The freedom of God means that black bodies are created to be free.

There is no one who articulated more clearly the moral mandate for enslaved men and women to rise up and to free themselves from the chains of slavery than Henry Highland Garnet. In his 1843 "Address to the Slaves of the United States," given in Buffalo, New York, Garnet called the enslaved to "resistance, *resistance! resistance!*"[25] He argued that slavery "hurls defiance in the face of [God]."[26] Therefore he said, "*neither God, nor angels, or just men, command you to suffer for a single moment. Therefore it is your solemn and imperative duty to use every means, both moral, intellectual, and physical that promises success*" in securing freedom.[27] Garnet told the slaves, "The forlorn condition in which you are placed, does not destroy your moral obligation to God."[28] This was an obligation to fight for the freedom that God intended for them. Garnet explained, "The humblest peasant is as free in the sight of God as the proudest monarch that ever swayed a scepter. Liberty is a spirit sent out from God, and like its great Author, is no respecter of persons."[29]

The enslaved Africans were clearly very aware that God did not intend their bondage. Such awareness provided another tool for resisting any human constructions that sought to make them chattel. This understanding of who they were created to be was enough to inspire creative ways to protest if not escape their enslavement. James

---

25. Henry Highland Garnet, "An Address to the Slaves of the United States of America, Buffalo, NY, 1843," p. 9, http://digitalcommons.unl.edu.

26. Ibid, 5.

27. Ibid.

28. Ibid.

29. Ibid., 6.

Cone explains, "Slave religion was permeated with the affirmation of freedom from bondage and freedom-in-bondage. Sometimes black religious gatherings were the occasions for planning overt resistance. At other times the reality of freedom was affirmed in more subtle ways."[30] One of those more subtle ways was, of course, through music. Testifying that they had not capitulated to even the chains of chattel, black people sang:

> We'll soon be free,
> We'll soon be free,
> We'll soon be free,
> When de Lord will call us home.

At other times they might signal through song that it was time to escape:

> Don't be weary, traveller
> Come along home to Jesus
> My head get wet with the midnight dew
> Come along home to Jesus
> Angels bear me witness too
> Come along home to Jesus.

Worth noting here is the repeated reference to "home." To the ears of their enslavers, home may have simply signified "the great by and by when they die." However, with an appreciation for the meaning and significance of being created in the image of a free God, to be called home is to be called to a "free space" where black bodies can live into the fullness of who they are. God is always calling a black body home, which means calling that body into freedom. The significance of this is profound in a stand-your-ground culture. For a stand-your-ground culture that denies black bodies a home in the world—in other words, a free space—is a culture that denies God's "purposes" for all human bodies. It is a culture that is contrary to the ways of God. In no uncertain terms, therefore, stand-your-ground culture and all that it spawns represents a sinful reality.

Recognizing home as the place to which God calls black bodies makes even more poignant Sybrina Fulton's observation that her son,

---

30. Cone, *The Spirituals and the Blues*, 30.

Trayvon, was simply trying to get home.[31] According to the black faith tradition this means Trayvon was simply trying to get to that space where he could be free—that is, to be the Trayvon God created him to be. He was trying to get to the space to which he was called by God. He was trying to get to where he belonged and had a divine right to be. On that fatal night in Florida, his killer refused to let him get home. He denied Trayvon a free space. In so doing, the killer violated the purposes of God.

The spiritual "Slavery Chain" seems to speak to the enslaved's overall understanding of the totality of God's freedom, and its implications for their condition. The point is, God means freedom, which means that slavery's chain is broken, whether in fact or ontologically. And so the enslaved sang:

> Slavery chain done broke at last, broke
>   at last, broke at last,
> Slavery chain done broke at last,
> Going to praise God till I die

Black Faith: A Narrative of Resistance

What is becoming clear in our discussion thus far is that the faith tradition forged by the enslaved provided a counternarrative to the grand narrative of Anglo-Saxon exceptionalism. In other words, the black faith tradition itself generates a discourse of resistance that allows black people to affirm their innate and created worth, even when everything around them suggests their utter worthlessness. This faith testifies to a way of seeing one's self that is not determined by the ideologies of Anglo-Saxon exceptionalism. Black faith provides the counternarrative to the sacred canopies and religio-science of white supremacy that graft constructed identities upon black bodies. Black faith testifies to a God that allows black people to maintain their sense of divine dignity and claim their strength in the face of a stand-your-ground culture that seeks to pervert their self-image and disrespects their bodies. Black faith allows black people to see themselves from beyond the "veil" of Anglo-Saxon whiteness. It frees black people

---

31. Sybrina Fulton, "Trayvon Martin's Parents Speak Out on Not Guilty Verdict," *Time,* http://newsfeed.time.com.

from the "sense of always looking at one's self through the eyes of [white] others."[32] This faith helps black people to develop an independent consciousness, and, thus, to claim their God-given, "inalienable" right to be free. It is in this way that black faith thwarts the very power of cherished white property to make chattel of black people. The power of black faith, which is found in the freedom of God, is more powerful than any human power that seeks to destroy black life.

To connect our black daughters and sons to the faith of their enslaved forebears is, therefore, to provide them with a faith that fosters self-definition and self-determination. It is to let them know they are created in the image of a God that is free from anything human beings can conceive or construct; thus, they too are meant to be free. Put simply, to connect our children to the black faith tradition is to give them the tools to know that "what white people say about [them] . . . what they do and cause [them] to endure, does not testify to [their] inferiority but to [white people's] inhumanity and fear."[33] To connect our children to black faith, therefore, is to provide them with a firm foundation on which to stand in the midst of the absurdities of black life without being overcome by them.

During one of her many speeches in her fight for black freedom, nineteenth-century black female activist Maria Stewart said this to her black audience, "Many think, because your skins are tinged with a sable hue, that you are an inferior race of beings; but God does not consider you as such. He hath formed and fashioned you in his own glorious image, and hath bestowed upon you reason and strong powers of intellect."[34] Maria Stewart clearly understood that if oppressed people are going to withstand the assaults against their lives and well-being then they must be equipped with the knowledge of their sacred humanity. This is why poet and essayist Audre Lorde says, "The true focus of revolutionary change is never merely the oppressive situations we seek to escape, but that piece of the oppressor which is implanted deep within each of us."[35]

---

32. W. E. B. Du Bois, *The Souls of Black Folks,* with an introduction by Arnold Rampersad (New York: Alfred A. Knopf, Inc., 1993; orig., 1903), 9.

33. Baldwin, "Letter to My Nephew," *The Price of the Ticket,* 335.

34. Maria Stewart, *Maria W. Stewart, America's First Black Political Writer: Essays and Speeches* (Bloomington: Indiana University Press, 1987), 29.

35. Audre Lorde, *Sister Outsider* (New York: Crossing Press, 1984), 123.

From the first day that my son was born I told him every morning, "You are a child of God. God loves you. There is no one greater
than you but God." I knew that my son would be growing up in a
society that would despise him for his blackness. Therefore, I wanted
to provide him with that piece of black faith that would not allow a
denigrating piece of America's Anglo-Saxon exceptional identity to be
"implanted deep within [him]." Howard Thurman perhaps says it best
of all. He says that the message of faith to the enslaved was, "You are
created in God's image. You are not slaves, you are not 'niggers'; you
are God's children. . . . He who knows this," Thurman says, "is able to
transcend the vicissitudes of life, however terrifying. . . ."[36]

In a stand-your-ground-culture war, black faith provides a powerful tool of resistance. This faith tradition makes clear that God is not
Anglo-Saxon and that black people are not chattel. In short, God's
ontological freedom affirms the ontological and existential freedom
of black bodies.

This brings us to a second aspect of God's freedom, namely, God's
movement in the world on behalf of freedom. Thus, we now turn to
the meaning of the exodus in the black faith tradition.

The Meaning of the Exodus for Stand-Your-Ground Culture

> Didn't my Lord deliver Daniel
> Deliver Daniel, deliver Daniel
> Didn't my Lord deliver Daniel
> An' why not-a every man.

Even as the enslaved crafters of the black faith tradition affirmed
the absolute freedom of God, that is, God's transcendence, they also
recognized that the power of divine freedom is expressed through
God's movement in the world. God's very freedom, they recognized,
was expressed in God's delivering others into freedom. The progenitors of the black faith tradition affirmed God's enduring presence and
movement in human history; in other words, they recognized God's
immanence.

Within African religious traditions this was the significance of the
lesser gods created by the Great High God. These lesser gods consti-

---

36. Thurman, *Deep River*, 18.

tuted the divine presence in African life. They testified to the fact that "God is not without the world, and the world is not without God." They reflected the ongoing divine activity of God in human history. These lesser gods served as mediators between the Africans and the Great High God. It is worth repeating that it is perhaps in this way that the African religious heritage laid the foundation for the enslaved African's acceptance of Christianity. Jesus is easily accommodated within this African theological framework as perhaps a lesser god, or perhaps even an ancestor. For sure, the lesser gods of the African religious tradition provided a theological foundation for another essential claim of black faith: God is in the world. Therefore, not only would a story such as the exodus, which reveals God's presence in history, be consistent with the African religious heritage, but undoubtedly it was this heritage that attracted the enslaved Africans to the exodus story in the first place. For the exodus was not just a story of God's presence in history, it was also a story about the freedom of God.

Reverend Reed, an ex-slave, said this: "The children of Israel was four hundred years under bondage and God looked down and seen the suffering of the striving Israelites and brought them out of bondage."[37] Reverend Reed's telling of the exodus story is instructive. Reverend Reed first makes clear that God is the one who initiates a relationship with the Israelites. This fact further affirms God's freedom. For the freedom of God means that God acts first. God's actions are compelled by who God is, by God's own essence. They are not dependent on human actions or anything external to God. The recognition that God acts first is consistent with the theological principle that God creates out of nothing: *creatio ex nihilo*. God's creative act was a free act, motivated only by who God is in God's self. The same is true of God's presence in human history. German theologian Karl Barth said this: God is "the free partner of humanity in a history which [God] inaugurated and in a dialogue ruled by [God]."[38] Reverend Reed makes it plain, "God looked down and seen." Reverend Reed goes on to specify what God saw: the bondage, suffering, and striving of the Israelites. Reverend Reed's witness to God's move-

---

37. Quoted in Hopkins, *Down, Up, and Over*, 1.
38. Karl Barth, "The Humanity of God," trans. James Strathearn McNab, in *Karl Barth: Theologian of Freedom*, ed. Clifford Green (London: Collins, 1979), 48.

ment clearly indicates that what moved God was not any exceptional aspect of the Israelites themselves. Rather, God was moved by their condition of bondage and suffering as well as their striving to be free. Consistent with who God is and who God created humans to be, God was moved to free the Israelites from their bondage. In so doing, God freed them to live into their divinely created selves. Reverend Reed's story accords with the biblical narrative that reads: "I have indeed seen the affliction of my people in Egypt. I have heard them crying out because of the taskmasters, and I am concerned about their suffering. So I have come down to rescue them from the hand of the Egyptians . . ." (Exodus 3:7-8).

The exodus story points to the fact that God chose to free a people from circumstances that were contrary to who God created them to be. God's choice was motivated by the very freedom that is God. God chose the Israelites because they were a people in bondage. The Israelite's particular historical circumstances serve as the historical context through which God reveals a universal concern for all people. The context itself is revelatory. For the context of God's revelation is consistent with the very nature of God. In this instance, it reaffirms the very freedom of God.

The point of identification with the exodus story for the enslaved did not lie in their exceptionalist claim to be the chosen people of God. Rather, the identification was based on the recognition that their historical condition was the same as that of the Israelites—a condition contrary to the freedom of God. So they reasoned if God freed the Israelites, God would free them. They understood the universal meaning of God's revelation through the particularity of the Israelite story. As Howard Thurman explains, the enslaved knew that "God is no respecter of persons, what He did for one race He would surely do for another."[39] Thus they sang that if God delivered Daniel, "why not-a every man." With particular reference to the exodus they sang,

> Go down Moses
> Way down in Egypt land
> Tell ole Pharaoh
> To let my people go

---

39. Thurman, *Deep River*, 21.

What the enslaved understood and testified to in song is that God's preferential option in the exodus story is for freedom. This is the way that we are to understand the centrality of the exodus story in black faith. It confirms that God's intention is for all people, including black people, to be free to live into the goodness of their very creation. It is only in freedom that people are able to reflect the very image of a God who is free from all human forms of bondage. This understanding has implications for the two faith claims in the stand-your-ground-culture war.

An Exodus Response to Conflicting Faith Claims

The faith claims of the nation rest on the notion that Anglo-Saxons are the "chosen" people of God. In this instance, as we have seen in our discussions, chosenness is connected to blood. This very fact betrays God's concern for all God has created. More particularly, it does not accord with the contextuality of God's revelation in the exodus story. In short, that God chose the Israelites is first an indication that God chooses to be in the world. Second, it indicates God's preferential option for freedom. What it does not indicate is God's choice for any particular people above all other people. The exodus story tells us that God's choice of the Israelites was not about blood, but about freedom. The story says that God looked down and saw that they were in bondage, not that they were Israelites. This is not to negate the fact that in the Old Testament (Hebrew scriptures) God enters into human history through the life, culture, and history of the Israelites. Nor is this to deny the special meaning this may hold for Jewish traditions. Nevertheless, the particularity of God's revelation is not the same as divine exclusivism. It does not suggest that there are only certain people who are deserving of God's care and freedom. To reiterate, it is through the particularity of the revelation of God that the universal meaning of God's freedom can be found.

Furthermore, any suggestion that God's identification with a particular people is a matter of blood ruptures the distance between human beings and God. What is most troubling, it allows for humans to see themselves as God and thus to equate their story and their history as being God's very story and history. God is reduced to a human creation, while humans are elevated to a divine status. The dangers of this are immense, as we have seen in the Manifest Destiny war. In this instance,

God is made into a "defender and guarantor of the presumptions" and brutality of America's Anglo-Saxon exceptionalism.[40] God's absolute transcendence and God's creative initiative are vitiated. The inherent difference between humanity and God is lost. For this reason the freedom of God must become the measure for all that is said about God. Indeed, God makes this clear in an interaction with Moses.

When God heard the cries of the Israelites and recognized their oppression, God commissioned Moses to go to the pharaoh and tell him to let the people of Israel go free. Unsure of who this God was, and by what divine authority he could make demands of the pharaoh or even speak to the people of Israel, Moses asked God who precisely God was. He asked for the name of God, to which God responded, "I am who I am. . . . Say this to the people of Israel, I am has sent me to you" (Exodus 3:14). In this proclamation the freedom of God is asserted. Even as God has proclaimed that the Israelites are God's people, God's identity is not attached to the Israelites. To know the Israelites is not to know God. God's identity is connected to God's very free movement in history. More importantly, God's identity is not a stagnant identity. God says: I am who I am. In the very use of a verb as a name, God clearly self-identifies as movement, an ongoing presence in history. In other words, God is to be known by the way in which God moves in the world. God is not to be known by being identified with any particular people. God may be with a people, and can best be seen from the vantage point that is theirs in a particular context, but God is not those people. That is, no one people can have an exclusive claim on God. In the end, the movement that is God's very identity is defined in terms of a deliverance from bondage into the freedom that is life. In giving Moses directions for setting the people of God free the identity of God is clarified. Essentially, the exodus story preserves the freedom of God, and as it does so it affirms the essence of God as freedom.

A Nonliberating God

There are, of course, other aspects of the exodus story that are problematic. The freeing of the Israelites from bondage is not the end of the

---

40. Howard Thurman, *Jesus and the Disinherited*, repr. ed. (Boston: Beacon Press, 2012), 43.

story. In choosing the Israelites, God promises not only to free them from bondage but also to bring them to an inhabited land. God says, "I have come down to deliver them out of the Egyptians and to bring them up out of that land to a good land, a land flowing with milk and honey, to the place of the Canaanites, the Hittites, the Amorites, the Perizzites, the Hivites and the Jebusites." It is with this promise of an occupied land, with a later promise to destroy the people who occupy the land, that a sanctified narrative of Manifest Destiny emerges. There is no one who speaks more to the problems associated with the exodus story, particularly for black faith, than womanist theologian Delores Williams.

Williams cautions against using the exodus story as an indication of God's commitment "to set the captives free." She argues that if one takes into account the full exodus story, and not simply the event of a peoples' deliverance from bondage, then it soon becomes clear that God does not show a concern for the freedom of all people. Williams points out that the God of the exodus event fails to liberate those who are not Israelite and those who are not male, suggesting perhaps that there is a certain exclusivity to God's movement in history. She says, "when non-Jewish people . . . read the entire Hebrew testament from the point of view of the non-Hebrew slave, there is no clear indication that God is against their perpetual enslavement."[41] Adding to the problem, Williams says, is the fact that the exodus story also reveals a God who permits victims to make victims of others. Addressing her concern for the centrality of the exodus event within black faith, Williams warns that the Israelite exodus from Egypt must be read as a "*holistic story* rather than an event."[42] Doing so, she argues, reveals a God who sanctions "genocide in the land of Makkedah, in Libnah and in the Promised Land."[43]

Williams is right. The exodus story does indeed reveal troubling contradictions in understanding the freedom of God. Moreover, it portrays a God who sanctions Manifest Destiny missions. These contradictions are not to be casually dismissed. Nevertheless, they are instructive.

---

41. Delores S. Williams, *Sisters in the Wilderness: The Challenge of Womanist God-Talk* (Maryknoll, NY: Orbis Books, 1993), 146.

42. Ibid., 150.

43. Ibid.

Ironically, as troubling as they are, they point to the freedom of God. That God is free means the way God moves through history sometimes may elude human understanding. Thus, the freedom of God is a reminder that the claims we make about God may not always be about God. In this regard, the exodus paradoxes are a reminder that the reality of God is always more complex and dynamic than our very faith claims about God. If we are going to take the freedom of God seriously, we must be reconciled to the fact that we may not always know what God is doing in the world. What must be trusted, however, is faith in the knowledge that God creates and intends all people to be free.

As important as the exodus story is to black faith, it does not provide the final word, and perhaps not the authoritative word, on who God is in history, especially for black people. The Jesus story serves as a "new exodus." Through this story God as freedom is confirmed, along with the manifestation of God's freedom as life, and, as we will see, as love. It is through the Jesus story that the justice of God becomes clear, perhaps providing a counternarrative to the promised-land narrative of Manifest Destiny.

Furthermore, the annihilation of a people in the promised land suggests the distance between God and the world. That is, while God is in the world, all that is in the world is not of God. It could always be the case that the biblical story of the takeover of Canaan says more about the people telling it than it does about God. This is what the enslaved recognized when they testified to the freedom of God, and thus realized that what their enslavers said about God was not true. Inasmuch as claims about God were incompatible with their experience of God, then those claims were rejected. Those claims did not have theological authority. The freedom of God that the enslaved experienced became the adjudicating principle of their very faith claims. This has implications for the black faith tradition.

The core of black faith, as we have demonstrated, is a belief in the freedom of God. The recognition of God's freedom contests the claims of ideologies that denigrate black bodies. It is an adjudicating principle of black faith. However, if the freedom of God serves as an adjudicating principle, then it must also serve as a principle for self-critique. Simply put, if the central claim of the black faith tradition is that God has a preferential option for freedom, then the black faith community must be held accountable to that claim. This means, as Williams suggests, that the black faith community must not be blind to the ways in which it is complicit or participates in denying certain bodies the freedom that God has given them.

Even with this said, there is no getting around the fact that there is, as Williams asserts, "a non-liberative strand" in the Bible.[44] There are biblical stories that are nothing less than "texts of terror" for some people.[45] One such story is that of the Israelites' divinely sanctioned takeover and conquest of the land and people of Canaan. Read from the vantage point of modern-day Canaanites in a Manifest Destiny war, this is the story of Native Americans. Such a story simply cannot be reconciled with a God who stands for freedom. Such a story suggests a God who is virtually demonic. Thus, if the norm of black faith is an understanding of a God who is freedom, then that also means there are certain stories within the Bible that cannot be given authority. If black faith means refusing to capitulate to or compromise with any situation that violates the very freedom of God, then this principle must be maintained even when it comes to the Bible. Therefore no story that compromises the freedom of God, and thus the freedom of those whom God created, can be given authority in the black faith tradition. It must be looked upon, at best, with suspicion. Indeed, the enslaved set this precedent as they refused to grant authority to the Pauline texts that suggested a God who sanctioned slavery. They did not accept as the "word of God" the dictate in Ephesians 6:5 that slaves were to obey their masters. In this instance they treated the Pauline texts as something that Paul believed, but not something that came from God. Such was the case for Howard Thurman's mother. She told her son,

> During the days of slavery . . . the master's minister would occasionally hold services for the slaves. Old man McGhee was so mean that he would not let a Negro minister preach to his slaves. Always the white minister used as his text something from Paul. At least three or four times a year he used as a text: 'Slaves, be obedient to them that are your masters . . . , as unto Christ.' Then he would go on to show how it was God's will that we were

---

44. Ibid.

45. See Phyllis Trible, *Texts of Terror: Literary-Feminist Readings of Biblical Narratives* (New York: Fortress Press, 1984).

slaves and how, if we were good and happy slaves, God would bless us. I promised my Maker that if I ever learned to read and if freedom ever came, I would not read that part of the Bible.[46]

For Thurman's mother, God was freedom. She would not grant authority to anything said otherwise about God, even if it was in the Bible. Moreover, even while she was not yet free, she still affirmed the freedom of God.

The point is made: God is always greater and more complex than our words about God. This is the meaning of God's transcendent freedom. If human understanding could capture God, then God would not be God. This brings us full circle in our attempt to understand the enduring meaning of black faith for a black people who are victimized by a stand-your-ground war.

The Paradoxical Meaning of Black Faith

The very black faith claim that because God is free so black people are to be free was made in the context of bondage. This was not a statement derived from black people's current situation. Rather, it was a statement about the truth of God. Black faith is, in this regard, by nature a paradoxical faith. It is a faith born in the cauldron of oppression and giving witness to the freedom of God. It does not resolve the contradictions of black living or the contradictions of faith. And perhaps this is not the point of faith at all. For it is not the case that faith promises to free black people from the suffering and pain of being black in a society saturated with the Anglo-Saxon myth. Rather, it is a testament to a God who is present even in the midst of the particular brutalities of "living while black." This is a God who calls and moves black people toward freedom. Moreover, this is a God that lets black people know that they are indeed meant to be free. The God that is no despiser of blackness has a "preferential option" for the liberation of black bodies from that which denies them a free life. The enduring meaning of black faith is that it allows black people to know that the "contradictions of life are not themselves final or ultimate."[47] It

---

46. Told by Thurman in *Jesus and the Disinherited*, 30-31.

47. Howard Thurman, *The Search for Common Ground* (Richmond, IN: Friends United Press, 1986; orig., Howard Thurman Books, 1971), 6.

helps black people to stand in the gaps between being free yet not free, without becoming lost in them.

Black faith, however, is not passive. It does not seduce black people to wait on the Lord to free them. This was not the testimony given voice in the spirituals. Rather, black faith empowers black people to claim the freedom of God that is theirs, knowing that God is fighting with them. The contradictions between black faith and black life have a radicalizing impact. To know that one is meant to be free yet is not free does not create a hopeless spirit but a restless one. This is why we have seen a long line of black people who, in the face of the stand-your-ground cultures of their day, were inspired by faith to destroy whatever impeded their "inalienable" right to be free. There is no one who exemplifies more the significance of black faith in the freedom of God than Ida B. Wells. It was no doubt the gap between the God she believed in and the reality of black lives that inspired her to carry on the fight against the stand-your-ground lynchings of her day. She was sure that God was with her in the sometimes lonely fight against lynching. She made this clear to a group of African Methodist Episcopal clergy who were debating whether they should issue a proclamation endorsing her work. They were reluctant to endorse the work of a "young woman of whom they knew nothing." Appalled at their response Wells retorted, "Why, gentlemen . . . I cannot see why I need your endorsement. Under God I have done work without any assistance from my own people."[48] She indeed made clear to others that a belief in the freedom of God should empower a people to fight for their freedom, not "wait on the Lord" to free them. This was the message she gave to twelve black men who were awaiting execution for a crime they did not commit. After spending an evening with them, where they "talked and sung and prayed about dying," she said to the men, "But why don't you pray to live and ask to be freed? The God you serve is the God of Paul and Silas who opened their prison gates, and if you have all the faith you say you have, you ought to believe that he will open your prison doors too."[49]

---

48. Ida B. Wells, *Crusade for Justice: The Autobiography of Ida B. Wells,* ed. Alfreda M. Duster (Chicago: University of Chicago Press, 1970), 222.

49. Ibid., 402-403.

As clear as Wells was about the meaning of black faith for black people, she was equally clear about what believing in a Christian God should mean for white people, and especially for a country that was presumed to be Christian. In a speech before an audience in Liverpool, she said lynching was "inconsistent with Christian character, and even incompatible with civilization."[50] Wells was confident in the stand-your-ground war that was hers to fight; the God of freedom would surely not be on the side of the lynchers, or even of those who remained silent in the face of it.

In terms of the Manifest Destiny war that is stand-your-ground culture, the meaning of black faith is also clear. This too is "inconsistent with Christianity." Moreover, as Wells suggests, it is inconsistent with the claims of exceptionalism. A nation that sustains a war in which children become its target is not exceptional in Anglo-Saxon "virtue or justice" at all. Indeed, such a war reveals a "depraved indifference," which racial chauvinism breeds, to the life of the "other." Without a doubt, such indifference is inconsistent with the freedom of God that fosters life. As for the black faithful, the best response is indeed a response of faith, which means being relentless in the fight to dismantle this culture of death. It cannot be said enough, the Manifest Destiny vision and its attendant narrative of Anglo-Saxon exceptionalism are as sinful as the stand-your-ground culture that they have spawned.

If black people are to respond to stand-your-ground culture with the strength of black faith then we must work to put an end to the laws of a stand-your-ground culture that rob black bodies of freedom and life. Like the Black Codes of the postemancipation era, laws such as Stop and Frisk, mandatory drug sentencing, Conceal and Carry, and the Stand Your Ground law itself must be brought to an end. They are a violation of the sacredness of all of God's creation, most notably black creation. For the black faith community to settle for anything less than an end to these laws is a capitulation to sin. In the end, the meaning of black faith is found in the very affirmation of the freedom of God. For a black person to know that he or she is created in the image of a free God is to be empowered to carry on the fight for free-

---

50. Ibid., 141.

dom in a world that tries at every turn to deny black bodies a space to be free.

There is a biblical story that perhaps makes even clearer God's presence in a stand-your-ground war that targets our children. It is a story about a father and his son, the story of the "Binding of Isaac."

In this story, Abraham responds to what he believes to be God's call for him to go to the land of Moriah and offer his son Isaac as a burnt offering. Following the command, Abraham leaves the home he shares with Isaac's mother, Sarah, without her knowledge, and heads off to sacrifice the life of his son. Just as "Abraham reached out his hand and took the knife to slaughter his son," an angel of the Lord called out and said, "Do not lay your hand on the boy or do anything to him" (Genesis 22:1-14). With this, God provides Abraham a ram to sacrifice at the altar.

This story has been controversial in Jewish, Islamic, and Christian traditions. It has been interpreted as a test of Abraham's faith as well as an example of how easy it is to confuse God's voice with other voices. Within the black faith tradition, this story is usually told to indicate that no matter how impossible a situation may seem, there is a ram in the bush—God will provide. Whatever the various renderings of this story may be, one thing is abundantly clear: God stopped the sacrifice. God did not desire that Abraham's son be put to death. This same God of black faith is one that does not require the sacrifice of our sons and daughters. Just as the God of Abraham demanded that Isaac be released from the bindings that were meant to take his life, God demands the same of our children. They are to be released from the bindings that are a stand-your-ground culture.

An Unshattered Faith

The Sunday After

The verdict in the case of Trayvon's killer was announced shortly after 10:00 P.M. on a Saturday night. That next morning I went to church. That Sunday was like no other that I had experienced at my church. It was crowded more than usual for a Sunday in the middle of July. People came in quietly, as if something was weighing very heavily upon their hearts and trying their souls. No words had to be exchanged. Each person knew what the other was feeling and think-ing. Prior to the service a time was set aside for people to express their feelings about the verdict. Numerous people got up to speak, men and women, young and old. Many people spoke through tears as they expressed their sadness, disappointment, fears, and incredulity. Many were bewildered by the verdict. Many questioned the nation's com-mitment to black freedom. Many expressed fears for their children. Young black men spoke about their own fears. Some told stories of the assaults and humiliations they had endured in this stand-your-ground-culture war. There was an overall sense of anger and frus-tration. But what struck me the most in all of the testimonies was that no one lashed out at God. No one doubted God. No one blamed God. At the end of several of the statements, there was a proclamation of faith. The congregation affirmed each of the proclamations. The people were sure that what happened to Trayvon betrayed the pur-poses of God, and so their faith, like that of Tracy Martin, remained unshattered.

I was scheduled to preach that day. I had prepared my sermon well before the verdict was announced. I was torn the night before. Should I rewrite my sermon to respond to the verdict? I decided against it, though I did change the ending. Ironically, on a day when no black bodies were feeling particularly at home in America, we were cele-brating "all states day," in an effort to celebrate people's roots. As it turned out, the sermon seemed to have been prepared for such a time as we were facing. I preached about how many of us moved from state to state looking for a home, for a place where we could be free. I spoke about the Great Migrations, which some have called a Great Exodus in black life. For it was a time when black people left the South to what they thought would be the promised land of the North. I said that what made this exodus even more compelling was that there was no Moses. Instead, black men and women left the South compelled by the call of God that they were meant to be free. And so I said, "The question of today is not a question concerning our regional or even national identity, but rather a question concerning our identity as people of God." This identity, I said, was defined by five things. First, there is the strength that comes from God to persist in doing what is the right and just and kind thing to do despite a world that does otherwise. Second, we are to be thoughtful, thus always looking out for and supporting the rights of one another to live fully into who God has called each of us to be, especially in a society that does not necessarily look out for black bodies. Third, I said we are to be aware of the life-giving force of God in our lives and never settle on anything that seeks to destroy life. Fourth, I said our identity as people of God meant that we were to always be true to ourselves and to who we were as children of God, and thus not to live into the lie that we are less than human. Ultimately, I said that we were to live into the truth of God. "The truth" I preached "is about the freedom of God, freedom from those things that would attempt to separate us from the righteousness, the justice, and thus the freedom that God has promised us." Finally, I said that we are to always be engaged in a movement toward the life, love, and freedom that is God's for us. I ended my sermon with these words: Church, I don't have to tell you we are living in disappointing, despairing, if not dangerous, times. They are times filled with self-righteous violence and immoral justice. They are times that indeed try our souls because the integrity of our very humanity is in peril. Last night, after the verdict, Trayvon Martin's father said, "Even though I am broken hearted my faith is unshattered." Let our faith not be shattered. Let us be strong, thoughtful, aware, true, and engaged. Let us be a witness to what it means to be a people of faith in a broken world.

After I preached that morning people responded with thanks for preaching just what they needed to hear. I realized that it did not matter that the sermon was not prepared for that day after the verdict, because I preached about black faith. And this is faith that finds its meaning in the absurdities and contradictions of black life.

Black faith cannot change the world. How we wish it could! Black faith cannot save our children's lives. How much we wish it could! It fundamentally gives us the "courage to be" free in a world that rejects our right to be free. And, ironically, it gives us the courage to believe in the very freedom of God. It does not take a great deal of courage to believe in the freedom of God, or even in God, when all is well. It is easy to proclaim that God is good, all of the time, when things are going well. Black faith was not born in a time when things were going well for black bodies. It was not born in a time when black people were even nominally free. That is the strength of the faith. Somehow, black people were still able to affirm their belief in God, and thus the freedom of God, when nothing around them said freedom. In the middle of the dehumanizing conditions of chattel slavery, God made Godself known to black people and called them to freedom.

There is an inherent absurdity in black faith. It speaks of freedom in the midst of bondage. It speaks of life in the midst of death. This, however, is what makes black faith indispensable in the midst of a stand-your-ground-culture war. For while black faith cannot change the world, black faithful can. Black faith enables black faithful to strive relentlessly to make this world a place of freedom, and hence safety, for our children. And so it is that in the wake of his own son's death, Tracy Martin, along with Trayvon's mother, Sybrina Fulton, tells the story of Trayvon and proclaims that he had a God-given right to be free. In so doing, he and Sybrina have brought attention to a stand-your-ground-culture war that threatens the lives of all of our children. This is what it means to have an unshattered faith. It means acting as if you really believe in the God of that faith, that is, a God that intends for black bodies to be free. To really believe is to live into that freedom, knowing that God is with you as you do. There is no doubt that the liberating movement of God is in the parents of the Trayvons and the Jordans of our world who have not been defeated by death but instead continue the fight to make sure that other black children do not become targets of a stand-your-ground war. In this stand-your-ground war the freedom of God is made manifest in the tears, the strife, and the fight of the black fathers and mothers whose children are casualities of this unholiest of wars.

Yes, perhaps black faith is absurd. Christianity itself is absurd. There is nothing more absurd than a religion that has a cross as its central symbol. But it is because of that cross that we know that Trayvon, Jordan, Renisha, and Jonathan, as well as Emmett, were not meant to die. It is because of the cross that we can be sure stand-your-ground culture will not have the last word over their lives. It is to the cross that we will now turn.

5

Jesus and Trayvon: The Justice of God

Both Jesus and Trayvon were members of despised minorities. Both were feared because of who they were. Both stood "beyond the reach of citizen security." Both offended the "lords of the land." Both were accused of sedition. Both were killed by the rule of "law and order." Both were victimized by a culture of lynching. Both were found guilty of their own deaths. Both deaths would shake a nation. Both deaths say something about God. In an interview prior to his trial for Trayvon's murder, Trayvon's killer was asked if he regretted getting out of the car and following Trayvon. He responded, "No sir." He was next asked if he regretted having a gun that night. He again responded, "No sir." He explained that he did not regret the fatal events of that night because "it was all God's plan," and he was not going to "second guess it or judge it."

The morning after this interview, Trayvon's mother and father appeared on NBC's *Today* show. Incredibly, the interviewer, Matt Lauer, asked Trayvon's parents if they thought the death of their son was God's plan. Without hesitation, Trayvon's mother said, "I really think that's ridiculous. I wish Trayvon was here to tell his side of the story. I don't believe that it's God's plan . . . to kill an innocent teenager."

As suggested above, the similarities between the stand-your-ground murder of Trayvon and the crucifying murder of Jesus are eerily striking. Trayvon and Jesus are indeed connected by the cross. Their connection, however, goes beyond the obvious similarities of their deaths, though those similarities are revealing. The parallels between the two deaths tell us something about the people with whom Jesus identified and are indicative of God's justice. Jesus' death on the cross at Golgotha provides us with a way not to explain but to at least gain some perspective on what happened to Trayvon.

The cross is at the center of black faith. The paradox of the cross helps black people to deal with the contradictions of black living. There is no greater contradiction than the senseless murder of a seventeen-year-old, young black adolescent denied an opportunity to go home. The cross affirms the faith of his mother that his death was not in God's plan. The absurdity of the cross reveals the "ridiculousness" of the assertion that God had something to do with Trayvon's death. This chapter seeks to understand precisely what the crucifixion of Jesus tells us about the murder of Trayvon.

This chapter will, therefore, explore the connection between Jesus' cross and Trayvon's murder. In so doing, we will engage the various issues raised in the previous chapters, such as redemptive suffering, violence, and the justice of God. This chapter will also address what the cross, as the central symbol of Christianity, implies for the way churches are to respond in a stand-your-ground culture. In the end, this chapter will answer the haunting question, "Where was God when Trayvon was slain?" Let us now turn to the cross of Jesus.

A Stand-Your-Ground Crime

Along with others, I have pointed out that Jesus' crucifixion amounted to a first-century lynching. No one has made this clearer than James Cone in his book *The Cross and the Lynching Tree*.[1] Through personal narrative, passionate telling of the stories of black lynching, and scrupulous attention to the way black literary artists have made the connection, Cone leaves no doubt that Jesus' crucifixion was a first-century Roman lynching. Thus, Cone says, "The cross helped [him] to deal with the brutal legacy of the lynching tree, and the lynching tree helped [him] to understand the tragic meaning of the cross." It is only in recognizing Jesus' crucifixion as a lynching that we can appreciate its significance in a stand-your-ground war, and, hence, the meaning of God's justice in stand-your-ground times.

---

1. James H. Cone, *The Cross and the Lynching Tree* (Maryknoll, NY: Orbis Books, 2011).

Lynching is one of the most heinous weapons of stand-your-ground culture. Whether the weapon of choice is a rope, a cotton-gin fan with barbed wire (Emmett Till), chains at the end of a car (James Byrd), or a gun, it is a lynching just the same. Lynching is about power standing its ground against anyone it deems a threat. It is meant to be a deadly reminder to a suspect community of its "proper" place in society. It is about the protection of Anglo-Saxon white supremacy. It attempts to safeguard the "wages of whiteness." The message of lynching is clear: you either go along with the Anglo-Saxon, white "social usages and customs of the day" or this too can happen to you. Lynching in any form is meant to strike fear in the black community.

At the same time, lynching strikes out at those whom the purveyors of white supremacy fear the most. Though not the only targets, black men have been its primary targets. As noted in the previous chapters, black men, cast as predatory and threatening criminals, are seen as the ultimate threat to Anglo-Saxon "purity" and domination. They become the body most feared by the guardians of cherished white property. Ironically, those who are lynched are typically the most powerless in society. That is why they are so vulnerable to being lynched in the first place. Though constructed by narratives of Anglo-Saxon exceptionalism as dangerous predators, black males are actually the defenseless prey. Historically, even those to whom they were considered most threatening, white women, were actually the greater threat to them. This was most evident in the lynching of Emmett Till. Simply being in the same space with a white woman who perceived him as a threat cost him his life.

In general, because black people continue disproportionally to represent the social, economic, and political underclass they are typically without access to the social, political, or legal resources to protect or defend themselves against such a crime as lynching, regardless of the various forms it takes. In the words of Thurman, they have "little protection from the dominant controllers of society. . . ." Moreover, as we have seen, laws have been constructed in such a way that black people are unable to defend themselves judicially. Thus, within the justice system they are defenseless. Even when dead they are viewed as such a threat that their character continues to be attacked. There is, therefore, a decidedly "lynched class" of people. These are the most vulnerable bodies in a stand-your-ground war.

They are black bodies and typically young black bodies—the most vulnerable of all.

In Jesus' first-century world, crucifixion was the brutal tool of social-political power. It was reserved for slaves, enemy soldiers, and those held in the highest contempt and lowest regard in society. To be crucified was, for the most part, an indication of how worthless and devalued an individual was in the eyes of established power. At the same time, it indicated how much of a threat that person was believed to pose. Crucifixion was reserved for those who threatened the "peace" of the day. It was a torturous death that was also meant to send a message: disrupt the Roman order in any way, this too will happen to you. As there is a lynched class of people, there was, without doubt, a crucified class of people. The crucified class in the first-century Roman world was the same as the lynched class today. It consisted of those who were castigated and demonized as well as those who defied the status quo. Crucifixion was a stand-your-ground type of punishment for the treasonous offense of violating the rule of Roman "law and order."

Jesus in the Face of Trayvon

That Jesus was crucified affirms his absolute identification with the Trayvons, the Jordans, the Renishas, the Jonathans, and all the other victims of the stand-your-ground-culture war. Jesus' identification with the lynched/crucified class is not accidental. It is intentional. It did not begin with his death on the cross. In fact, that Jesus was crucified signals his prior bond with the "crucified class" of his day. There is perhaps no story that reveals this more than the story of Jesus' interaction with the Samaritan woman at the well.

Jesus: The "New Exodus"

In the social-religious context of Jesus' day, there was a long history of conflict between Jews and Samaritans. Jews had constructed images of Samaritans as an indecent and ritually impure people. Samaritan women were considered the most impure of all. Multiple narratives of power intersected on the bodies of Samaritan women—ethnic, gender, and cultural. Put simply, they represented, at once, an inferior "race," gender, and religion. In this regard, the relationship between Jewish men and Samaritan women was one of extreme opposition. This relationship reflects in the first-century Roman world the antagonistic opposition between white bodies and black bodies in a context of Anglo-Saxon exceptionalism. Thus, the social spaces of Jewish men and Samaritan women were to remain separate. The Jewish male space was a protected space. Samaritan women were not to encroach upon it, and Jewish men were not to interact with Samaritan women, especially not in public. Jesus violates this separation of space by entering into the "demonized" space of the Samaritans.

By most accounts, Jesus did not have to pass through Samaria on his journey from Judea to Galilee. This was considered a circuitous route. It was also considered a dangerous route, given the antagonism between Jews and Samaritans. Samaritans were considered violent enemies of the Jews. However, Jesus crossed the boundaries into Samaritan space anyway. By going into Samaria, Jesus placed himself in the midst of those most denigrated and marginalized, if not feared, in the Jewish world. He ignored all of the prevailing caricatures of Samaritans as an unclean and dangerous people. He flagrantly dismissed the social-religious narratives about Samaritans by going out of his way to enter their space. If this was not violation enough, Jesus interacts with the most worthless of all the Samaritans, a woman. Not only did Jesus ask this woman for a drink of water, but he also engaged her in a long conversation.

Jesus' transgression of the "law and order" established between Jews and Samaritans characterizes his ministry. It shows his intentional solidarity with a "crucified class" of people. It is worth noting that it was Jesus who entered Samaritan space, not the other way around. Jesus initiated the relationship. Practically speaking, this was the only safe way for the interaction between the Samaritan woman and him to have occurred. For while Jesus received ridicule from his disciples for the interaction, had it been the Samaritan woman who violated Jewish male space, the consequences might have been deadly. Theologically speaking, Jesus, as the incarnate reality of God, further reveals God's utter freedom. Not only is God not a respecter of persons; God is not a respecter of social-religious boundaries and constructs. God simply does not recognize them. They do not define God, and they certainly do not thwart God's movement of freedom in the world. Neither do they negate the goodness of all creation.

By going into Samaritan space and interacting with a Samaritan woman, Jesus (again as God incarnate) is affirming the sacred worth of this woman. In other words, any human narratives and constructs that suggest otherwise do not vitiate her status as a "good creation." This is further substantiated by the fact that Jesus grants the woman salvation. Salvation in this context is not simply a "heavenly" reward. Rather, it is a restoration of the woman to her value and worth as a child of God. Again, Jesus frees her from the social-religious constructs that deemed her an offense, and restores her sacred identity. It is for this reason that the woman who came to the well at noon, no doubt to avoid the stares of people (she was also ridiculed for having many husbands), is able to leave and go among the people to tell her story.

The historical particularity of who Jesus is as a Jewish male is also revelatory. For in this instance, Jesus frees himself and the Samaritan woman from constructs that deem certain bodies as superior and others as inferior. If Jesus is to be considered the "New Exodus," the exodus that takes place in this story is his. He is the one who departs the space of the privileged class. In so doing he enters into solidarity with the most put-upon bodies of his day. In the end, his social-religious status is diminished, while the Samaritan woman's status is elevated. Jesus rejects any notion of "exceptionalism" that may be attached to Jewish maleness. He and the Samaritan woman virtually become equals. Hence, "The first are last and the last are first," because there is no hierarchal subordination.

It is also worth noting that, according to the Gospel of John, the first time Jesus reveals himself as the Messiah is in this conversation with the Samaritan woman. More will be said about this fact later. The point of emphasis now is Jesus' intentional association with the most scorned and marginalized bodies of his day. He initiates a salvific relationship with the body that is constructed as the one most opposed to his, those whom Thurman called the "disinherited." In stand-your-ground culture today these are black bodies. In making such an alliance, Jesus repudiated the narratives and constructs of power. During his ministry he effectively becomes one of the crucified class. His crucifixion is, therefore, inevitable.

The Kenosis of Jesus

At the time of his crucifixion Jesus further demonstrates his solidarity with the crucified class of people and concomitantly his opposition to crucifying forces. One sees this when he goes before his accusers.

Jesus refuses to answer their questions. His silence is not a sign of consent, but rather a refusal to grant them any authority over him. The same is true regarding his silence when he is spat upon and mocked by the crowds. Most significantly, Jesus does nothing to save himself from the fate of crucifixion. "If you are the King of the Jews, save yourself," the soldiers shout. In his silence, Jesus neither saves himself nor complies with the way in which his identity has been constructed. He does not in any way recognize the rule of his crucifiers. His silence is resistance at the same time as it indicates his unwavering solidarity with the crucified class of the Roman world. This did not go unnoticed by the enslaved, who testified in song:

> Dey crucified my Lord
> An' He never said a mumblin' word
> De crucified my Lord
> An' He never said a mumblin' word
> Not a word, not a word, not a word.[2]

On the cross, Jesus fully divests himself of all pretensions to power, privilege, and exceptionalism, even as the incarnate revelation of God. What is clear is Jesus' free and steadfast identification with crucified bodies. It is no wonder then that the Christ hymn in Philippians (2:5-11) is a text often recited in various black churches. Growing up in the black church, I learned this text well before I knew where it came from because members of my congregation so often quoted a version of it. "Jesus thought it not robbery to be equal with God," they would say, "he humbled himself, and became obedient unto death, even unto the cross."[3] Theologians have referred to Jesus' self-emptying as *kenosis*, which indicates his sacrificial obedience to God. However, when understood in the context of Jesus' full ministry as it led to his crucifixion, this self-emptying indicates his "letting go" of anything that would compromise his absolute alliance with those of the crucified class.[4] Jon

---

2. All spiritual lyrics come from http://www.negrospirituals.com unless otherwise indicated.

3. This quote is based upon the King James Version because that is the way it was handed down to me in my church.

4. I take this concept of "letting go" from Rosemary Radford Ruether, who suggests that those of privilege in any context must develop a "theology of letting-go." See Ruether, "A U.S. Theology of Letting Go," in *The Reemergence of*

Sobrino puts it this way, "The cross, for its part, tells of God's affinity with victims; nothing in history has set limits to the closeness of God."[5] That Jesus empties himself of not simply his divinity but his worldly status and privileges was not lost on the enslaved. Thus, they knew that they could count on him even unto death. They sang,

> Oh when I come to die
> Give me Jesus
> Give me Jesus
> You may have the world
> Give me Jesus.

Thurman describes the significance of Jesus' death on the cross for the enslaved this way: "[the] death of Jesus took on a deep and personal poignancy." There was, he says, "a quality of identification in experience."[6] The same can be said of the black faith community today. Because of Jesus' death on the cross, there is no doubt that Jesus would have a "deep and personal" identification with the black pain, heartache, suffering, and death that is exacted by stand-your-ground culture. Just as black people identify with the cross of Jesus, the cross of Jesus means he identifies with them. Implied, therefore, in the song "Were You There when They Crucified my Lord?" is the way the boundaries of time are crossed by both black people and Jesus. For not only are black people with Jesus at the cross, but Jesus is with black people in stand-your-ground times.

Jesus Loves Me

When we were growing up my mother would sing to my siblings and me, "Jesus loves me, this I know, for the Bible tells me so." She would sing this song to us often because she knew that the world we were growing up in would not always treat us in a loving way. She knew that because our bodies were black, her children would be treated too often with disdain and hate. She wanted us to know that no matter how others treated us, Jesus loved us—and that was all that mattered.

Liberation Theologies: Models for the Twenty-First Century, ed. Thia Cooper (New York: Palgrave Macmillan, 2013).

5. Jon Sobrino, *Christ the Liberator: A View from the Victims* (Maryknoll, NY: Orbis Books, 2001), 88.

6. Thurman, *Deep River,* 27.

There is no greater testament to the love of Jesus, and thus God's love for God's creation, than the cross. It reveals the extent to which God will go to show that God loves and "recognizes the value of— each and every piece of creation."[7] On the cross God takes on the very extremity of human hate to show the enormity of God's love. God's love has no bounds. It seeks to preserve the integrity and goodness of all creation regardless of how far God must reach down into the con-structs of human hate to do so. The freedom of God that is expressed through life is always connected to love. It is God's very love for life that serves as the motivating force for all that God does. Because of God's love for God's creation, God has entered human history. God's very movement in human history is defined by the love of God. Daniel Day Williams puts it this way: God's love is "nothing other than the meaning of God's historical dealing with [humans]."[8] The freedom of God is inextricably related to the life and love that God is. Simply put, to know the freedom of God is to know the life and love of God. In one respect, the love of God means that God freely chooses to free human beings from all that would deny them life in any way. In this regard, God loves people into freedom and thus into life. In another respect, freedom signifies the love and life of God. The point is, to know God is to know God as life, love, freedom at once. They are intertwined aspects of God. They reflect the very essence of God. Each relies on the other and is defined by the other.

The freedom/love/life of God that was expressed through the exo-dus of the Israelites from Egyptian bondage is expressed on the cross of Jesus as the triumph over all that denies life. It reveals that this love knows no bounds, as it reaches down into the vilest realities of human hate and evil. This love has particular meaning in a stand-your-ground culture.

Jesus on a Florida Sidewalk

In the stand-your-ground war today, crucifixion comes in the form of gun violence. The Matthean question today might be, "But Lord,

---

7. Sallie McFague, "Human Dignity and the Integrity of Creation," in *Theology That Matters: Ecology, Economy and God* (Minneapolis: Fortress Press, 2006), 202.

8. Daniel Day Williams, "Love in Our History," in *The Spirit and the Forms of Love* (Lanham, MD: University Press of America, 1981-), chap. 1.

where did we see you dying and on the cross?" And Jesus would answer, "On a Florida sidewalk, at a Florida gas station, on a Michigan porch, on a street in North Carolina. As you did it to one of these young black bodies, you did it to me." The tragedy of the cross is the tragedy of stand-your-ground war. It is in the face of Trayvon dying on a sidewalk that we see Jesus dying on the cross. To know the extent of God's love, one must recognize the face of Jesus in the face of Trayvon.

The Cross and Stand-Your-Ground Crucifixion

The Evil of the Cross

There is another side of Jesus' cross that says something about stand-your-ground culture itself. The cross reflects the lengths that unscrupulous power will go to sustain itself. It is power's last stand. It is the "extinction" side of the Manifest Destiny ultimatum: be assimilated or become extinct. The cross reflects power's refusal to give up its grip on the lives of others. It is the refusal of power to retreat. Essentially, the cross represents the height of humanity's inhumanity. It shows the extent to which humans defile and disrespect other human bodies. It represents an absolute disregard for life. It reveals "human beings' . . . extraordinary capacity for evil."[9] It is the pinnacle of the human opposition to God.

There is no doubt that the guns of stand-your-ground culture are today's crosses. In many respects, in the Stand Your Ground law itself as well as the Conceal and Carry law, one can hear echoes of "crucify them, crucify them." The crucifying shouts echo in lobbyists for these laws as they proclaim that they must protect themselves from those who would encroach upon their rights. On the other side of those self-righteous proclamations are the human bodies that are believed to be a threat to the rights of "cherished white property." Unquestionably, the laws of stand-your-ground culture reflect a community's desire to protect its way of life from those they find most threatening. These laws were constructed to protect the "inalienable rights" conferred upon white bodies by America's narrative of Anglo-Saxon exceptionalism. These laws thus negate the very humanity of those deemed the

---

9. "Interview with Archbishop Desmond Tutu," http://www.egonzehnder.com.

oppositional other, those for whom the "inalienable rights" were never intended. These are the bodies on the other side of the stand-your-ground gun. They are the crucified of the twenty-first century.

Just as slavery was a negation of the sacredness of God's creation, so too are Stand Your Ground laws. To be sure, they cheapen black life. These laws perpetuate death, not life. As they are construed to defend cherished white property, they are actually nothing less than instruments of death. It is telling that the Stand Your Ground law was originally called the "Shoot First" law. The fact that perpetrators of stand-your-ground-culture murders can easily proclaim their lack of regret reveals the crucifying malevolence of these laws. They grant a person the power to take the life of another, with impunity.

It should not be that easy to deny the life of another human being. To do such a thing certainly does not reflect "the plan" of a God who creates life. The God who freely grants life is not a commissioner of death. Ironically, it is through the cross that God's commitment to life is undeniably demonstrated. In order to appreciate this we must turn back to the ministry of Jesus.

Freed to Live

Just as Jesus' ministry showed his intimate bond with the demonized outcasts of his day, it also shows his commitment to fostering and nurturing life. In this regard, he is the embodied reality of the freedom of God that is expressed as a life-giving force. Throughout his ministry, Jesus frees people from the clutches of death and returns them to a full life. This is evident in the stories of him restoring sight to the blind, making the lame to walk, or even casting out demons. He simply does not hand human bodies over to the powers of death. There is not one story reported in the four Gospels in which Jesus cooperates with death. He takes on the powers of death and defeats them. The story of Jesus restoring Lazarus to life is the best illustration of Jesus doing this in his ministry.

The Gospel of John reports that an ill Lazarus died after Jesus had left him. Hearing the report of his death, Jesus returns only to discover that Lazarus had been dead for four days. When Jesus was led to the tomb where Lazarus lay, "Jesus wept." Nevertheless, Jesus did not resign himself to the death of Lazarus. Rather, "he cried out with a loud voice, 'Lazarus, come out.'" With that, Lazarus came out of his tomb and was restored to life (John 11:1-44). It is revealing that the two times it is reported in the Gospels that Jesus wept are in the face of death. According to the Gospel of Luke, Jesus wept when he saw how Jerusalem has been consumed by a culture of death (Luke 19:41-44). It is the powers of death that stand in stark opposition to what Jesus cares about and represents, that is, life itself. Thus, Jesus takes death on and defeats it by restoring Lazarus to life. It is telling that the Gospel of John places this story prior to reporting the plot to kill Jesus. For it is on the cross that Jesus takes on the powers of death for the final time.

In his own day these powers were both religious and political. The political leadership, represented by Pontius Pilate, and the religious leadership, represented by Caiaphas, the Jewish high priest, as well as the Sanhedrin, collaborated in Jesus' crucifixion. They all came together to put an end to Jesus' life and all that he stood for. Pontius Pilate, Caiaphas, and even the Sanhedrin all served as commissioners of death. The cross they erected to destroy Jesus epitomizes human opposition to all that God stands for as one who gives life. As such, it symbolizes the depth of human sin, and thus the height of human evil. As Delores Williams rightly notes, "The cross . . . represents historical evil trying to defeat good."[10] By going silently to the cross, not saving himself from it, Jesus takes on this evil. He takes on and defeats the power of death. Again, Jesus does so by remaining silent and not granting to the power of death any authority over him. At the same time, he does not respond in kind, by adopting the methods of this power. The final triumph over the death of the cross is the resurrection of Jesus.

The Force of Resurrection

The resurrection is God's definitive victory over crucifying powers of evil. Ironically, the power that attempts to destroy Jesus on the cross is actually itself destroyed by the cross. The cross represents the power that denigrates human bodies, destroys life, and preys on the most vulnerable in society. As the cross is defeated, so too is that power. The impressive factor is how it is defeated. It is defeated by a life-giving rather than a life-negating force. God's power, unlike human power, is not a "master race" kind of power. That is, it is not a power that dimin-

---

10. Williams, *Sisters in the Wilderness*, 165.

ishes the life of another so that others might live. God's power respects the integrity of all human bodies and the sanctity of all life. This is a resurrecting power. Therefore, God's power never expresses itself through the humiliation or denigration of another. It does not triumph over life. It conquers death by resurrecting life. The force of God is a death-negating, life-affirming force. This is significant in two ways.

The black feminist literary artist and social critic Audre Lorde once said, "*The master's tools will never dismantle the master's house. They may allow us to temporarily beat him at his own game, but they will never enable us to bring about genuine change.*"[11] What the crucifixion–resurrection event reveals is that God does not use the master's tools. God does not fight death with death. God does not utilize the violence exhibited in the cross to defeat deadly violence itself. As Lorde suggest, while this may bring a temporary solution, it does not bring an end to the culture of death itself. Rather, one stays entrapped in that very culture. The culture of death is thus granted power over life. As such, "only the most narrow parameters of change are possible and allowable."[12]

If indeed the power of life that God stands for is greater than the power of death, then this must be manifest in the way God triumphs over death-dealing powers. The freedom of God that is life requires a liberation from the very weapons utilized by a culture of death. In other words, these weapons cannot become divine weapons. This liberation was foreshadowed by Jesus' refusal to cooperate with the powers of death at the time of his crucifixion. The culmination of this liberation is Jesus' resurrection. Moreover, that God did not defeat the cross with weapons of death further illustrates the fact of God's transcendent freedom. For again, it reveals that God is not constrained by the ways of the world to accomplish God's ends.

This brings us to a second, interrelated aspect of God's resurrecting power. It is nonviolent. There is no doubt that the cross reflects the depth and scope of human violence. The cross in this respect represents the consuming violence of the world. It points to a world that is saturated with violence. This violence includes not simply the phys-

---

11. Lorde, "The Master's Tools Will Never Dismantle the Master's House," in *Sister Outsider*, 112 (emphasis in original).

12. Lorde, "The Master's Tools," 111.

ical brutality meant to harm bodies, but also the systems, structures, narratives, and constructs that do harm. Anything that would devalue the life of another is violent. God enters into this world of violence, yet God does not take it into God's self. Thus, God responds to the violence of the world not in an eye-for-an-eye manner. Instead, God responds in a way that negates and denounces the violence that perverts and demeans the integrity of human creation. Thus, through the resurrection, God responds to the violence of the cross—the violence of the world—in a nonviolent but forceful manner. It is important to understand that nonviolence is not the same as passivity or accommodation to violence. Rather, it is a forceful response that protects the integrity of life. Violence seeks to do another harm, while nonviolence seeks to rescue others from harm. It seeks to break the very cycle of violence itself. The forces of nonviolence actually reveal the impotence of violent power. Ironically, the nonviolent power of God is revealed through the violence of the cross. But this is essential. That God could defeat the unmitigated violence of the cross reveals the consummate power of the nonviolent, life-giving force that is God.

No one recognized the power of the nonviolence of God in a fight against a stand-your-ground culture more than the Reverend Dr. Martin Luther King Jr. He showed this in the fight against the manifestation of stand-your-ground culture in his time.

To be sure, King recognized the practicality of nonviolent resistance for the black community. As Cone points out, he understood that "a 10 percent Negro minority with no access to the weapons of warfare [could] [n]ever expect to wage a successful violent revolution against a white majority with the military technology of the United States."[13] As previously noted, the stewards of Anglo-Saxon exceptionalism actually enlisted military forces during the civil rights struggle in the form of Operation Garden Plot. Thus, King was right in his assessment concerning the practical futility of adopting a violent strategy against the force of the military. Notwithstanding his appreciation for its practicality, King's commitment to nonviolence was a reflection of his black church faith and hence his belief in the resurrecting power of God.

---

13. James Cone, *Martin & Malcolm & America: A Dream or a Nightmare* (Maryknoll, NY: Orbis Books, 1991), 78.

King believed that the only way to break the cycle of violence was through nonviolence. As King said, "[Violence] ultimately destroys everybody." He said that he could not adopt the "eye-for-an-eye philosophy . . . [because] it ends up leaving everybody blind." "Somebody," he said, "must have sense and somebody must have religion."[14] King believed, as Cone points out, that "in the long run of history destructive methods cannot bring about constructive ends . . . ends are preexistent in the means."[15] King's commitment to nonviolence was, as Cone recognizes, based on a commitment to "communicating God's life-giving force to the 'least of these.'"[16]

Within the profoundest moments of evil and hence of death, the utmost power of God is made known. There is nothing that symbolizes the worst realities of evil more than the cross. Ironically the cross, which was to be a sign of Jesus' weakness, actually reveals his power, and it exposes the impotence of those who would put him to death. This irony is expressed this way in one of the spirituals:

> High up on de mountain
> De stone done roll away
> De soljahs dere a-plenty standin' by de do'
> But dey could not hinder
> De stone done roll away
> Ol' Pilate an' his wise men didn't know what to say
> De miracle was on dem
> De stone done roll away.

While the message of the cross in relation to the death of Trayvon and other victims of stand-your-ground culture is becoming evident, there is another aspect of Jesus' death on the cross that must be explored. This is the matter of redemptive suffering.

Making Meaning out of Death?

One of the ways to cope with senseless and unnecessary death is to try to find meaning in it. Peter Berger argues, "The need for meaning

---

14. Quoted in ibid.
15. Quoted in ibid.
16. Quoted in ibid., 248.

is as strong as or even stronger than the need for happiness."[17] There is no greater need for meaning, he says, than in the face of "tormenting illness" or needless, unwarranted death. Thus, people develop theodicies, in this instance as a way to make sense of the death. He says, "It is not happiness that theodicy primarily provides, but meaning."[18] One such theodicy is heard in the words, "He/she did not die in vain." The problem with theodicies of senseless death is that they too easily give way to notions of redemptive suffering, that is, the notion that some good can come from the suffering of another. In this regard, suffering and senseless death appear to be divine instruments through which God brings forth good. This, for some, is the inherent problem with finding meaning in the cross.

Delores Williams has been unrelenting in her criticism of theological and faith traditions that find meaning in the death of Jesus on the cross. In no uncertain terms Williams asserts, "I don't think we need folks hanging on crosses and blood dripping and stuff."[19] She explains, "Jesus came for life and to show us something about life and living together and what life was all about."[20] Williams points out that an undue emphasis has been placed on the salvific and redemptive power of Jesus' crucifixion. With particular concern for the way in which black women have been compelled into surrogacy roles, Williams argues that finding redemptive meaning in Jesus' crucifixion allows for a justification of the oppressive surrogacy roles that black women have been forced to play.[21] She suggests that Jesus is virtually viewed as a surrogate for human sin, thus giving legitimacy to surrogacy roles. More broadly speaking, Williams's argument implies that any interpretation of Jesus' crucifixion that finds redemptive meaning in it leads to finding redemptive value in human suffering. As Williams says, "Christians . . . cannot forget the cross, but neither can they glorify it. To do so is to glorify suffering and to render . . . exploitation

---

17. Berger, *Sacred Canopy*, 58.

18. Ibid.

19. Quoted in Kelly Brown Douglas, *What's Faith Got to Do with It?* (Maryknoll, NY: Orbis Books, 2005), 90.

20. Ibid.

21. For an understanding of black women's surrogacy roles, see Williams, *Sisters in the Wilderness*, esp. chap. 3, "Social-Role Surrogacy: Naming Black Women's Oppression."

sacred. To do so is to glorify the sin of defilement."[22] Williams ultimately argues that meaning must be found in the resurrection apart from the cross. She says, "The resurrection does not depend upon the cross for life. . . . The resurrection of Jesus and the flourishing of God's spirit in the world as the result of the resurrection represent the life of the *ministerial* vision gaining victory over the evil attempt to kill it."[23]

There is no doubt that an emphasis on Jesus' crucifixion has perpetuated human suffering physically and otherwise. It has also unquestionably led to the unnecessary acceptance of suffering. Williams is correct to warn against any notion that unwarranted suffering is to be tolerated. Suffering is not to be glorified. Neither are suffering and death to be legitimated with claims of their redemptive value. She is right to assert that there is "no power in the blood" of one who is victimized by crucifying realities. However, this is not what the crucifixion–resurrection event suggests. And it certainly has not been the prevailing meaning of the cross within the black faith tradition, even though it is the cross that has provided black people with a full understanding of the presence of God in their lives.

Maintaining the connection between the cross and the "empty tomb" is essential to the meaning of the resurrection itself. It grounds the resurrection in history. It makes clear that the evil that God overcomes is historical, that is, that God really defeats the powers of this world. Understanding the resurrection in light of the cross prevents the resurrection from becoming an otherworldly triumph over cosmic evil. Again, it is about God's triumph over the "principalities and powers" of this world. It is the connection between the cross and resurrection that has enabled black people to know that God, as revealed in Jesus, intimately understands their suffering and pain. It also lets them know that God can and will overcome it. Because God overcomes the "historical evil" of the cross, black people are assured that the "historical evil" they endure will not have the last word.

The resurrecting power of God is made fully manifest in the defeat of the ultimate power of evil represented by the cross. The resurrection is God's definitive response to the crucifying realities. It clarifies the essential character of God's power—a power that values life. The res-

---

22. Williams, *Sisters in the Wilderness*, 167.
23. Ibid., 165.

urrection of the one who died such a hideous and ignominious death firmly establishes that God does not in any way sanction the suffering of human beings. The resurrection asserts the sanctity of human life as it overcomes all the forces that would deny it. The resurrection in effect makes plain the "wrongness" of the crucifixion, and thus of all crucifying realities. It shows that death does not have the last word. It is in understanding the crucifixion–resurrection event in relation to each other that allowed black people to sing, "He arose, he arose from the dead, An' de Lord shall bear my spirit home."

Yes, there is a danger in trying to make meaning out of senseless deaths. What the resurrection points to, however, is not the meaning of Jesus' death, but of his life. It is revealing that in the Gospels of Mark and Matthew the resurrected Jesus instructs the disciples to "go to Galilee" where he will be. Galilee was the site where Jesus' life-affirming ministry began. As Jon Sobrino points out, "Galilee is the place of the poor and the despised."[24] The resurrection of Jesus thus solidifies God's commitment to the restoration of life for the "crucified class" of people. It reveals that there are "no principalities or powers" that can frustrate or foil God's power to overcome the crucifying death in the world that not only targets but also creates a "crucified class" of people. To restore to life those whose bodies are the particular targets of the world's violence is to signal the triumph over crucifying violence and death itself. It is also noteworthy that none of the stories of Jesus' resurrection takes the disciples back to Golgotha, the site of his death. The crucifixion–resurrection event points to the meaning found in Jesus' life, not his death. By understanding the resurrection in light of the cross, we know that crucifying realities do not have the last word, and, thus, cannot take away the value of one's life. The meaning of one's life, in other words, is not found in death, and it is not vitiated by it.

If the crucified Jesus is seen in the face of Trayvon dead on a Florida sidewalk, then the resurrected Jesus is seen in the faces of his parents testifying to the meaning of Trayvon's life beyond his crucifying death.

Resurrected Realities in Stand-Your-Ground Death

There was perhaps no one more vilified after his murder than Trayvon Martin. The constructs of Anglo-Saxon narratives that no doubt led to

---

24. Sobrino, *Christ the Liberator,* 14.

his being followed and confronted in the first place shaped his identity in death. Instead of being seen as a seventeen-year-old teenager coming home from a store with Skittles and ice tea, he was portrayed as a "thug" looking to commit a crime. That he was wearing a hoodie over his head was portrayed as a sign of criminal intent, as opposed to an attempt to protect himself from the falling rain. Commentator and talk show host Geraldo Rivera said that the "convenience store surveillance tape" showing Trayvon purchasing Skittles and ice tea revealed that he was dressed in "thug wear." Explaining why Trayvon was victimized that night, Rivera said, "I think what's far more significant is what Trayvon Martin looked like on that night . . . he's dressed in that thug wear." Reinforcing his point that Trayvon's killing was perhaps unavoidable, even if unjustified, Rivera said, "Trayvon Martin looks just like the people who had been burglarizing and victimizing that neighborhood for the last six months."[25]

Despite the fact that he had no prior encounters with the criminal justice system, unlike his killer, Trayvon was repeatedly portrayed as a delinquent looking for trouble. He was depicted as a "gangsta wannabe." Throughout the coverage of Trayvon's murder, leading up to his killer's trial and after the verdict, Trayvon's character and life were demeaned. The ignominious crime that caused his death was used to mark his life. His death became the defining parameter of his life. Because the way he died was presumably a death reserved for criminals, then certainly he was a criminal. The life of Trayvon was overshadowed by his crucifying death. So complete was the crucifixion of his life, there was little if any coverage of the Trayvon before his encounter with his killer that night; the encounter, itself, was portrayed through the eyes of the killer. Trayvon's life was stripped of meaning. It was crucified along with his body. It fell to his parents to assume the task of resurrecting their son's life. This monumental resurrecting task of Tracy Martin and Sybina Fulton was poignantly revealed in interviews with Matt Lauer, host of the *Today Show*.

The first of three interviews occurred prior to the arrest of their son's killer. During that interview, as pictures were displayed of Trayvon that portrayed him as the young teenager he was, Lauer conjec-

---

25. Comments made by Geraldo Rivera in March 2012 interview on Fox News *O'Reilly Factor*, http://www.huffingtonpost.com.

tured that it was easy to look at those pictures and want to comfort the parents, but "with all the public outcry," he asked the parents if they believed that there had been "a rush to judgment" in regard to Trayvon's killer. Lauer suggested that the killer should be given the presumption of innocence until proven guilty. It was notable that Lauer did not extend to Trayvon such a presumption. Indeed, there seemed to be urgency in Lauer's comments to dispute the image of Trayvon that the pictures portrayed. The pictures revealed a young man who enjoyed the life of a cared-for and beloved son. That life went unacknowledged by Lauer. During the interview, Trayvon's father attempted to restore dignity to Trayvon by repeatedly referring to him as "my son," as if to make clear to Lauer and the viewing public that this was not simply a crucified body.[26]

Not only did Lauer ask Trayvon's parents if they believed their son's death was in God's plan, he further succumbed to crucifying caricatures. Lauer repeated the killer's accusation that Trayvon had threatened him with expletive-laced language. Lauer asked the parents, "Can you imagine your son saying something like this . . . ?" Trayvon's mother said, "No, he's a child. He's a seventeen-year-old child." Once again, refusing to let go of the image shaped by crucifying constructs, Lauer quickly retorted, "I understand, but you are answering that question through a parent's love and unconditional approval. Is it possible that Trayvon said those words?" Clearly it was impossible for Lauer to accept an image of Trayvon other than that of a sinister "thug." For him, Trayvon's life had no meaning beyond that night on the sidewalk. He discounted his parents' testimony that Trayvon was not simply a crucified body but their seventeen-year-old child. As if to have the final say on Trayvon's life, Lauer repeated the killer's assertion that there had been a "rush to judgment" concerning the events of that fatal night. Lauer asked the parents, "Would you agree [the killer] deserves to be treated as an innocent man until proven otherwise?" Lauer assumed the humanity of the killer. He refused to allow the killer to be defined by the events of that crucifying night. Not so for Trayvon. Lauer's question implied that Trayvon was not an innocent child. Tracy Martin quickly defended his son by saying, "There was a rush to judgment for [the killer] to think that Trayvon

---

26. See *Today Show* interview, March 21, 2012.

was suspicious, for him to think we're rushing to judge, he rushed to judge Trayvon."

In a final interview after the trial, the contest between crucifying and resurrection realities continued. Lauer defended the jurors and called attention to the rare show of violence in response to the verdict, ignoring the many nonviolent protests. Discounting that their child was murdered because someone perceived him to be a criminal outcast who did not belong in the neighborhood, Lauer virtually begged Trayvon's parents to sympathize with the killer who said he felt like an "outcast" after the trial. Astoundingly, Lauer asked the parents, "Do you think that's what the system intends for someone who is acquitted of charges like these?" Trayvon's mother quickly retorted,

> We sit on the victim's seat. So, is this the intent for the justice system to have for victims? I mean, it's sending a terrible message to other little black and brown boys that you can't walk fast, you can't walk slow. So what do they do? I mean, how do you get home without people knowing or either assuming that you're doing something wrong? Trayvon wasn't doing anything wrong.[27]

Notably missing from the three interviews that Matt Lauer conducted with Tracy Martin and Sybrina Fulton was the typical question that the *Today Show* hosts ask parents who have lost a child to a senseless act: Is there anything that you want us to know about your child? As I watched each interview I listened for that question, though I was not surprised when it was not asked. It became evident throughout the interviews that Lauer was wittingly or unwittingly influenced by the narratives that suggest a free black body, especially a male body, must be guilty of something. In Lauer's mind, Trayvon had no life beyond the one defined by his stand-your-ground crucifixion. However, for the parents, the crucifixion of Trayvon would not have the last word on their son's life. That it has not is evident not only in the ways in which attention has been drawn to stand-your-ground-culture laws, but also in the nonprofit Trayvon Martin Foundation his parents founded after his death. This foundation seeks to help other families of victims of violent crime, to increase "public awareness of

---

27. *Today Show* interview, July 18, 2013.

all forms of . . . profiling," and to "educate youth on conflict resolution techniques" in order to reduce the occurrence of deadly confrontations with strangers. On the foundation website Tracy Martin says in an interview, "I won't let the verdict sum up who Trayvon was." Under the heading "Meet Trayvon Martin" are these words:

> Who he is; he has awakened us to go forward with faith, courage and empowerment . . .
>
> Trayvon Benjamin Martin (February 5, 1995–February 26, 2012) was the son of Sybrina Fulton and Tracy Martin. He was a junior at Dr. Michael M. Krop High School and lived with his mother and older brother in Miami Gardens, Florida. At age 9, Trayvon pulled his father from a burning kitchen, saving his life. Trayvon was our hero. He loved sports, repairing his bikes, listening to music and horseback riding. At only 17, he had a bright future ahead of him with dreams of attending college and becoming an aviation mechanic or pilot. On the day Martin was fatally shot, he and his father were visiting his father's fiancée and her son at her townhouse in Sanford, Fl. where the shooting occurred.[28]

Trayvon's parents have not sought to derive meaning from his death, but rather to restore the meaning of his life. Jordan Davis's parents have sought to do the same. They have continually spoken of their son beyond what happened on that night. They have refused to allow his crucifying death to have the last word on his life. And thus, following the verdict of Jordan's murderer, Jordan's father, Ron Davis, proclaimed, "Jordan was a good kid." This is the meaning of the resurrection. It is not a theodicy to explain or make meaning out of a death Rather, the resurrection restores life to those who have been crucified. It calls attention to the meaning of a life. Because of the resurrection, victims of the world's crucifying violence are able to overcome the "absolute indignity" of their crucifying death.[29] The resurrection is nothing less than a refusal to allow the final verdict on a person's life to be a crucifying verdict. Moreover, the resurrection fosters and nur-

---

28. Trayvon Martin Foundation, http://www.trayvonmartinfoundation.org/aboutus.html.

29. Sobrino, *Christ the Liberator*, 88.

tures a culture of life, even in the midst of death. Such is the case with the Trayvon Martin Foundation, as well as the fight that continues to end the crucifying laws.

Stand-Your-Ground Culture: A Culture of Sin

The meaning of the cross for a stand-your-ground culture becomes clear. It indicates first that God is present in the harsh realities of black living. This is a God that freely takes on the depth of the pain, heartache, and suffering of black bodies navigating life in the stultifying context of Anglo-Saxon exceptionalism. The black enslaved testified to this in song:

> Slavery chain done broke at last, broke at last, broke at
> last, . . .
> Way down in-a dat valley
> Praying on my knees
> Told God about my troubles,
> And to help me ef-a He please.
>
> I did tell him how I suffer,
> In de dungeon and de chain,
> And de days were with head bowed down,
> And my broken flesh and pain.
>
> I did know my Jesus heard me
> 'Cause de spirit spoke to me
> And said, "Rise my child, your chillun,
> And you shall be free."

Essentially, this spiritual reveals a faith that God would free them, because God understood the depth of their oppression. This song is addressed to one who suffered the brutality of the cross. In this regard, any divine meaning to be found in the act of crucifixion itself relates to God's loving solidarity with the crucified ones—those on "the victim seat" of stand-your-ground war. God is where the crucified are. The cross, therefore, becomes a profound indictment on stand-your-ground culture. As this culture is antithetical to life, it is a negation of all that God stands for. The cross exposes stand-your-ground culture as a culture of sin.

Sin is that which alienates humans from the very ways and will of God. It is that which contests the freedom of God as a loving, life-giving force. It essentially reflects a breach with God. Stand-your-ground culture reflects such a breach both individually and systemically.

Stand-your-ground culture alienates people from the very goodness of their own creation. It essentially turns people in on themselves as it sets people against one another. This culture promotes the notion that one life has more value than another life. This is a culture that thrives on antagonistic relationships as signaled by the very idea of "standing one's ground." A stand-your-ground culture does not value dialogue, mutuality, respect, or compassion. Stand-your-ground culture thrives on what Howard Thurman might call "understanding that is strikingly unsympathetic."[30] This is when a person is not able to put him/herself in the place of another. Such was blatantly on display in the series of interviews conducted by Matt Lauer with Trayvon Martin's parents. It was with an "unsympathetic understanding" that Lauer asked Trayvon's parents if they thought their son's death was God's plan. There was certainly a lack of sympathy when he all but asked them to consider their son's killer a victim. "Unsympathetic understanding" is a product of a culture of sin.

As a sinful construct, stand your ground is sustained by a notion of "not belonging." Certain human beings are assumed to not belong in certain spaces and to not belong to God. Stand-your-ground culture disengages perpetrators from their humanity and most significantly disengages victims from their lives. The person on the other side of the stand-your-ground gun is not seen as a human being or as having a life worth living. One only needs to be reminded that the Stand Your Ground law was initially called "Shoot First," suggesting that whatever was on the other side of the gun had no real value. Behind the myth of "self-protection" is a disdain for certain lives—most notably, as Trayvon's mother points out, the lives of "black and brown boys." In effect, stand-your-ground culture empowers people to deny the sacredness of God's human creation. Both the lack of regret for the taking of a life and the refusal to acknowledge the meaning of a life beyond a crucifying death are inevitable outcomes of stand-your-ground culture.

---

30. Thurman, *Jesus and the Disinherited*, 76.

If the freedom of God is expressed as God's love for life, then we meet God in the places where life is "sustained and enhanced" as well as "where all that jeopardizes life and its fulfillment is resisted and set under [the] judgment" of the God who is creator.[31] Inasmuch as individuals engage in the despoiling of life in any way, then they have sinned. It is in this way that stand-your-ground culture fosters individual sin.

Stand-your-ground culture also nurtures systemic and structural sin. Laws such as Stand Your Ground, Stop and Frisk, Conceal and Carry speak for themselves. They objectify life. They are meant to oppress and humiliate. They devalue life. Other aspects of stand-your-ground culture such as the Prison Industrial Complex are structures and systems of sin because they thrive on denying life to others.

There is no getting around it: stand your ground is a reflection of a culture of death. It degrades humanity and destroys life. Sallie McFague is right when she says, "The dignity of human beings and the integrity of creation rests, first of all, on our willingness to affirm the value of life, not just our own, or our own tribe or religion or country or class or species. . . ."[32] As she further suggests, we need to be able to look at one another and see the "good" that is God. Since stand-your-ground culture does not allow for people to see the goodness of God in one another, it is a culture of sin.

This brings us to the meaning of salvation in a stand-your-ground culture, which is nothing less than the justice of God. Salvation, as Gustavo Gutiérrez states plainly, "is a cure for sin in this life."[33] Essential to Gutiérrez's definition of salvation is the cure *in this life*. If sin is not simply an otherworldly construct, but rather is that which impacts the quality and condition of one's historical life, then salvation must not refer simply to an otherworldly state. The double meaning that is characteristic of the spirituals attests to this. When the enslaved sang about salvation they were also referring to their earthly freedom. So they sang, "Children, we shall be free/When the Lord shall appear." Salvation

---

31. Daniel L. Migliore, *Faith Seeking Understanding: An Introduction to Christian Theology*, 2nd ed. (Grand Rapids: Wm. B. Eerdmans Publishing Co., 2004), 133.

32. McFague, "Human Dignity and the Integrity of Creation," 202-203.

33. Gustavo Gutiérrez, *A Theology of Liberation*, 15th Anniversary Edition (Maryknoll, NY: Orbis Books, 1973, 1988), 84.

means freedom from sin as it is manifested in the very realities of one's historical existence. Salvation in the context of stand your ground is a freedom from this very culture that exacts death upon black bodies. This freedom requires more than the eradication of certain laws.

Stand-your-ground culture is itself a product of a sinful narrative that values certain lives above others—that is, America's grand narrative of exceptionalism. Salvation in the context of stand your ground requires naming and calling out the very narratives, ideologies, and discourses of power that indeed promote the culture of stand-your-ground sin. Without its radical naming—literally, going to the root of the stand-your-ground sin itself—this sin will simply reappear in other forms. If our discussion has revealed anything, it has shown that stand-your-ground culture is not a twenty-first-century phenomenon. Rather, it is part and parcel of America's narrative of Anglo-Saxon exceptionalism. This narrative is nothing other than America's original sin.

America's Original Sin

The doctrine of original sin is not meant to suggest the origins of sin itself. Rather, it signals the fact that the human condition is defined by a captivity to sin. To recognize America's narrative of Anglo-Saxon exceptionalism as the nation's original sin is to realize that the unspoken but palpable identity of the nation itself is a sinful identity. Essentially, the way in which the early Americans, as well as the founding fathers, constructed the identity of the nation is consequential. It has virtually meant that the nation has been held captive to sin. There have been those who have considered the inhumane treatment of Native Americans as America's original sin. Others have claimed it to be the enslavement of African Americans. Both are the sins that sin produced. They are a reflection of the web of sin created by America's grand narrative. This is a web of discourse, ideologies, constructs, and ultimately Manifest Destiny wars that attempt to disengage people from the goodness and sacredness of their humanity. This narrative inherently devalues the lives of those who are not viewed as members of Tacitus's "unmixed race." Until this myth of exceptionalism is called out and its debilitating impact on America's culture and values is recognized, then ours will be a nation forever trapped in the web of sin. The stand-your-ground culture will continue to appear and reappear in various forms.

In his Second Inaugural Address Abraham Lincoln lamented that "American slavery" was an offense against God. It was in his estimation a sin. He conjectured that the Civil War, which had torn the nation apart, was a result of that sin. He feared the "judgments of the Lord" if the sin of slavery were not removed. Lincoln was right in naming slavery as a sin. What he did not understand was the original sin that produced slavery: the very exceptionalism upon which the nation was built.

Some one hundred and fifty years later, our nation is still a nation divided by war. It is divided by a stand-your-ground-culture war. It cannot be said enough that such a war will reinvent itself throughout history until the original sin of America's Anglo-Saxon exceptionalism is forthrightly addressed and eliminated. The salvation of the nation depends upon it. The manifestation of this salvation will be nothing less than the justice of God.

The Justice of God

As Daniel Day Williams says, "God's justice is manifest in [God] working to put down the unrighteous, expose idols, show mercy, and achieve reconciliation in a new order which expresses [human beings'] dignity as the bearer of the divine image."[34] God's justice means a restoration of the sacred dignity of all people. This begins with the crucified class of people.

The context through which God enters human history is revelatory. It matters that Jesus died on the cross, just as it matters that God freed the Israelites from bondage. For it is only when the least of these are free to achieve the fullness of life that God's justice will be realized. The profound meaning of God's preferential option for freedom is seen in God's solidarity with the crucified class. Their freedom will mark an eradication of all that separates people one from another and thus disengages all people from the goodness of their humanity. Thus, the justice of God also begins from the bottom up. Put simply, it is in the freedom of those who are crucified that one can see the justice of God working in the world.

---

34. Williams, "Love and Social Justice" (chap. 12), in *The Spirit and Forms of Love.*

God's justice is freedom from the bondage of sin. In the context of a stand-your-ground culture this means the sin of setting one's self above or against another. Hence, it again means exposing the myths, the narratives, and hence the sense of American exceptionalism. This narrative is a violent narrative that creates and maintains a cycle of violence. Justice therefore represents the peace of God. This peace is freedom from the violence that distorts the human person. It is the elimination, in other words, of systems, constructs, and all actualities of violence. God's peace thus requires a radical restructuring of a political, social, and economic order that is sustained by and thus creates "crucified classes of people." These again are the systems and structures that maintain the myth of America's Anglo-Saxon exceptionalism. As Gutiérrez rightly points out, "All injustice is a breach with God."[35] The very identity of a nation that claims to be "a city on a hill" reflecting the glory of God actually reflects a breach with God. God's justice is the healing of that breach. In a stand-your-ground-culture war this begins with the victims of that very war. Recognition of this has implications for the church.

Being Church in Stand-Your-Ground Culture

> The stench from your houses of worship is wafting its way across this country, polluting citizenship, demoralizing parents and families, mocking accountability and blaspheming the Holy God whom you say you love and worship. . . . Speak up for justice. Stand up and demand that this license for murder be removed from your books, from your lives. Stop defending it. It is but a few steps removed from lynching. And you recall, do you not, that the center of the Gospels is the story of the passion of our Lord who was lynched by Romans who perceived him as a threat?[36]

These are the words of a white Baptist minister, Michael Bledsoe, to the "white churches" of Florida. He was responding to the verdict

---

35. Gutiérrez, *A Theology of Liberation*, 139.

36. Michael Bledsoe, "Dear White Christians of Florida: An Open Letter," Riverside Baptist Church, Washington DC, February 26, 2014, http://www.riversidesedc.org.

in the trial of Jordan Davis's killer. As mentioned earlier, although his killer was convicted of attempted murder, the jury was hung on whether or not his killer actually murdered him. Recognizing the connection between Jesus' crucifixion and the stand-your-ground lynching of Jordan, Pastor Bledsoe called out the white churches of Florida for remaining silent. He rebuked them for not demanding that Florida's Stand Your Ground law "be removed from [the] books and from [the] laws." Recognizing the specter of race, he suggested that if the victims of these stand-your-ground crucifixions were white, he had no doubt that the white churches would speak up. Remaining silent, he said, was to cooperate with evil. He pronounced, "Shame. Shame. Shame."

Harriet Martineau, often cited as the first female sociologist, said the white clergy during the debate over slavery were "the most backward and timid class in the society in which they live; self-exiled from the great moral question of the time."[37] Perhaps this same claim can be made of white clergy in this time of stand your ground. To be sure, it was not simply the white churches of Florida who remained silent in the face of the murders of Jordan Davis and Trayvon Martin. There were far too many other churches that did the same. There is a long history of churches, particularly white churches, being on the wrong side of crucifying realities in their own time. James Cone recognized this in relationship to the lynching that terrorized black American's in the nineteenth and twentieth centuries. He said, "The lynching tree has no place in American theological reflections about Jesus' cross or in the proclamation of Christian churches about his Passion."[38] When I asked a white clergyman why there was such silence coming from the white church community concerning the verdict in the Trayvon Martin murder case, he responded that the situation was "too controversial." In hearing that, I was reminded of the white religious leaders of the South who issued a public statement condemning Martin Luther King Jr. for involving himself in "controversial social justice issues." They suggested that the role of the minister was to "save souls." This statement prompted King's "Letter from a Birmingham Jail." The

---

37. Harriet Martineau, *Society in America*, vol. 2 (New York: Saunders & Otley, 1837), 244.

38. Cone, *The Cross and the Lynching Tree*, 30.

concern to save souls is precisely what Ida B. Wells said prevented white churches of her day from engaging in the fight against lynching.

Throughout history there has been a variety of reasons for the silence or antagonism of the white religious community when it comes to black peoples' struggles against the oppressions generated by Anglo-Saxon exceptionalism. As we have seen throughout this discussion, some among the white clergy class have been Anglo-Saxon chauvinists themselves. They have believed that white people were indeed superior to black people. There were no doubt those who believed, as Protestant theologian and church historian Philip Schaff did, that blacks were the punished descendants of Ham and thus doomed to be slaves. Thus, they reasoned, it was God's business, not theirs, to free black people from their oppressed condition. Schaff put it this way: "Should we then not have patience and forbearance and wait the time which Providence in its own wisdom and mercy has appointed for the solution of a problem which thus far has baffled the wisdom of the wisest of statesmen."[39] Evangelical clergy typically have maintained that their duty is indeed to save souls. Consequently, their focus has been on the sins of the individual as opposed to the sins of society. Evangelical churches have therefore been under "no commission to reconstruct society." In general, many white churches have too often "lived with 'white and black' as an apparently predestined distinction."[40] For whatever the justification may be, historically the white religious community has been reluctant to respond, if not antagonistic in their responses regarding matters that pertain to race.

What cannot be forgotten is that these churches are not separate from the social historical context that exudes the ideology of cherished white property. It cannot be said enough that American society is infused with the Anglo-Saxon myth. We have seen how this myth has distorted both notions of democracy and understandings of Christianity throughout American history. It is no wonder, therefore, that the connection between Jesus' crucifixion and the stand-your-ground murder of black bodies might be a particularly difficult connection for many in the white religious community to make.

---

39. Philip Schaff, *Slavery and the Bible: A Tract for the Times* (Chambersburg, PA: M. Kieffer & Co.'s Caloric Printing Press, 1861), 31.

40. Marty, *Righteous Empire*, 72.

The cross has indeed been a "stumbling block" for many churches when it comes to matters of race. In this instance, it prevents far too many white churches from seeing the reality of Jesus' crucifixion in their very midst. They "stumble" when it comes to recognizing the face of the crucified Jesus that is not white. What this means is that the crucified Jesus is virtually ignored. For in a context brimming with Anglo-Saxon white supremacy, the crucified Jesus is simply not white.

Whiteness is an oppositional construct. It opposes the freedom of God that is life and love for all of God's creation. In opposing the reality of blackness, it actually opposes the crucified Jesus. Whiteness signifies a crucifying reality. The challenge for white churches is to step out of the space of cherished white property to be where Jesus is, with the crucified class of people. This is the significance of Jesus entering into the space of the Samaritans. He let go of his privilege of Jewish maleness in order to show forth the full measure of God's love. The church must follow Jesus in this regard. It must cross over into the space of the Samaritans in its own time. If Jesus crossing over was an exodus event, then for white churches it would be *ekstasis*, a stepping outside of themselves. Such a stepping out is the first requirement in pointing the way to the salvation that Jesus offered to the Samaritan woman. Such salvation is about the life of the body as much as it is about the life of the soul. It is the way of justice.

During what has come to be known as the Last Supper, Jesus instructed his disciples, "Do this in remembrance of me." The Greek word for "remembrance" used in this instruction is "anamnesis." This word means more than simply a mental recollection of past events. It means to bring the past into the present. Anamnesis is perhaps best understood as the reenactment of past events. During the Last Supper, Jesus was calling his disciples to remember him through their actions—that is, to act in their present as he did throughout his life and ministry. One of the fundamental tasks of the church is to bear the memory of Jesus. This means being in the world as he was. To do this requires entering into solidarity with the crucified class in any given context. In the context of stand-your-ground-culture war, this necessitates understanding this war from the vantage point of its victims.

The church is compelled as a bearer of the memory of Jesus to step into the space of the Trayvons and Jordans who don't know whether to walk slow or walk fast in order to stay alive. To step into their space is what it means for the church to bring the past, which is Jesus, into the present crucifying realities of stand-your-ground culture. Moreover, it is only when one can enter into the space of the crucified class, with sympathetic understanding, that one is able to realize what is required for the salvation of God, which is justice, to be made manifest in our world.

As Daniel Day Williams says, "Justice is the order that love requires."[41] The love of God that comes through the cross demands an unflinching solidarity with the crucified ones. For the church to be anywhere else is to be in the crucifying crowd, and thus to betray the very memory of the one who died on the cross, the memory of the one whom Christian churches are to bear.

This brings us back to the haunting question, "Where was God when Trayvon was slain?"

The Life That Is God

A Mother's Pride

Weep no more, Marta,
Weep no more, Mary,
Jesus rise from de dead,
Happy Morning.[42]

Renisha McBride worked for Ford Motor Company. She loved cars and shopping. "She loved to be around family and friends—and to have fun." She had been a cheerleader in high school.[43]

Jonathan Ferrell was an "athlete and scholar who inspired others without drawing attention to himself." He was a former football player at Florida A&M University where he majored in chemistry and psychology. At the time of his death he was working two jobs. He

---

41. Williams, "Love and Social Justice" (chap. 12), in *The Spirit and Forms of Love.*

42. Quoted in Cone, *Spirituals and the Blues.*

43. Taken from Tammy Stables Battaglia, Bill Laitner, and Niraj Warikoo, "Renisha McBride funeral mourns 'tragedy that didn't have to happen'; shooter 'torn up', *Detroit Free Press*, http://www.freep.com.

believed "there was no substitute for hard work." He was engaged to be married. His favorite toy growing up was a Winnie the Pooh doll.[44]

Jordan Davis was a junior at Wolfson High School in Jacksonville, Florida. He had hopes of becoming a Marine. His friends said there was nobody who didn't like Jordan. If you didn't like Jordan, they said, something was wrong with you.[45]

Trayvon Martin loved sports, repairing his bikes, listening to music, and horseback riding. At only seventeen, he had a bright future ahead of him, with dreams of attending college and becoming an aviation mechanic or pilot.

Renisha, Jonathan, Jordan, and Trayvon were the pride of their mothers. They were daughters and sons. They were all children of God. They had lives that were not defined by the stand-your-ground realities that killed them. Their lives were defined by who they were as children of God. Because of Jesus' resurrection the crucifying realities of their deaths will not have the last word over their lives.

The Question Answered

God is freedom. God is love. God is life. And so it is that God is with our black sons and daughters as they live into the freedom, love, and life that is theirs to claim. God is with them as they resist the sinful realities of a stand-your-ground war that tries to demean and destroy their very lives. God is with them on their journeys to be the best people they can be—fun-loving, hard-workers on their way to becoming Marines, aviation mechanics, or pilots. Where was God when Trayvon was slain? What we know for sure is that God was not a part of the crucifying mob. Thus, on the night when Trayvon was slain, God was where life was crying out to be free from the crucifying death of stand-your-ground culture.

Yet a question remains: "O Lord, how long?" To this question, we now turn.

---

44. Taken from Michael Gordon, "Hundreds gather for Jonathan Ferrell's Funeral," http://www.charlotteobserver.com.

45. Denene Miller, "Jordan Davis' Father on Son's Senseless Death," *Jet* http://www.jetmag.com; "Remembering Jordan Davis at Georgia Memorial," *News4Jax*, http://www.news4jax.com.

6

Prophetic Testimony:
The Time of God

"It is important to recognize that the African American community is looking at this issue through a set of experiences and a history that doesn't go away." We have come full circle in this discussion. These are words that President Obama also spoke in the July 19, 2013, speech after the verdict of Trayvon's killer. As we have shown, what happened to Trayvon was not an isolated event in history. His murder, along with the acquittal of his killer, represented a continual pattern of disregard for black life that is endemic to America's grand narrative of Anglo-Saxon exceptionalism. When the first Americans arrived believing they were the chosen Anglo-Saxon remnant meant to build a "city on a hill," the groundwork was laid for a stand-your-ground culture. Because of its malleability this culture has been persistent. It adapts to the social-historical climate of the day. Whether in the form of slavery, Black Codes, lynching, Jim Crow, restrictive covenants, or a gun, its primary targets remain the same—black bodies. This is a culture that stubbornly refuses to respect the free black body. It serves to perpetuate the construct of the black body as chattel. The free body is perceived as an inferior, guilty black body that must be prevented from encroaching upon the space of cherished white property. As for the white body, stand-your-ground culture serves to protect its free space. Constructed in opposition to the black body, the white body is perceived as a superior, innocent body.

Essentially, stand-your-ground culture is a perennial part of America's history. It is crucial to America's grand narrative of Anglo-Saxon exceptionalism. It functions to secure this narrative by safeguarding the customs and conventions of white supremacy. Navigating the realities of stand-your-ground culture shapes the history of black life in America. As long as black people have been in America, they have understood the limits of their rights as citizens. What the 1857 Dred Scott decision made official, black people have long understood: that at any given moment in time, they have "no rights that the white man is bound to respect." The decision regarding Trayvon's killer was a reminder of this.

At some point in the life of every black woman and man they must face the "shock," James Baldwin says, "that the flag to which you have pledged allegiance, along with everybody else, has not pledged allegiance to you. It comes as a great shock," he continues, "to discover that the country which is your birthplace and to which you owe your life and identity has not, in its whole system of reality, evolved any place for you."[1] For many young black men and women coming of age some fifty years after the civil rights era and during the time of a black president, they faced this shock as they came to grips with what happened to Trayvon. Again, for older generations of black Americans this was, as someone said to me in response to the verdict, "the same ole, same ole." This "same ole, same ole" is the history that black people carry with them, the history referenced by President Obama.

However, this history does not belong to black people alone. It is America's Anglo-Saxon white history as well. It is the white American resolve to protect the "wages of whiteness" that has determined the course of America's racial history. These cherished wages, however, do not free white bodies from confronting the burden of the history that is theirs. Baldwin minces no words in reminding white Americans of this fact. He shouts out,

> White man, hear me! History, as nearly no one seems to know, is not merely something to be read. And it does not refer merely, or even principally, to the past. On the contrary, the great force of history comes from the fact that we carry it within us, are unconsciously controlled by it in many ways, and history is literally *present* in all that we do. It could scarcely be otherwise, since it is to history that we owe our frames of reference, our

1. Baldwin, "The American Dream and the American Negro," in *The Price of the Ticket*, 404.

identities, and our aspirations. And it is with great pain and terror that one begins to realize this.[2]

In the same July 19, 2013, speech, President Obama asked, "Now,
the question is . . . where do we take this? How do we learn some les-
sons from this and move in a positive direction?" How, in fact, do we
write a new history?

After the events surrounding the murder of Trayvon, one thing
was clear to me: this time in the life of the country is a *kairos* time.
Kairos time is the right or opportune time. It is a decisive moment in
history that potentially has far-reaching impact. It is often a chaotic
period, a time of crisis. However, it is through the chaos and crisis
that God is fully present, disrupting things as they are and providing
an opening to a new future—to God's future. *Kairos* time is, therefore,
a time pregnant with infinite possibilities for new life. *Kairos* time is
God's time. It is a time bursting forth with God's call to a new way of
living in the world. It is God calling us to a new relationship with our
very history and sense of self, and thus to a new relationship with one
another, and even with God.

Interestingly, the very biblical paradigm that has been central to
both the nation's faith and black faith, the exodus, reveals a *kairos* time
in the life of the Israelites. Once again we discover that the exodus
story is about more than the event of liberation and about more than
the conquest of the Promised Land. As the Israelites began to thrive
and build a nation, they began to betray what it meant for them to be
chosen. Perhaps they believed that their very blood was exceptional.
For whatever reason, they lost sight of the fact that they were chosen
to be free. They had entered into a covenant relationship with a God
who was free and had called them into the very freedom of God. This
meant nothing less than being a people free from all of the social-cultural customs and conventions that would prevent them from living
into the freedom that was theirs to claim. If they were to inhabit the
land of "milk and honey," showing forth the glory of God to all the
nations, then that land had to be a land where all were free. As we
know, this was not to be. It became a land where power "trample[d]
the head of the poor into the dust of the earth and turn[ed] aside the
way of the afflicted" (Amos 2:7 NEV). Instead of being a land that

---

2. Baldwin, "White Man's Guilt," in *The Price of the Ticket*, 410.

showed forth the God that was freedom, it had become an "abomination" to God (Jeremiah 2). Into this time of crisis, God brought forth prophets. These prophets held Israel accountable for its very history, that is, a history of being led from bondage into freedom. The prophets reminded the Israelites that they had a responsibility as a nation to live into the very freedom for which they were chosen. The prophets, in effect, turned the sense of chosenness back upon the Israelites and took them to task. The time of the prophets was no less than a *kairos* time in the life of the Israelites in which God was calling them into a new relationship with their history, with one another, and with God.

Within the context of the stand-your-ground-culture wars that have violated the freedom and imperiled the lives of black people, prophetic black voices have emerged to hold the nation accountable for its own self-proclaimed history. These black voices have turned the narrative of "exceptionalism" back upon the nation and called it to live into its very claims to be that "city on a hill" shining forth divine virtues of morality and freedom. In so doing, these prophetic black voices have held the nation accountable for its faith in itself as a people chosen to "follow the sun" in spreading democracy across the globe.

Martin Luther King Jr. was one of those voices. In the stand-your-ground-culture war that was his to fight, he confronted America with its chauvinism. There is no greater testament to the prophetic black tradition than King's "I Have a Dream" speech. In this speech King turned the dynamics of power in on itself. He spoke of America's identity of exceptionalism, but with a difference. In so doing, he brought together the two faith claims that have emerged in the stand-your-ground-culture war: America's faith in itself and black faith in the freedom of God. Through this prophetic declaration, King tried to break the persistent pattern of stand-your-ground-culture realities.

Chapter 1 answered the question of how we got here to this particular stand-your-ground moment, with Trayvon gunned down on a Florida sidewalk and his killer set free. This chapter will attempt to address how we get beyond this point. How might we break the cycle of stand-your-ground realities? King's "Dream" will be the lens through which we attempt to answer this question. Through this particular prophetic protestation, King points a way forward beyond the stand-your-ground cycle. At the same time, he steps into a history of black prophetic testimony that has consistently called the nation to account for its own history. This testimony has been more than a counternarrative to America's narrative of Anglo-Saxon exceptionalism. It has been a "signifyin' narrative."

Signifyin' has been an ongoing tool within the black culture of survival and resistance to the oppressing power of cherished white property. Signifyin' takes a variety of forms, with each generation adding its own nuances. It has come in the form of double talk or coded language, as seen in the spirituals and the blues. Sometimes it is simply "repetition with a difference."[3] In the main, signifyin' is one of the ways in which black people have spoken truth about and to power. Black prophetic testimony in many respects is a part of this signifyin' tradition. It speaks truth to power, often by repeating the narrative of America's exceptionalist identity, but with a difference. As this chapter enters the history of black prophetic testimony through King's "Dream" speech, it seeks to discern what we can learn from this testimony in this time of stand-your-ground-culture wars. The underlying assumption of this chapter is that this is indeed a *kairos* time. In this stand-your-ground-culture war that is ours, God is calling us to a new way of being with one another and with God. We are being called to write a new history. In the end, therefore, this chapter is a response to President Obama's question: "Can we move in a more positive direction" after what happened to Trayvon? That response begins with the stand-your-ground time that was King's.

A History-Making Moment

I remember it like it was yesterday. I was six years old. It was a hot Wednesday afternoon in August. My brother, two sisters, and I were playing in our bedrooms while my parents were sitting on the living room couch watching something on television. Out of nowhere, with a sense of urgency, my mother called the four of us to come quickly to see what they were watching. We all ran in, not quite knowing what to expect. When we got there my parents told us to sit down and watch because history was being made. I was not quite sure what they meant by that, but I followed their instructions. I remember watching and wondering why so many people, especially black people, were all

---

3. Henry Lewis Gates Jr., *The Signifying Monkey: A Theory of African American Literary Criticism* (New York: Oxford University Press, 1988), xxiv.

gathered listening to a man give a speech. My parents told me they were gathered in Washington, DC, and they were listening to Martin Luther King Jr. As I listened, my six-year-old mind was not taking in what he was saying. What I *was* taking in, however, were my parents' reactions to what was on the screen. Both were silent and noticeably moved by King's words. Occasionally one of them would utter, "That's right." The one television image that captured my attention was seeing the mass of people all singing, "We Shall Overcome." My parents even joined in from their place on the couch. This was the first time I had heard this song. After hearing it that day, I never forgot it. Even as a six-year-old child the words stuck with me. Still today, anytime I hear that song, I am transported back to that moment in time, sitting in front of the television with my family watching "history being made."

What I did not realize then was that for my parents the "history being made" was the hope they had for their children. As they listened to King, his dream was their dream for my siblings and me. They too wanted their four children to live in a world where they "will not be judged for the color of their skin but by the content of their character." My father and mother sat on the couch that day hoping that the history-making moment was the beginning of a new history being written. They hoped that the stand-your-ground culture of their day was coming to an end.

That day in front of the television was of course August 28, 1963, when King delivered his "I Have a Dream" speech to over 250,000 people gathered at the Lincoln Memorial. This was the speech that for many defined King's historical significance. It was certainly the speech that "allowed" America to admit King into its pantheon of heroes and to integrate him into the "American" story. It would become for many his signature speech. And perhaps it is. For in that moment and in that speech King took on America's stand-your-ground culture at its very root. This is what my parents understood. In that moment in history, King provided a prophetic signifyin' response to America's grand narrative of exceptionalism. He turned the nation's identity back upon itself. He held the nation accountable to its own religiously legitimated chauvinistic claims. He repeated its history, but with a prophetic difference. In order to appreciate the significance of what King did in that moment, we must appreciate the stand-your-ground culture that King was confronting—the *kairos* moment to which he was responding. In so doing, we will appreciate not only the extent to which this culture is entrenched in the very soil of America but also the prescient insight of black prophetic testimony.

Two Warring Souls

Characteristic of stand-your-ground culture, King's time was a particularly divided time in America. It was truly a war, replete with guns and even bombs. In various corners and on various levels of society, the stewards of America's Anglo-Saxon identity seemed to call upon its full arsenal to defend and protect the free space of cherished white property. Just eight months before King's signature speech Alabama Governor George Wallace declared in his inaugural speech, "Segregation now, segregation tomorrow, segregation forever!" In an attempt to make good on those words, two months before King stood in front of the Lincoln Memorial, Wallace stood in front of the doors of the University of Alabama administration building to prevent black students from entering. Wallace was standing his ground in order to protect the "educational" space of cherished white property. Wallace was one of many across the country who stood their ground to prevent black bodies from coming together with white bodies to learn. Quality education was deemed a "wage" of whiteness.

Five months before King stood at the podium on the Memorial mall, he sat in a Birmingham jail writing a letter to the religious leaders who told him that his job was to save souls and not to involve himself in social justice matters. These religious leaders were standing their ground to preserve what they believed to be a sacred status quo, one that maintained separate racial spaces. In a manner similar to the stand-your-ground-culture war today, King could not count on the religious community to support him in the fight against it.

In May, four months before the images of black people singing "We Shall Overcome," different images played across television screens— the images of firemen using the force of water and policemen using the ferociousness of dogs to stop singing protestors, many of them children, in their tracks. On that day, the stand-your-ground weapons of choice were firehoses and dogs. Two months before that day in August, civil rights leader Medgar Evers was gunned down in his Mississippi driveway in front of his wife and children. This was a stand-your-ground lynching delivering the message to all who would dare to think black bodies should be free: this too will happen to you. Unfortunately, Medgar Evers was not the only one to fall victim to the deadly stand-your-ground violence of the civil rights era.

In the wake of the increasing violent and hateful resistance to black people's demands for their rights as citizens, on June 11, 1963, President John F. Kennedy delivered perhaps his most significant speech on civil rights. In this speech he called civil rights a "moral issue." Kennedy said this issue was as "old as the scripture and as clear as the American Constitution." With that phrase, President Kennedy was tapping into America's collective religious consciousness. As we have seen, America's defining identity is as a religious nation. The Constitution for all intents and purposes is considered an extension of the scriptures. It is sacred, as the scriptures themselves are sacred. Kennedy, therefore, played upon this connection in his attempt to call America to a new relationship with its black citizens by grounding this call in scriptures and the Constitution. In effect, he was suggesting that the "moral issue" was actually a sacred concern.

Kennedy continued to draw upon the history of the nation by connecting to another war in which the freedom of black bodies was at stake. "One hundred years of delay have passed since President Lincoln freed the slaves," he said, "yet their heirs, their grandsons, are not fully free. They are not yet freed," Kennedy explained, "from the bonds of injustices. They are not yet freed from social and economic oppression. And this Nation, for all of its hopes and all of its boasts, will not be free until all of its citizens are free." Recognizing that the plight of black bodies was a threat to America's self-proclaimed exceptionalism as a "city on a hill," Kennedy warned, "We preach freedom around the world . . . and we cherish our freedom here at home, but are we to say to the world, and much more importantly, to each other that this is a land of the free except for the Negroes, that we have no second-class citizens except Negroes; that we have no class or caste system, no ghettoes, no master race except with respect to Negroes?"[4] Indeed, in the Manifest Destiny war of Anglo-Saxon exceptionalism, this was exactly the point. Only the white body was meant to be free. Kennedy, however, attempted to rewrite that narrative.

---

4. All references to this speech are from John Fitzgerald Kennedy, "Address on Civil Rights" (June 11, 1963), Miller Center University of Virginia, http://www.millercenter.org.

Kennedy was describing the profound contradiction of a nation proclaiming to be an exceptional steward of "liberty" yet standing its ground against the rights of the black body to share in that liberty. As in the time of President Lincoln, the nation stood to rise or fall depending upon its decision surrounding the freedom of the black body. Kennedy was, for all intents and purposes, challenging America to determine its true identity. Was it going to be defined by an Anglo-Saxon or a democratic exceptionalism? Was its exceptional identity about the "blood" or the institutions? Stand-your-ground culture reveals a nation that is actually at war with itself.

The warring soul of the black American, which Du Bois so poignantly described, provides an apt description for America itself. In the words of Du Bois, America has been a nation defined by "two thoughts, two unreconciled strivings, two warring ideas."[5] Is the nation striving to be a slave nation or a free nation? Is it going to be a nation torn asunder by differences of race or a nation unified by a commitment to freedom? Is it to be a nation separate and unequal by lines of color or a nation dedicated to the declaration that "all men are created equal"? The problem of the twentieth century, Du Bois declared, was the problem of the color line. As we have seen, the purpose of stand-your-ground culture is to maintain the color line. But ironically, as it does this it threatens an essential feature of America's exceptional identity, and thus signals a nation divided against itself. Stand-your-ground culture is the sign of the nation's two warring souls. President Lincoln recognized this. So too did President Kennedy, and so too did Martin Luther King Jr.

Two Faith Traditions

This was the significance of King delivering his "Dream" speech at the Lincoln Memorial. In so doing, he was signaling to the nation that once again it was in a war with itself. With this homage to Lincoln, he was confronting the nation with the reality of surviving or being destroyed by a war over the color line. Even though Lincoln was not resolved in his own mind that black people were equal to whites, he was clear that the nation could not survive divided against itself, and it could not endure "permanently half slave and half free."

---

5. Du Bois, *The Souls of Black Folks*, 9.

Lincoln firmly believed that slavery was the great sin of the nation and that perhaps the Civil War was God's punishment for this sin. Therefore, in his First Inaugural Address Lincoln implored the nation to be "touched by its better angels" and to find a way to resolve the problem of slavery—the stand-your-ground issue of his day.

One hundred years later, King recognized that this issue had not yet been resolved. He recognized that the stand-your-ground war he was facing was much like the Civil War Lincoln faced. While not officially slaves, black bodies were still not free. This stand-your-ground war defined as a battle for civil rights would determine the nature of black freedom. This was obvious. Perhaps not so obvious to many was that beyond black freedom, the nation's very sense of self was also at stake. King tried to make this obvious. He turned the stand-your-ground-culture war against itself. In so doing, he ingeniously and seamlessly brought together two faith claims, that of the nation and that of the black community. One provided the foundation for King's dream; the other was that upon which he prophetically "signified." To appreciate how this was the case, let us look more closely at the impact of the black faith tradition on King's dream.

To listen to King, especially when he was before black audiences, was to know how significant the black faith tradition was to his thoughts and actions. Drawing upon the faith claims of this tradition, King consistently referred to God as the "God of history." King was clear that God moved and acted in human history. As the enslaved had done in their time, King asserted that God identified with black people in the same way that God had once identified with the Hebrew slaves. King's God was a God who had a "preferential option" for freedom. This is why King could announce with passionate resolve to the people gathered at Mason Temple Church of God in Memphis Tennessee, the night before his assassination, "I've seen the Promised Land. I may not get there with you. But I want you to know tonight, that we, as a people, will get to the Promised Land!"[6]

King in fact believed that Jesus' liberating ministry, and certainly his crucifixion and resurrection, challenged all Christians to identify with the crucified classes of people in their own contexts and to

---

6. Martin Luther King Jr., "I've Been to the Mountaintop" (April 3, 1968), http://www.americanrhetoric.com.

protest any form of injustice. This was clear when King said in his first public address, delivered at the beginning of the Montgomery bus boycott, "We are not wrong in what we are doing. . . . If we are wrong, God Almighty is wrong. If we are wrong, Jesus of Nazareth was merely a utopian dreamer that never came down to earth. If we are wrong, justice is a lie."[7]

Without a doubt, King's involvement in the civil rights movement was not just a matter of politics. It was a matter of faith. It was this black faith that brought King to the Lincoln Memorial and informed his dream. It was this faith that resonated with black people and brought many of them with him to the Lincoln Memorial, just as it inspired them to fight for their rights as free children of God. Therefore, it was fitting that King ended his "I Have a Dream" speech with a testimony of black faith: "And when we allow freedom to ring . . . we will be able to speed up that day when all of God's children . . . will be able to join hands and to sing in the words of the Old Negro Spiritual, 'Free at last, free at last, thank God Almighty, we are free at last.'"

As important as black faith was to King and to the black community in general, King knew that it alone would not prick the conscience of America. While black faith allowed black people to survive and to fight against stand-your-ground culture, this was not the faith that could change it. King understood that he would have to call upon the nation's faith in itself. So he did, but with a signifyn' difference. King drew upon America's belief that it was God's city on a hill to call it to task for its treatment of its black citizens, in essence for not being that city.

In his "Dream" speech, King reminded the nation of its most sacred documents, the Constitution and the Declaration of Independence. These documents represented the covenant the nation had made with itself, if not with God. King said the "architects" of these sacred documents were "signing a promissory note to which every American was to fall heir." He explained that this note promised all of its citizens their God-given rights of "Life, Liberty, and the pursuit of Happiness." Like the prophets to the Israelites, King charged the "chosen nation" of dishonoring its "sacred obligation." He proclaimed, therefore, "America has defaulted on this promissory, insofar as her citizens of

---

7. MIA Mass Meeting at Holt Street Baptist Church, Papers of Martin Luther King Jr., http://mik-kpp01.stanford.edu.

color were concerned." Pointing to the white persons who were in the crowd, King reminded the white community that their freedom was "bound" to black freedom. Perhaps recognizing the prophetic nature of his own testimony, King recalled words from the prophet Amos when told the audience that they should not be satisfied until in America, "justice rolls down like waters, and righteousness like a mighty stream." King then masterfully linked the hope of black faith for freedom with the American sense of exceptionalism. He said, "I still have a dream. It is a dream deeply rooted in the American dream."

King's dream is actually the fusion of two faith traditions. To hear King's dream of a nation where "every valley shall be exalted, and every hill and mountain shall be made low . . . and the glory of the Lord shall be revealed and all flesh shall see it together" is to hear the black faith tradition. At the same time, as he articulates his dream, it is the black faith tradition holding America accountable to its faith in itself as a divine land of democracy. This tradition is virtually signifyin' upon America's sense of exceptionalism. This is most evident when King says, "I have a dream that one day this nation will rise up and live out the true meaning of its creed: 'We hold these truths to be self-evident, that all men are created equal.'" After describing his dream in more detail, King utilizes the language of faith. At this point, King is at once alluding to both the faith of a black people and the faith of a nation. He connects them, making clear to all listening that they are both about freedom. Again illustrative of the black prophetic tradition of signifyin', King accomplishes this by turning America's faith back upon itself. Thus, he quotes one of its most sacred hymns, "My country 'tis of thee, sweet land of liberty, of thee I sing/Land where my fathers died, land of the Pilgrim's pride/From every mountainside, let freedom ring!" After quoting these lines he pronounced, "And if America is to be a great nation, this [freedom ringing] must become true."

Through his "Dream" speech King confronted head-on the stand-your-ground culture that shapes America's history and reifies the color line. In so doing, he provides the parameters for perhaps moving beyond it. Before looking at what those are it is important to recognize that he was not the first to do this. As earlier mentioned, others have provided prophetic testaments in response to the stand-your-ground wars they fought.

Over one hundred years before King, Frederick Douglass did the same in his now much-quoted Fourth of July speech of 1852. Invited to speak at an Independence Day celebration in Rochester, New York, Douglass begins by extolling the history of the nation and its fight for freedom from the tyranny of the British government. In recognizing the nation's identification with the exodus tradition, he says of the Fourth of July, "It is the birth day of your National Independence, and of your political freedom. This, to you, [is] what the Passover was to the emancipated people of God. It carries your minds back to the day, and to the act of your great deliverance; and to the signs, and to the wonders, associated with that act, and that day."[8] With prophetic signifyn' intent Douglass says to the audience, "The 4th of July is the first great fact in your nation's history—the very ringbolt in the chain of your yet undeveloped destiny." He tells them to stand by the principles extolled in the Declaration of Independence, those of justice and liberty. He further affirms the claims of the Declaration that these are "eternal principles" in which the architects of the Declaration had "sublime faith." He then proclaims that as significant as the past may be, the "accepted time with God and His cause is the ever-living now." With this Douglass turns the faith of the nation on its head.

"This Fourth of July," he tells his audience, "is yours not mine." In "the severest language" at his command, he says "America is false to the past, false to the present, and solemnly binds herself to be false to the future." Making clear that God's cause is with the "crushed and bleeding slave," he says America has "trampled" upon both the Constitution and the Bible. Like those after him, Douglass recognizes the sacredness of the Constitution. Thus, he makes clear that to betray the Constitution, according to the narrative of America as a chosen people, is to betray the Bible. It is essentially a sin. In what are perhaps the most quoted lines of this speech, Douglass perceptively and prophetically "signifies" on the nation's exceptional identity. He says,

> What, to the American slave, is your 4th of July? . . . To him, your celebration is a sham: your boasted liberty, an unholy license; your national greatness, swelling vanity; your sounds of rejoicing are empty and heartless; your denunciation of tyrants,

---

8. Frederick Douglass, "The Meaning of July Fourth for the Negro," Rochester, NY, July 5, 1852, http://www.historyisaweapon.com.

brass fronted impudence; your shouts of liberty and equality, hollow mockery; your prayers and hymns, your sermons and thanksgivings, with all your religious parade and solemnity, are to Him, mere bombast, fraud, deception, impiety, and hypocrisy—a thin veil to cover up crimes which would disgrace a nation of savages. There is not a nation on earth guilty of practices more shocking and bloody than are the people of the United States, at this very hour.

From beginning to end, Douglass's speech "signifies" on America's faith and identity. He repeats its proud history with the intention of calling it out. In his final analysis he mocks the notion of exceptionality. In effect, he proclaims that the exceptionalism of the nation is found in its crimes against black bodies, not in its demonstrations of liberty. He makes clear that this national hypocrisy is a betrayal of its very faith and thus an affront to God. He calls out slavery, the expression of stand-your-ground culture in his day.

In this same vein, Mary Church Terrell also "signified" on America's sense of exceptionalism though her own prophetic testimony. In a 1906 speech before the United Women's Club in Washington, DC, Terrell responds to the notion that "the national capital" is "the Colored Man's Paradise." After reciting the numerous Jim Crow indignities she faced in the nation's capital as a "colored woman," she said, "surely nowhere in the world do oppression and persecution based solely on the color of the skin appear more hateful and hideous than in the capital of the United States, because the chasm between the principles upon which this Government was founded, in which it still professes to believe, and those which are daily practiced under the protection of the flag, yawn so wide and deep."[9]

Terrell, like Douglass before her, scoffs at the nation's exceptional identity. It is exceptional, she suggests, only in the measure of oppression it doles out upon black bodies. The greatest hypocrisy of it all is that the citadel of its "democracy," Washington, DC, is one of the worse betrayers of democracy itself.

---

9. Mary Church Terrell, "What It Means to Be Colored in the Capital of the United States" (1906), http://www.americanrhetoric.com/speeches/marychurch terellcolored.htm.

In her fight against the stand-your-ground war of lynching that was hers to fight, Ida B. Wells was just as relentless in calling America out for its hypocrisy when it came to the black body. She "signified" on both its exceptional and its Christian identity. Obviously speaking well before the Nazi holocaust against Jewish people, she said, "No other nation, civilized or savage, burns its criminals; only under the Stars and Stripes is the human holocaust possible. . . . Why is mob murder permitted by a Christian nation . . . [lynching] is . . . a blight upon our nation, mocking our laws and disgracing our Christianity."[10] In an attempt to get the nation to act to end the brutality of lynching, she tried to shame it with its own self-proclaimed identity.

While not in the form of a speech, there is probably no greater black prophetic testimony than that found in the letters of Phillis Wheatley and Benjamin Banneker to the founding leaders of the nation. Wheatley formally requested that "His Excellency General Washington, who fought for colonial America's freedom," fight also for black freedom from slavery. She wrote "we demand/The grace and glory of thy martial band."[11]

Banneker made his appeal to the "Father of Democracy," Thomas Jefferson. That Banneker wrote this letter to Jefferson has as much prophetic symbolism as King standing in front of the Lincoln Memorial. Banneker literally takes on one of the crafters of America's identity. Jefferson's response is just as telling. It reflects the shrewdness of stand-your-ground culture and exposes the insidious nature of its myth of origin. In a letter written on August 19, 1791, Banneker reminded Jefferson of "that time in which the Arms and tyranny of the British Crown were exerted with powerful effort, in order to reduce [him] to a State of Servitude." He beckoned him to recall how he felt and the "variety of dangers to which you were exposed." Reminding Jefferson of the fact that when the nation fought for its freedom from the British Jefferson "clearly saw into the injustice of a State of Slavery," he called upon Jefferson not to permit the nation to "counteract" the "benevolence of the Father of mankind" by maintaining the "most

---

10. Ida B. Wells, "Mob Murder in a Christian Nation" (1901), http://www.factmonster.com/t/hist/mob-murder/

11. Phillis Wheatley, "His Excellency General Washington," http://www.poets.org.

criminal act" of slavery.[12] Banneker appealed to Jefferson, "I hope you cannot but acknowledge, that it is the indispensable duty of those who maintain for themselves the rights of human nature, and who profess the obligations of Christianity, to extend their power and influence to the relief of every part of the human race, from whatever burthen [*sic*] or oppression that may unjustly labour under."

Standing his ground firmly against the notion of a free black body, Jefferson made this short reply:

> No body wishes more than I do to see such proofs as you exhibit that nature has given to our black brethren, talents equal to those of other colors of men . . . I can add with truth, that no body wishes more ardently to see a good system commended for raising the condition both of their body & mind to what it ought to be as fast as the imbecility of their present existence, and other circumstances which cannot be neglected, will admit.[13]

Jefferson's response reveals what we have already uncovered in our discussion, the way in which the Anglo-Saxon myth penetrated his consciousness, and hence shaped America's identity. This myth, as we also have seen, distorts the meaning of democracy as well as Christianity. This brings us back to King's "Dream" speech and what black prophetic testimony tells us about breaking the pattern of stand-your-ground culture.

There is much to be learned from black prophetic testaments, especially as they responded to the harsh realities of stand-your-ground culture. To be sure, their very witness confirms the terrifying relentlessness of this culture. Once again, it is clear, as long as America's narrative of exceptionalism has not been "debunked" then this culture will be a consistent part of America's historical landscape. This fact makes the black prophetic tradition even more important. For this tradition points not simply to a new way of being in the world, but to a different history that black America also carries within it.

---

12. "Letter from Benjamin Banneker, &c.," August 19, 1791, http://www.factmonster.com/t/hist/banneker-jefferson/1.html.

13. "Thomas Jefferson to Benjamin Banneker," August 30, 1791, http://www.factmonster.com/t/hist/banneker-jefferson/2.html.

As much as black life may be circumscribed by a stand-your-ground culture, it is not defined by it. In many respects, the black prophetic tradition, especially as it is shaped by black faith, reflects the crucifixion–resurrection realities of black living. In the midst of a crucifying culture, black women and men have forged a life that defies this culture. At the same time, they have acted against this culture. In short, black life continues another history. It carries forth the history of the Hebrew prophets and the Christian resurrection. In many respects, the resurrection is a prophetic response to the crucifixion. The resurrection calls a people back to who they are supposed to be as children of God. It calls them to a life beyond the crucifying death.

As black people have lived into their identity as free beings, they have mocked with their very living the narratives of Anglo-Saxon testimony that betray the creation of God. Black people, as they defy Anglo-Saxon narratives, have been embodied realities of a prophetic resurrection tradition. Black prophetic testimony, therefore, puts into words the history that black people have lived. President Obama was right to proclaim that black America sees what happened to Trayvon "through a set of experiences that doesn't go away." These experiences, however, are not in the main defined by how this culture has acted upon black bodies. They are defined by the way in which black bodies have responded as embodied prophetic testimony. This is also the history "we carry within us," as Baldwin says. This history is a testament of hope to a new way of being in the world. Let us now look more closely at the prophetic protestation of King to discern precisely what it suggests to us about breaking the pattern of stand-your-ground-culture realities.

Moral Memory

The tradition of prophetic testimony that King stepped into and carried forth is one that indeed takes seriously the past that continues to shape America's racial history. That it has become a cliché does not make Edmund Burke's observation any less true. "Those who don't know history," he said, "are doomed to repeat it." Stand-your-ground culture continues to reassert itself in increasingly violent ways because of a failure to take seriously the very history that has fostered it. This is the history that King forced the nation to confront in that prophetic moment at the Lincoln Memorial. This is not simply the history of an idea. Rather, it is a history of an idea derailed. To be sure, as we have seen, the idea of

"Life, Liberty and the pursuit of Happiness" was never meant to extend to nonwhite bodies. And perhaps this is the weakness of King's prophetic testament as well as those of Douglass, Terrell, Wells, Banneker, and others brave enough to speak truth to power—the failure to come to grips with that fact. But the point is this: black bodies and white bodies are bound together in one American history. This King recognized. It is this history that he confronted. He essentially called upon white Americans to assess the price they paid to be white. This, as he made clear, is the price of giving up on an idea of being a beacon of democracy. Perhaps it is a price they are willing to pay. The persistent nature of stand-your-ground culture suggests as much. However, if this is the case, then the prophetic testimony exemplified by King compels white America to own that truth. Baldwin puts it this way: "Go back to where you started, as far back as you can, examine all of it, travel your road again and tell the truth about it."[14] If this is the truth that is to be told, then the prophetic black tradition demands that it be told. To do so is at least the beginning of "white" America taking responsibility for the past that it carries within it, and thus responsibility for the persistent racialized violence against black bodies.

In many respects, we have arrived at this particular stand-your-ground moment because of our nation's inability to be honest with itself and to face the hard truths of its own story. It is a story about the vicissitudes of America's narrative of Anglo-Saxon exceptionalism and ideology of cherished white property. The nation will certainly continue to be held captive to that narrative until it honestly confronts it and the history it has created. Prophetic black testimony thus calls the nation to a moral memory.

Moral memory is nothing less than telling the truth about the past and one's relationship to it. Moral memory is not about exonerating ourselves for the past. Rather, it is taking responsibility for it. To have a moral memory is to recognize the past we carry within us, the past we want to carry within us, and the past we need to make right. Righting the past is about more than facile apologies or even guilty verdicts for killers of innocent black children. Rather, to right the past is to acknowledge the ways in which our systems, structures, and ways of being in society are a continuation of the myths,

---

14. Baldwin, *The Price of the Ticket*, xix.

the narratives, the ideologies of the past and then to transform these present realities. A moral memory recalls the story of America's chosen identity, the way it is shaped by the Anglo-Saxon myth, and thus recognizes how that continues to play itself out in our current reality. A moral memory does not ignore but recognizes the racial contract that is America's democracy, and the way that racial contract continues to be enacted. A moral memory uncovers the relationship between the slavocracy and the Prison Industrial Complex. A moral memory reveals the laws of stand-your-ground culture as a reincarnation of the Black Codes. A moral memory allows one to see that what happened to Renisha, Jonathan, Jordan, and Trayvon are legalized twenty-first-century lynchings. As President Obama said, invoking the words of William Faulkner, in another speech that addressed the racial history of America, "The past is never dead. It's not even past." A moral memory allows one to recognize how, in fact, the past is not past, but continues to shape present realities. Undoubtedly, it is only with the help of moral memory that the connection between America's very sense of itself and a stand-your-ground culture will come to light. Until that occurs, stand-your-ground culture will be an ever-present part of American reality. Baldwin put it bluntly: "One wishes that Americans—white Americans—would read, for their own sakes, this record, and stop defending themselves against it. Only then will they be enabled to change their lives. The fact that they have not yet been able to do this—to face their history, to change their lives—hideously menaces this country. Indeed, it menaces the entire world."[15]

It was this truth of the American story that King, along with other black prophetic voices, sought to tell. They called the nation to a moral memory. At the same time they exposed the travesty of America's exceptional identity. In each of the prophetic testaments we have examined, the notion of exceptionalism was ridiculed. King went a step further. Recognizing that America's exceptional identity was grounded in the Anglo-Saxon myth—this nation's version of God's presumed partiality for a particular people over all other people—King insisted that whiteness did not matter to God. King proclaimed, in much the same way as his enslaved forebears, that God was only partial to freedom. This meant that all of God's people were created

---

15. Baldwin, "White Man's Guilt," in *The Price of the Ticket*, 410.

to enjoy the gift of divine freedom. King, therefore, called upon the American people to recognize this divine truth. He did this as he spoke of a faith that compelled a people to "stand up for freedom together." It is in that way that King called the nation to a moral identity.

Moral Identity

A moral identity recognizes, as Paul Tillich says, "that every human soul has infinite value." A moral identity is what Tillich calls the "courage to be oneself."[16] To be oneself is to be the child of God that one is, nothing more and nothing less. A moral identity, therefore, is free from any "social usages and customs" that distort the integrity of another's creation. A moral identity is one that is relieved of pretensions to superiority. It lets go of any myths that suggest one people is more valuable than another or that one people is chosen by God while another is not. A moral identity affirms the shared humanity of all human beings. Essentially, it is with a moral identity—as King suggested—that one lives into the image of a God who is freedom.

It is this identity that makes possible "sympathetic understanding." It frees one from moving through the world as if entitled, because of "blood," to certain "wages" such as life, liberty, and the pursuit of happiness. At the same time, it opens one to move through the world with empathy, thus feeling the suffering, the heartache, the hunger of others for life, liberty, and happiness. In many respects, a moral identity is the human response to Jesus' *kenosis*, that is, the way in which he emptied himself of anything that would set him apart from humanity, especially crucified humanity. It is only with a moral identity that one is able to enter into solidarity with the crucified class of one's own time. And thus, it is a moral identity that allows one to recognize the face of Jesus in the victims of a stand-your-ground-culture war.

Moral Participation

Each of the black prophets engaged in the struggle to end the stand-your-ground-culture realities of their day. For Douglass and Banneker it was a call to participate in the abolition of slavery. For Wells it was a call to end lynching. For Terrell and King it was a call to eliminate Jim

---

16. Paul Tillich, *The Courage to Be*, 2nd ed., with an introduction by Peter J. Gomes (New Haven: Yale Nota Bene, 2000; Yale University Press, 1952), 87.

Crow laws. Black prophetic testimony calls people to moral participation. This is a participation marked by a commitment to freedom,
love, and life. Such participation is a matter of faith.

The Greek word for faith, as used in the Gospels, is *pistis*. This
word does not suggest a way of thinking about who God is or reflecting upon God's relationship to us. Rather, it points to a way of acting
in light of our relationship to God. Put simply, faith is not about loy-
alty to a certain doctrine, dogma, or set of beliefs. Instead, it involves
commitment to a certain way of "living and moving and having our
being" in the world. Gustavo Gutiérrez puts it this way:

> Faith is the total human response to God. . . . In this light, the
> understanding of the faith appears as the understanding not
> of the simple affirmation—almost memorization—of truths,
> but of a commitment, an overall attitude, a particular posture
> toward life."[17]

This posture, which I have identified as moral participation, is what
Gutiérrez calls "praxis," having an "active presence in history."

Faith recognizes that God acts first, thus inviting human beings
into a relationship. It is important to recognize that this invitation
comes in the form of God acting in the world to make real the freedom of God, which is love and life. Thus, God's call to faith is an invitation to become a partner with God in "the mending of creation."
That is, God invites human beings to join with God in creating a world
where "justice is cherished and where freedom, [life] and love flourish."[18] To have faith is to accept the invitation to be an "active presence
in human history." It is in this way that black prophetic testimony
reflected the black faith tradition. It certainly was the case in terms of
King's testimony. Again, it was his understanding of the commitment
of faith that compelled him into the civil rights struggle. The only way
to change the realities of the world is through moral participation in
history. In the words often attributed to Mahatma Gandhi, "You must
be the change you wish to see in the world." Moral participation is,
in effect, bearing the memory of Jesus in the world. It is, therefore,
reflecting the already/not-yet reality of God's kingdom. It is being the
change that is God's heaven.

---

17. Gutiérrez, *A Theology of Liberation*, 6.
18. Migliore, *Faith Seeking Understanding*, 246, 247.

This brings us to perhaps the most significant aspect of King's dream and the black prophetic tradition. It is not bound by the past, or even by the present. It is driven by the future. In the midst of the harshest realities of a stand-your-ground culture, King spoke of a dream for a different world. He did not surrender to the crucifying realities of the world. He did not permit it to have the last word. This was the power of his black faith. It enabled him to live into the resurrection promise of new life. In this regard, the future was that which shaped his life, and hence his vision for America. King's dream was not born from the possibilities that the past offered but rather from the promise of God's future. Recognizing the nation's religious identity, King called the nation to this future. King often proclaimed that the "arc of the universe is long, but it bends toward justice." King's dream was a testament to this arc. Therefore, though the past was significant in shaping the present reality, because it was a crucifying past, King did not allow it to have authority over his future dreams, or his present actions for that matter. As the cross took seriously the harsh and brutal realities of human evil, so too did King. However, a new history had to be written. The only way for that to occur was from the vantage point of the future, not the past. King's dream reflected the in-breaking of God's future into the present. It was about a moral imagination.

Moral Imagination[19]

A moral imagination is grounded in the absolute belief that the world can be better. A moral imagination envisions Isaiah's "new heaven and new earth," where the "wolf and the lamb shall feed together," and trusts that it will be made real (Isaiah 65). What is certain, a moral imagination disrupts the notion that the world as it is reflects God's intentions.

With a moral imagination one is able to live proleptically, that is, as if the new heaven and new earth were already here. This means one's life is not constrained by what is. It is oriented toward what will be. Moral imagination allows black bodies to live as free black bodies, despite the forces that would deny that fact. A moral imagination

---

19. While this concept of "moral imagination" was arrived at independently, it is worth noting that Elizabeth S. Fernandez speaks of "A Household of Moral Imagination" in "The Church as a Household of Abundant Life," in *Theology That Matters*, 180.

defies the power of stand-your-ground culture. It recognizes this culture as a human construct that does not reflect God's "eternal law."

A moral imagination is nothing other than the hope of black faith. Such hope trusts that the arc of God's universe does in fact bend toward justice. As we know, black faith was the source of King's moral imagination. It was unquestionably a moral imagination that enabled King to proclaim that, with or without him, black people would get to the promised land, and to close his "Dream" speech with the confidence that one day black people would be "Free at last."

Beyond Stand Your Ground

A Grandmother's Dream

My grandmother moved from Georgia to Ohio during the Great Migration. After a couple of stops along the way she finally landed in Columbus, Ohio. With only a sixth-grade education, she was able to get a job as an elevator operator. At that time elevators ran by pulleys. A person would ring a bell, and the operator, sitting inside the elevator, used a hand crank to bring the elevator to you. My grandmother was the one sitting inside the door.

My grandmother had her own dream. She dreamed that her four grandchildren would one day finish high school. As an investment in that dream, she put money from every paycheck into an account for each of her grandchildren to receive after their graduation. What of course she could not dream was that her grandchildren would not only complete high school, but go well beyond in their educational achievement. What is striking, however, is that in the midst of the stand-your-ground culture that was hers, one marred by Jim Crow and lynching, she was still able to dream. Moreover, she worked to make her dream come true. She believed the world would be a better place for her grandchildren and that the realities of stand-your-ground culture as she experienced them would come to an end. Her dream was shaped not by the history and limitations of stand-your-ground culture but by the history of black prophetic testimony.

The Question Answered

One of the tools of our own stand-your-ground culture is the narrative that we are now living in a postracial time. Such a narrative discards what happened to Trayvon, Jordan, Renisha, and Jonathan. Their stand-your-ground deaths were all about race. Suffice to say, the only thing postracial about this time in the nation's history is the refusal to talk about race. The subject has almost become taboo. To paraphrase Audre Lorde, "Our silence does not protect us."[20] Martin Luther King put it this way: "Our lives begin to end the day we become silent about things that matter." Not talking about race does not make the matter of race disappear. It only sustains the culture of race that continues to take the lives of our children. Indeed what makes stand-your-ground culture so dangerous is the "major desire not to [speak] of it at all."[21]

During his remarks following the verdict of Trayvon's killer, President Obama also said, "It is important for all of us to do some soul-searching." This is indeed a *kairos* time. It is a time for the nation to engage in soul searching to discern how we have gotten to this place in our society so that we can get to a better place. "The time has come, God knows," Baldwin says, "for us to examine ourselves, but we can do this only if we are willing to free ourselves of the myth of America and try to find out what is really happening here."[22]

This *is* a *kairos* time. It is the time for each of us to be embodied realities of a black prophetic tradition and with moral memory, moral identity, moral participation, and moral imagination begin to create the world we "crave for our daughters and sons."[23] There are other Trayvons, Jordans, Renishas, and Jonathans. Their grandmothers and mothers are dreaming of the fun-loving, hard-working Marines, aviation mechanics, or pilots that they can become. Fifty years ago, when King stood at the Lincoln Memorial, he said, "Now is the time to make justice a reality for all of God's children." Now *is* the time. It is the time to live into God's time and to create that new heaven and new earth where the time of stand-your-ground culture is no more.

---

20. Paraphrase of Audre Lorde, "The Transformation of Silence into Language and Action," in *Sister Outsider*, 41

21. Baldwin, "The Dangerous Road of Martin Luther King," in *The Price of the Ticket*, 247.

22. Baldwin, "The Discovery of What It Means to Be Black," in *The Price of the Ticket*, 175.

23. Lorde, "Man Child: A Black Lesbian Feminist's Response," in *Sister Outsider*, 78.

EPILOGUE

A Mother's Weeping for Justice

"A voice was heard, weeping and loud lamentation, Rachel weeping for her children, she refused to be comforted, because they are no more." It was the time of Jesus' birth. After discovering that he had been betrayed by the wise men, Herod demanded that "all the male children in Bethlehem and in all that region who were two years old and under" be killed. Herod was standing his ground of power. It is in speaking of the edict from Herod that the Matthean Gospel writer speaks of Rachel, who centuries earlier was weeping for her lost children.

Rachel died giving birth to her son Benjamin. She was buried in Ramah, presumably somewhere on the way to Bethlehem. Centuries later, Rachel's offspring, the children of Israel, would be killed and led off into exile in Babylon. As Jeremiah recalls the children of Israel being led off, he tells of Rachel weeping and refusing to be consoled. In both Matthew's Gospel and the prophecy of Jeremiah Rachel's weeping is at once a sign of deep grief and great hope. Her children are gone, and she refuses to be consoled by any justice that the world might offer, particularly as it continues to take her children. She can only be consoled by God. Thus, it is fitting that her weeping is recalled at the time of Jesus' birth, not simply because Bethlehem is weeping over the loss of its children, but because the Christ child is born. Into the midst of a mother's deepest pain and suffering God is present in the world bringing hope. One thing is made clear as Rachel's weeping is juxtaposed with the birth of Jesus: there is no power that can stand its ground against God, not even the power of death.

After the acquittal of her son's killer, Trayvon's mother said, "At the end of the day, God is in control." As the weeping of Rachel signals, there is a persistent dark side to God's world. It is a world filled with a mother's grief, which nothing in the world can console. This is a grief that does not go away. It is not to be dismissed or taken lightly. And God does not. For it is in the midst of this great suffering and grief that God comes. It is, thus, through a mother's weeping that we can see the measure of the hope in the world that is God's. It is in knowing the deep grief of a mother for her children that we can understand the extent of hope for the justice of God. Feminist and womanist theologians often proclaim God as mother. To know God as mother is for us to see God in the weeping mothers of Trayvon, Jordan, Jonathan, and Renisha as they refuse to be consoled until there is justice for their children.

As I have mentioned throughout this book, there has simply been no story in the news that impacted me more deeply than the murder of Trayvon—and then there was Jordan, then Jonathan, then Renisha, and then, during the writing of this book, there was Michael Brown.

It happened just after noon on August 9, 2014, on a street in Ferguson, Missouri. Michael was walking down the middle of the street with a friend. A white police officer approached both of them, apparently ordering them onto the sidewalk. What happened next is unclear. Two starkly different versions of the story have emerged. Numerous witnesses say that Michael was walking with his hands up when the officer opened fire on him. While the officer's version of events has not been fully revealed, it suggests that he perceived Michael as a threat, and thus claims to have been justified in shooting him to death. While the precise details of what occurred on that Saturday afternoon are as yet unclear, there is no disputing the fact that Michael Brown was unarmed when he was shot at least six times. Also undisputed is the fact that Michael's lifeless body was left to lie uncovered in the middle of the street for several hours. In response to this noonday slaying, the streets of Ferguson were filled with protests for nine nights, interrupted occasionally by looting and violence. The police met the protestors, even when they were not aggressive, with the kind of military force typically reserved for battlefields.

As I watched the events in Ferguson unfold, it was as if I were seeing the arguments of this book play out before me. Once again, an unarmed black teenager was killed because he was presumed "guilty of something." As if to substantiate his "guilt," a video was released of Michael allegedly shoplifting cigars from a local convenience store. In the reporting of this incident various media outlets described Michael as being involved in a "strong-armed robbery," a far cry from shoplifting. Moreover, the reason for releasing the video was unclear. The chief of police, Thomas Jackson, admitted that there was no relationship between what happened in the store and the officer's pursuit of Michael and his friend. As the police chief explained, the "robbery does not relate to the initial contact between the officer and Michael Brown." He was stopped, the police chief continued, for "walking down the middle of the street and blocking traffic" [though the presence of traffic is also disputed].[1] At play, it seems, in the release of the video was the persistent need of stand-your-ground culture to criminalize the black victim—again, to make clear that such a body is always guilty of something worthy of pursuit, if not death. To be sure, the decision to leave Michael's body in the middle of the street for several hours was meant to send a warning to his community. Upon watching the CNN footage of the spectacle made of Michael's lifeless body for hours in the middle of his neighborhood street, I was reminded of nineteenth- and twentieth-century "spectacle lynchings," where black bodies (mostly males) were left hanging from trees for hours, if not days. The spectacle made of black bodies, no matter in what century, is meant to send the same message: this too can happen to you. The militarized assault on the protestors of Ferguson only reinforced this message, while also making it clear that a war has been declared on the black body

Recognizing that Michael was a victim of the same war that took the life of her son, Trayvon's mother, Sybrina Fulton, wrote an open letter to Michael's family. Warning the Brown family of the attempts that would be made to criminalize Michael, she said:

> You will . . . unfortunately, hear Michael's character assassinated.
> . . . Honor your son and his life . . . no one will ever convince me

---

1. Police Chief Thomas Jackson, quoted in Greg Botelho and Don Lemon, "Ferguson police chief: Officer didn't stop Brown as robbery suspect" (August 15, 2014), http://www.cnn.com.

that my son [Trayvon] deserved to be stalked and murdered. No one can convince you that Michael deserved to be executed.[2]

Even as Sybrina Fulton warned them of the "character assassination" that in fact would follow, she also sounded a resurrection call. She essentially encouraged Michael's family not to permit Michael to be defined by the crucifying realities of his death. Rather, she counseled that they remember the resurrecting realities of his life. Michael's parents, Michael Brown Sr. and Lesley McSpadden, indeed proclaimed that "Michael was a good boy. He didn't deserve this."[3]

Michael Brown Jr. was an eighteen-year-old young man. He graduated from Normandy High School eight days before his slaying. Teachers said he "loomed large and didn't cause trouble." He was described by many as a "gentle giant." Michael was scheduled to start Vatterott College on August 11, three days after his death. He wanted to become a heating and cooling engineer.[4] His life had meaning apart from the crucifying death he endured.

Sybrina Fulton's letter reminded me of something else. As shaken as I was by the senseless deaths of Trayvon, Jordan, Renisha, Jonathan, and now Michael, I have been even more moved by a mother's faith. These are mothers who refuse to be consoled until they get justice for their children. "We need justice for our son," declared Michael Brown's parents.[5] Ironically, two days before Michael's death, on August 7, a jury found the killer of Renisha McBride guilty of second-degree murder along with other gun-related charges. On October 1, 2014, during a retrial, Michael Dunn was found guilty of Jordan Davis's murder. Jordan's mother said that this verdict "represented justice" for "Trayvon and for all the nameless faces and children and people that will never have a voice."[6] The convictions of Renisha's and Jordan's killers, while certainly a just end in these cases, is not the full justice

2. Sybrina Fulton, "If They Refuse to Hear Us, We Will Make Them Feel Us," *Time*, September 1, 2014, 29.

3. Quoted in "Dad of Slain Unarmed Missouri Teen: 'We Need Justice for Our Son,'" *Good Morning America*, http://www.abcnews.go.

4. Information taken from the obituary of Michael Brown Jr. (1996–2014), http://www.legacy.com/obituaries/delawareonline/obituary.aspx?pid=172213385.

5. See "Dad of Slain Unarmed Missouri Teen."

6. See Elliott C. McLaughlin and John Couwels, "Michael Dunn found guilty of 1st-degree murder in loud-music trial," http:/www.cnn.com.

that Michael's mother or the others' mothers demand. This is not the justice for which mothers weep. Theirs is a justice that goes beyond the conviction of their children's killers. They weep for divine justice. God's justice means an end to the very culture that has declared war on innocent, young black bodies. This means an end to the systemic, structural, and discursive sin of Anglo-Saxon exceptionalism, which makes black bodies the target of war.

In her letter to Michael Brown's parents, Trayvon's mother said, "We will bond (as parents of slain children), we will continue our fight for justice and make them remember our children in an appropriate light."[7] We must all bond with these mothers by joining Rachel and refusing to be consoled until there is no longer a culture that perpetuates, as Trayvon's mother says, "racial profiling and stereotypes [that] serve as the basis for illegitimate fear and the shooting and killing of young teenagers." We must refuse to be consoled until this world is safe for our black children.

"God is in control," Sybrina Fulton said. And so God is. Left for each of us is to act like it, and thus to be where God is, standing up to stand-your-ground culture so that our sons and daughters might live. This book is my refusal to be consoled until the justice that is God's is made real in the world.

---

7. Fulton, "If They Refuse to Hear Us," 29.

Acknowledgments

While writing a book is often a solitary process, it cannot be done without the support and encouragement of many. This book would not have been possible without the Summer Faculty Research Grant that I received from my academic institution, Goucher College. I thank my student researcher, Sara Harris, for her assistance throughout this process. I am indebted to Eric Key for bringing the cover art to my attention and coordinating the process to make it a reality.

I thank Michele Hagans, who recognized even before I did that this project needed a sacred space to come to fruition. She provided me the space to write in the company of those Harlem Renaissance Voices of the Inkwell.

I am thankful to Seble Dawit, my true sister–friend, who throughout this writing process nurtured me with the right measure of solitude, company, conversation, and laughter, sustaining me through a summer of writing. I am appreciative to Salem and Kebe, whose comings and goings were a timely source of encouragement.

I am deeply grateful to Angelo Robinson, my "brother," for taking time from his own writing project to read and reread this book from proposal to completion, always offering valuable edits and insights. Most importantly he offered his friendship, without which this book could not be possible.

Robert Ellsberg, editor-in-chief and publisher at Orbis Books, has been invaluable to this entire project. He believed in it when it was just an idea. Without his editorial expertise and his unwavering friendship this book would have remained an idea.

I am blessed and inspired by my son, Desmond. I thank him for being who he is.

Finally, words are not enough to thank my life-partner, Lamont, for his unconditional support and steadfast belief in me. Without these things none of this would be possible.

Index